Death of the
Scharnhorst

Death of the
Scharnhorst

John Winton

CASSELL&CO

Cassell
Wellington House, 125 Strand
London WC2R 0BB

First published in Great Britain by Antony Bird in 1983
This paperback edition published in 2000

A CIP catalogue record for this book is available from the British Library

ISBN 0-304-35520-8

Printed and bound in Great Britain by
Cox & Wyman Ltd., Reading, Berks.

Contents

Illustrations

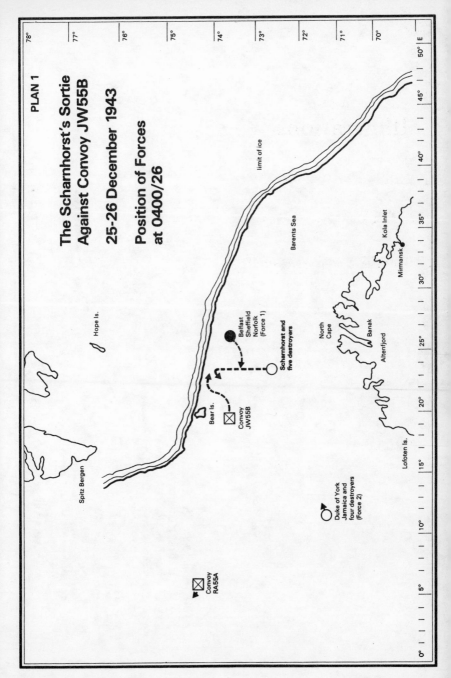

PLAN 1

The Scharnhorst's Sortie
Against Convoy JW55B

25-26 December 1943

Position of Forces
at 0400/26

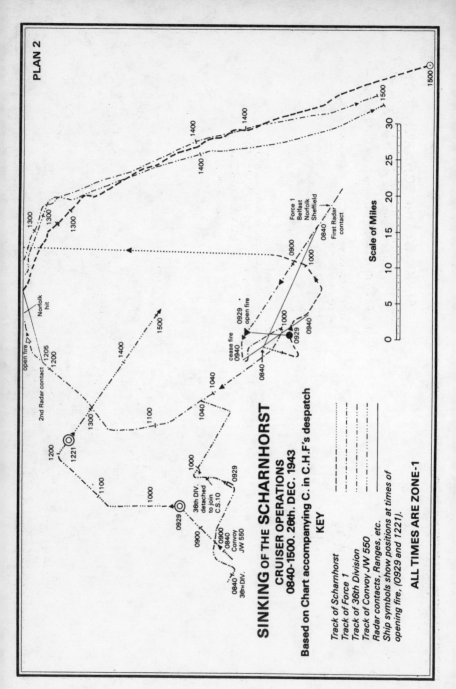

PLAN 2

SINKING OF THE SCHARNHORST
CRUISER OPERATIONS
0840-1500. 26th DEC. 1943
Based on Chart accompanying C. in C.H.F's despatch

KEY

Track of Scharnhorst
Track of Force 1
Track of 36th Division
Track of Convoy JW 550
Radar contacts, Ranges, etc.
Ship symbols show positions at times of
opening fire, (0929 and 1221).

ALL TIMES ARE ZONE-1

Scale of Miles

0   5   10   15   20   25   30

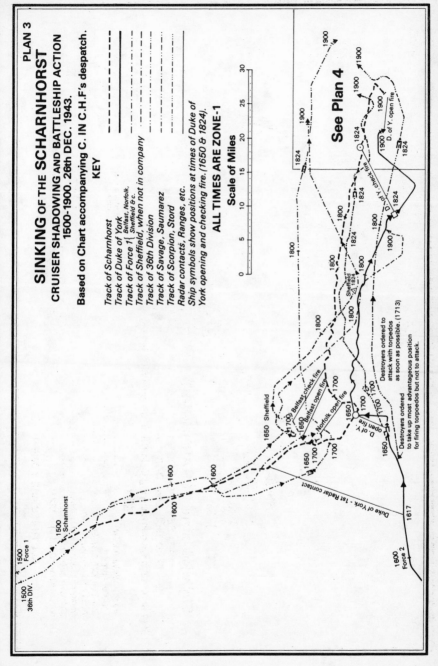

PLAN 3

SINKING OF THE SCHARNHORST

CRUISER SHADOWING AND BATTLESHIP ACTION
1500-1900. 26th DEC. 1943.

Based on Chart accompanying C. IN C.H.F.'s despatch.

KEY

Track of Scharnhorst	
Track of Duke of York	
Track of Force 1	Belfast, Norfolk.
	Sheffield & c.
Track of Sheffield, when not in company	
Track of 36th Division	
Track of Savage, Saumarez	
Track of Scorpion, Stord	
Radar contacts, Ranges, etc.	
Ship symbols show positions at times of Duke of York opening and checking fire. (1650 & 1824).	

ALL TIMES ARE ZONE -1

Scale of Miles

0   5   10   15   20   25   30

See Plan 4

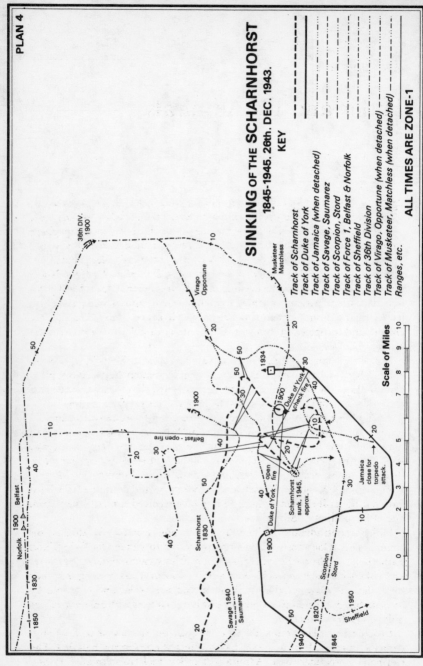

SINKING OF THE SCHARNHORST
1845-1945. 26th. DEC. 1943.

KEY

Track of Scharnhorst

Track of Duke of York

Track of Jamaica (when detached)

Track of Savage, Saumarez

Track of Scorpion, Stord

Track of Force 1, Belfast & Norfolk

Track of Sheffield

Track of 36th Division

Track of Virago, Opportune (when detached)

Track of Musketeer, Matchless (when detached)

Ranges, etc.

ALL TIMES ARE ZONE-1

Scale of Miles

1 0 1 2 3 4 5 6 7 8 9 10

CHAPTER 1

Hitler and his Admirals

EVERY time we hit her, it was just like stoking up a huge fire, with flames and sparks flying up the chimney. Every time a salvo landed, there was this great gust of flame roaring up into the air, just as though we were prodding a huge fire with a poker. Tremendous, unforgettable sight.' So said Lieut. Vernon Merry RNVR, the admiral's flag lieutenant, watching from the flag bridge of the battleship *Duke of York*, off the North Cape of Norway, late in the evening of 26th December 1943. It had been a long day, which was just reaching its climax, when ships of the Home Fleet, led by their Commander-in-Chief Admiral Sir Bruce Fraser, had sighted, chased, and trapped and were now finally about to sink the German battle-cruiser *Scharnhorst*.

It was a curiously old-fashioned naval engagement, like a head-to-head combat between maritime dinosaurs, a 'slogging match' between two giant capital ships, in which aircraft played no part. It was also a classical demonstration of two widely different national views of sea power.

Adolf Hitler, a 'land animal' and a very successful one, had only a limited grasp of naval affairs. He always wanted his Navy to triumph in battle, but not to suffer any losses. He took each success as a personal compliment, each loss as a private affront. It is significant that both *Bismarck* and *Scharnhorst*, in their last hours, transmitted personal signals to the Fuhrer; His Majesty King George VI, though himself a naval officer, would doubtless have been flattered but still extremely surprised to have received similar signals from one of His Majesty's Ships in action.

Hitler's contradictory philosophy of sea power naturally affected his commanders. Constantly being urged onwards to victory for Fuhrer and Fatherland, whilst at the same time being strictly cautioned against taking any risks with their ships, Hitler's admirals seemed easily depressed. For them the line between glory and gloom was very thin, and one unlucky torpedo hit, as with *Bismarck*, or one crushing salvo, as with *Scharnhorst*, was quite enough to breach it.

In *Scharnhorst*'s last action, the German ships put to sea with a very sound strategic purpose, but they were feebly directed and ineptly handled. The German commander, Rear Admiral Erich Bey, took his ships out knowing very well what he was supposed to do, but evidently with little idea of how to do it. He had more than one chance to accomplish his purpose. While trying to find his target he was counter-attacked by smaller but determined opponents and allowed himself to be driven off. Finally, in trying to evade, he chose the very course which was sure to take him almost directly into the arms of his most powerful adversary — of whose approach he had been quite unaware.

The Royal Navy, on the other hand, has always known that the price of Admiralty is very high indeed, in blood and treasure. But one setback does not lose a war. In Bruce Fraser the Home Fleet had a commander, on the day, at the top of his considerable form. He had always known who his opponent would be, sooner or later, and he had had ample time to think over what he was going to do and how he should do it. When the chance came, Fraser handled his forces with a sure touch. He knew when to break radio silence with advantage. He was well served by an able cruiser admiral in Robert Burnett, by the bravery of his destroyer captains, by professional and technical excellence in his ships and by a good personal staff, by ample and timely intelligence, and, finally, by the heavy guns of his flagship *Duke of York*. Fraser's reward was a model action, in which a fast and formidable enemy, actually better suited to the weather conditions that day than any other warship present, was methodically hunted down and brutally dispatched.

Scharnhorst and her sister-ship *Gneisenau* — 'Salmon and Gluckstein' as they were sometimes popularly called — were two of the most famous ships of the Second World War, on either side. They were built after the lifting of the limitations imposed on the German Navy by the Treaty of Versailles, and were originally intended for a war in which France was envisaged as Germany's only opponent; these two ships were designed to intercept and destroy the convoys bringing troop reinforcements back to France from West Africa.

Scharnhorst was laid down at the Marinewerft, Wilhelmshaven, on 16th May 1935, launched on 3rd October 1936, and commissioned, under her first commanding officer, Kapitan zur See Otto Ciliax, on 7th January 1939. She displaced 38,900 tons full load, of which some 12,500 tons was Krupp armour, in places nearly 14 inches thick. She had nine 28 cm. (10.92 inch) guns in three dual turrets, twelve 15 cm. (5.85 inch) guns, fourteen 10.5 cm. (4.095 inch) guns, and numerous 37 mm and 20 mm. anti-aircraft guns, with six 53.3 cm. (20.8 inch) torpedo tubes in two triple mountings. She carried four aircraft. Her three shafts gave her a top speed of 32 knots and she had an operational range of some 10,000 miles at 17 knots. She was 770.5 feet long, 98.4 feet in the beam and drew nearly thirty feet at full draught. The Germans called her a battleship, the Allies termed her a battle-cruiser; with her bows fully lengthened and flared, she was one of the most beautiful naval ships ever built.

Scharnhorst and her 'partner in crime' as the British public thought of

Gneisenau were both in the headlines from the earliest days of the war. On their first war cruiser in November 1939, it was *Scharnhorst* who sank the hopelessly outmatched armed merchant cruiser *Rawalpindi*, on the Northern Patrol, south of Iceland; this was an episode which *Scharnhorst*'s crew, who had already begun to think of themselves as an elite, did not consider as redounding to their credit. One of *Scharnhorst*'s survivors said 'it left an unpleasant taste in my mouth'.

In April, off Norway, they were both in action again, against the battle-cruiser *Renown* and later, in June, they sank the aircraft carrier *Glorious* and both her two escorting destroyers *Ardent* and *Acasta*. In January 1941, their teamwork reached its peak when they sailed on an extended raid on commerce. By the time they returned in March, two months later, they had brilliantly carried out their main purpose as raiders, having sunk or captured 22 ships, of 115,622 tons, and totally disrupted Allied convoy schedules for some time and over a very wide area. They had also tempered valour with discretion, having adroitly withdrawn on three occasions when they sighted an opposing capital ship with a convoy.

But this cruise was the summit of their achievements. At Brest, where they reached harbour on 23rd March 1941, both ships were subjected to harassing air attacks. In February 1942, *Scharnhorst* and *Gneisenau*, with the heavy cruiser *Prinz Eugen*, who had joined them after her own cruise with *Bismarck*, with an escort of destroyers, made their celebrated 'Channel Dash' and returned home to Germany in a boldly conceived and skilfully executed operation which greatly alarmed the people of Great Britain that enemy heavy ships could pass so close to their coastline. Certainly the German squadron had 'wiped the Allies' eyes' in passing through the Dover Straits almost unscathed, but the ships were far less dangerous to the Atlantic convoys in Germany than they had been at Brest.

The 'Channel Dash' was their last joint sortie. For *Gneisenau* the war was over. She had always seemed the unluckier partner; the crew of *Scharnhorst* actually called her their 'poor relation'. She was damaged by *Renown*'s gunfire in April 1940; torpedoed by the submarine *Clyde* off Trondheim in June; hit by a torpedo dropped from a Beaufort of 217 Squadron RAF in Brest in April 1941 (for which exploit the pilot Fl.Lt. K. Campbell RAFVR received a posthumous Victoria Cross); hit by four bombs in dock four days later; and mined during the passage back to Germany.

In Kiel, later in February 1942, *Gneisenau* was bombed again and damaged so badly that almost her entire bow was blown off. Afterwards, she burned for three days, and 180 mangled corpses were removed from her shattered forward compartments. She was moved to Gdynia in April and paid off in July. From 1943 onwards work on her gradually came to a halt, due to lack of labour and materials. By the end of 1944, only a small party of men was left on board, to keep watches, do damage control rounds and prevent her actually flooding and sinking. At last, on 27th March 1945, she was scuttled in the entrance to Gdynia hardbour, to prevent the advancing

Russians making any use of her. Her hulk was salvaged after the war, in an operation lasting from 1947 to 1951.

Meanwhile, *Scharnhorst* had become 'Lucky' *Scharnhorst,* regarded by the people of Germany as a symbol of naval power and eminence, rather as *Hood* was by the people of Great Britain. In fact, she suffered as many reverses and almost as much damage as *Gneisenau.* She was hit by one torpedo from *Acasta,* abreast 'C' (Caesar) Turret, and shipped some 2,500 tons of water; later, the bodies of 38 men were taken from the flooded magazine; bombed by Skuas in Trondheim in June 1940 and hit by one 500 lb. bomb which did not explode; bombed and hit five times by Halifaxes off La Pallice in July 1941, but was able to return to harbour at 27 knots, although she had taken on some 7,000 tons of water; and was mined twice during the 'Channel Dash'.

Scharnhorst's ship's company had been lucky enough to stay together through all the alarms and excursions of the earlier years of the war and they had developed a great pride in their ship. *Scharnhorst Immer Voran!* (*Scharnhorst* Ever Onwards!) was the ship's motto, and theirs. They were lucky, too, in their commanding officer, Kapitan zur See Kurt Caesar Hoffman, who had relieved Ciliax in September 1939 and had since become a figure almost of legend, beloved by his crew only just this side of idolatry.

In the spring of 1942, when *Scharnhorst* was in Kiel for repairs, Hoffman was promoted Rear Admiral. On 2nd April, he was relieved in command of *Scharnhorst* by Kapitan zur See Friedrich Huffmeier. It would have been very difficult for any man to have followed Hoffmann. But it took only a short time for *Scharnhorst*'s ship's company to decide, to a man, that 'Poldi' Huffmeier was a walking disaster area. They believed he owed his appointment more to social influence than to ability, and he quickly showed himself a poor seaman, with almost no talent at all for ship-handling. Every movement to sea required the maximum number of tugs, sometimes, as they said 'so many that there was no room for them all alongside.'

With or without tugs, 'Poldi' began to give his ship's company some exciting moments. He began by running *Scharnhorst* aground off Hela at 26 knots, and had the greatest difficulty in refloating her. An aircraft was inadvertently shot off the catapult before everybody was ready; only the observer survived. Leaving Gdynia, where *Scharnhorst* had gone for working-up trials, 'Poldi' contrived to wrap a buoy wire round the starboard screw and the ship had to be docked for repairs (she had only just left dock after making good the damage due to grounding). On another day leaving Gdynia, a tanker just ahead hit a mine and sank so swiftly that only her masts were visible by the time 'Poldi' had reacted, and another scrape was only just avoided. However, early in August 1942, *Scharnhorst* went to sea for tactical exercises with U-boats from Kiel and was soon in underwater collision with U.523, thus needing yet another docking. It was no wonder that by Christmas 1942, when there were rumours that *Scharnhorst* might be going to Norway, the crew were convinced that 'Poldi' was behind it, 'determined to win his Knight's Cross, First Class'. In fact, there were excellent strategic reasons why *Scharnhorst* should go north.

When, in A.P. Herbert's words, Hitler 'leaped upon his largest friend' and attacked Russia in June 1941, it was soon decided that it was necessary for the Allies to send supplies to Russia, by sea, round the North Cape. Whatever political and moral justifications there may have been for the convoys to north Russia, as naval undertakings they were always basically unsound. The merchant ships and their escorts had to make their way to and from the north Russian ports along a route often restricted by polar ice, and always within easy reach of enemy air, U-boat and surface force bases, where Allied heavy ships could not protect them. To the dangers of the appalling Arctic weather and the cold and the violence of the enemy was added the indifference, often shading into actual hostility, of a suspicious and ungrateful ally.

Yet, in spite of their sombre reputation, the Arctic convoys were in fact extremely successful and, by and large, safe for the ships who took part. Convoy after convoy crossed without any loss at all. Of the 58 outward-bound ships lost, 43 were from only three convoys, PQ.16, PQ.17 and PQ.18, which all sailed in the perpetual daylight hours of the summer of 1942. Of those 43, 23 were from PQ.17, ordered from London to scatter (the convoy had lost only two ships before it scattered). The rest were sunk whilst sailing independently.

The disaster to PQ.17 was to some extent counter-balanced by one splendid victory in the Barents Sea, on New Year's Eve, 1942, when convoy JW.51B was threatened by the German pocket battleship *Lutzow,* the heavy cruiser *Hipper,* and six large destroyers. The German Navy had promised Hitler a resounding victory, and he should have got it. The German ships accomplished a perfect 'pincer' movement. By all the rules of naval warfare, both convoy and escort should have been massacred. But the German commanders, no doubt recalling their frequent orders to exercise discretion and avoid risks, were deterred by a sublimely brave show of agression by the convoy's escort of five destroyers, led by Captain R.St. V. Sherbrooke in *Onslow.* They turned away when they should have closed, hesitated, and lost their chance. *Hipper* was damaged and one German destroyer, *Friedrich Eckholdt,* was sunk. The escort lost the destroyer *Achates* and the minesweeper *Bramble.* Sherbrooke lost an eye and won a Victoria Cross. The convoy was untouched.

This battle in the Barents Sea had a long-term effect upon the German Navy out of all proportion to the damage actually inflicted at sea. There was a (perhaps understandable) delay in reporting back to Hitler. The first news in fact came from the Allied side and was not at all what Hitler wanted, and expected, to hear: far from being annihilated, the convoy had escaped almost scot-free and, far from falling upon their opponents like wolves on the fold, the German ships had been shamefacedly driven away.

His fury fuelled by frustration, Hitler summoned Vice Admiral Theodor

Krancke, the representative of Grand Admiral Raeder at the Fuhrer's 'Wolfsschanze' H.Q., and informed him of his, the Fuhrer's, 'unalterable resolve' to pay off all the heavy ships and reduce them to scrap, because they were a 'needless drain on men and materials'. The guns would be removed and mounted on land, for coastal defences. Warming to his subject, Hitler told Krancke that the Navy was nothing but a source of constant embarrassment. Every operation they undertook ended in ridicule. They were not the cause of victories, only of vexation. The Navy was, said Hitler, utterly useless.

With considerable courage, Krancke eventually replied that the course of action the Fuhrer was ordering would be the cheapest victory that Great Britain could possibly gain. It would be the equivalent of a major naval engagement won without any exertion at all. Hitler repeated his 'unalterable resolve' and demanded to see the Commander-in-Chief Raeder himself.

Perhaps prudently, the Grand Admiral pleaded sickness and it was five days, in which he had time to gather together all the information available and to prepare his own case in mitigation, before Raeder saw Hitler at the Wolfsschanze. In the event, he need not have bothered. The Fuhrer did not wish to be troubled by counter-arguments. His wrath had not abated, indeed it had been fanned by Goering, who never neglected a change to denigrate the Navy and to boost the Luftwaffe. For (a reported) ninety minutes without stopping for breath, Hitler subjected Raeder to a humiliating harangue; he condemned the Navy's spirit, courage, morale and tactics. The recent failure to press home an attack on that Russian convoy was 'typical' and, in Hitler's opinion, 'just the opposite of the British who, true to their traditions, fought to the bitter end'.

Raeder himself, quite simply, thought it beneath his dignity to try and answer this attack, which was entirely unjust and untrue. It was a gross libel on the German Navy. In Raeder's own phrase, it was 'completely spiteful' and a 'completely fabricated story'. When he did at last have a chance to intervene, Raeder offered his resignation.

This appears to have disconcerted the Fuhrer. It was not quite what he had intended. He seems to have tried to moderate his tone, even to have tried to mollify Raeder. But Raeder had heard enough, and more than enough. He felt that his authority had been irretrievably damaged. He absolutely declined to stay in office.

On that, Raeder should have left at once, but there was some further discussion when it was agreed that Raeder would resign his appointment (which he had actually held since 1928) on 30th January 1943, which would be the tenth anniversary of the founding of the Third Reich. The choice of his successor lay between Admiral Rolf Carls, Flag Officer Gruppe Nord, and Admiral Karl Doenitz, commanding the U-boat branch. Hitler chose Doenitz.

But before he went, Raeder prepared a statement on naval policy which was in a way, his own professional *nunc dimittis*. He submitted it to Hitler on

15th January. It was an admirable exposition of the principles and practice of sea power. Raeder pointed out the support the surface fleet had given to the U-boat arm, by tying down large numbers of enemy destroyers and minesweepers. The big ships were a constant threat to the enemy, wherever they were, merely by existing, and compelled him to allocate large naval forces to guard against a break-out.

Scrapping the big ships, Raeder argued, would free very few men for other purposes. Most of them would be employed dismantling the heavy naval guns. As for using the guns for 'coastal defence', the guns would only at best provide defence at thirteen batteries — along a coastline of several thousand kilometres! By far the best 'coastal defence' along such a coastline was the ships themselves.

If the big ships were scrapped, the whole strategic picture in the Atlantic would change at once. The enemy would be able to move large naval forces elsewhere, to the Mediterranean or the Far East. The German Navy would no longer present any threat at all. Scrapping the big ships would present the enemy with a tremendous naval victory on a plate, without any effort at all on his part. It would give enormous encouragement to the enemy, whilst at the same time depressing the German people and disillusioning their Japanese allies. Above all, it would show the enemy that Germany clearly had not the faintest idea of the importance of sea power. That in itself would be the biggest defeat of all.

But it was no use. Hitler had never really understood sea power and he was not about to learn now. The big ships must go. However, the German Navy appears to have decided, deep down in its corporate fibres, that if Hitler could not be moved by argument, then he must be defeated by recalcitrance. For instance, all work was stopped, for ever, on the two 60,000 ton, 16-inch-gunned super battleships 'H', (reportedly named *Friedrich der Grosse*) and 'J' *(Gross Deutschland)*, both laid down at Blohm & Voss at Hamburg in 1939. But, on 7th January, on the very day after Hitler had decided to scrap all the big ships, one of those ships began to make preparations to move out of the Baltic, just as though Hitler had never spoken.

On 7th January 1943 the Allied Special Intelligence decrypting service, codenamed ULTRA, revealed that *Scharnhorst* had returned to Gdynia after exercising in Danzig Bay. On 9th, several 'Officer Only' signals were exchanged between the German Admiralty and the C-in-C Fleet, Admiral Otto Schniewind, embarked in *Scharnhorst*. They were not actually de-cyphered, but one of them, marked 'Emergency Priority', was repeated to *Prinz Eugen* and three destroyers *Paul Jacobi*, *Friedrich Ihn* and *Z.24*. On 8th, two destroyers left Trondheim and steered south; it seemed likely they were steaming towards a rendezvous with *Scharnhorst* and *Prinz Eugen*. A move out of the Baltic by one or more big German ships was clearly possible.

The signs of something about to happen began to multiply. The two southbound destroyers were sighted by a reconnaissance aircraft off Stadtlandet at 2 pm. on 9th and were later identified as *Karl Galster* and *Z.25;*

they were due to refuel at Kristiansand at 1 pm on 10th. By then, the C-in-C Home Fleet, all other interested flag officers and Bomber and Coastal Commands, had been warned that *Scharnhorst* and *Prinz Eugen* might pass through the Skagerrak on 10th. Emergency orders for sweeping the Great Belt had been decrypted; the fairway was to be swept by 4 pm on 10th, after which the fairway was to be kept clear of shipping.

Just after 7 pm on 10th January C-in-C Home Fleet sent a 'Hush Most Secret' signal warning that there were 'immediate possibilities' of *Scharnhorst* leaving the Baltic for Trondheim. Flag Officer Submarines was asked to divert two submarines to patrol to the north. The Eighth Destroyer Flotilla, of *Faulknor* (D.8) and six destroyers was brought to immediate notice. Orders were intercepted for two German patrol vessels, normally stationed one at each end of the Great Belt, to be ready for 'a certain operation' on 10th January. A German 'Sperrbrecher' minesweeper reported at 10 am on 11th that the speed of the formation she was escorting was 19 knots. Finally, just after 1 pm on 11th, a Britain reconnaissance aircraft reported one battleship, one cruiser and one destroyer off the Skaw steering 280° at 10 knots.

There was a drill for such occasions, which now swung into action. The 8th Destroyer Flotilla, supported by two cruisers, sailed to sweep the waters south of Stadlandet (the most westerly point on the Norwegian coast). Six flare-carrying and twenty torpedo-bombers took off to attack between 3.15 and 4.30 that afternoon. No.18 Group Coastal Command mounted a strong reconnaissance effort. The number of patrolling submarines was increased to six.

It was all to no avail. Of the attacking aircraft two were lost and the rest returned having sighted no shipping. The destroyers had sailed on 11th but at 10.40 pm that night very bad weather forced them to turn back. A continuous reconnaissance and air patrol maintained for the next twenty-four hours failed to sight anything. However, *Scharnhorst* had been informed by a German aircraft that she had been sighted and she had at once turned about. The German ships were reported by ULTRA as being due back in Gdynia on the evening of 13th. Their arrival was confirmed early on 15th.

Scharnhorst and *Prinz Eugen* resumed their trials and exercises in Danzig Bay until 23rd January, when they were both warned of a 'forthcoming operation' later revealed by ULTRA. The same flurry of activity took place. Two 'Sperrbrechers' were ordered to be off Arkona at 6.30 on 'Day X Plus One', to repeat the operation of 10th January. The destroyers *Erich Steinbrinck* and *Z.37* were ordered to be ready to leave Kiel on the morning of 24th (suggesting that 'Day X' was probably 23rd).

All the signs began to point to 23rd. *Scharnhorst,* with Schniewind embarked, was due to rendezvous with *Prinz Eugen* in Danzig Bay at 4 pm that day. *Scharnhorst* requested the radio beacon at Swinemunde to be activated from 7 pm on 23rd until 7 am on 24th. The two Sperrbrechers reported they were in position off Arkona, *Erich Steinbrinck* reported her departure from Kiel at 12.30 pm on 24th, *Paul Jacobi, Z.24* and *Z.25* were ordered to stand by from 6.30 am on 25th off Kristiansand, ready to 'join the formation'. ULTRA carried on reporting all this traffic, as though the British admirals were on the German distribution list.

The three destroyers were reported leaving Kristiansand by an aircraft on photographic reconnaisance at 9.45 am on 25th. At 2.15 pm another aircraft 40 miles west of the Skaw reported *Scharnhorst, Prinz Eugen* and five destroyers, and began to shadow. At 2.35 the German ships were seen to turn about.

A force of forty bombers and torpedo-bombers took off to attack but they were thwarted by the weather and sighted nothing. Air patrols over south and south-west Norway, maintained during the night, also saw nothing. Several attempts to photograph the area on 26th also failed. Meanwhile ULTRA revealed that Luftwaffe orders for reconnaissances off Narvik and Trondheim had been cancelled as the operation concerning *Scharnhorst* and *Prinz Eugen* had been 'broken off'. Both ships were due to arrive back in Gdynia at 1.30 pm on 27th.

For the second time in a month major German ships had been sighted and twice they had turned back unscathed. Admiral Sir John Tovey, the C-in-C Home Fleet, and Air Marshal Joubert, of Coastal Command, discussed methods of improving shadowing and reporting tactics. In fact, the German ships had been sighted and shadowed, but on both occasions it was the very bad weather which had prevented any effective action being taken against them. On 31st there were slight indications that *Scharnhorst* and *Prinze Eugen* might be making yet another attempt but the rumours turned out to involve the transfer of an armed merchantman. The two big ships stayed at Gdynia, still carrying out exercises.

The comings and goings of *Scharnhorst* and *Prinz Eugen* made no difference to the continuing need to pass convoys through to Russia. Even without *Scharnhorst* and *Prinz Eugen,* the German Navy still had *Tirpitz* and *Lutzow* the damaged *Hipper,* two light cruisers *Koln* and *Nurnberg,* eight destroyers and some 20 U-boats, all in bases in northern Norway, threatening the convoy routes. On the other hand, Luftwaffe strength in bombers and torpedo-bombers had been greatly reduced from its 1942 levels and, most important, there were in January still long hours of sheltering darkness. So, despite the surface ship threat, if convoys were to be sailed it were best they were sailed quickly.

Convoy JW 52, of 14 ships, left Loch Ewe on 17th January 1943, escorted by the destroyer *Onslaught* (Cdr. W.H.R. Selby), seven other destroyers, two corvettes, a minesweeper and two trawlers. This was a comparatively light escort but there was also a covering force of three cruisers, *Kent, Glasgow* and *Bermuda,* to go right through to Russia with the convoy, and, in the deep field, a distant escort including the battle ship *Anson,* flying the flag of Vice Admiral Sir Bruce Fraser, Flag Officer Second in Command Home Fleet.

One ship had to be sent back to Iceland because she could not keep up with the convoy, but the rest enjoyed unexpectedly good weather, and made a fast passage in which the U-boats' attacks were well contained by the escort. Selby and his fellow-captains used their High Frequency Direction Finding (H/F D/F) equipment with great success. The U-boats were loquacious opponents, being required to transmit frequent and lengthy signals to their bases. An escort could obtain a bearing of a transmission and steer down it to find the U-boat, or, better still, two or more escorts' H/F D/F bearings could give a 'fix' of a U-boat's position. Selby and his ships several times ran down bearings, found U-boats at the end of them, and counter-attacked.

On 23rd January, a Blohm & Voss Bv.138 flying boat reported the convoy. Next day, four out of a strike of five Heinkel He.115 torpedo-carrying seaplanes found and attacked the starboard column of merchant ships. They sank no ships, and two of them were shot down. Using H/F D/F bearings, the convoy made several adroit emergency turns to evade U-boats so that only one, U.622, made one unsuccessful attack. U-625 attacked *Bermuda* and *Kent* but missed. The convoy was sighted again by aircraft on 25th but reached Kola Inlet safely on 27th.

Selby and his ships were allowed only a respite of two days before setting out again on 29th January with the return convoy, RA52, of 11 'empties'. They were reported by U.625 south-west of Bear Island on 1st February and two days later U.255 sank the 7,460 ton steamer *Greylock*. The rest arrived without further serious incident in Loch Ewe on 8th February.

As time passed, the convoy route became ever more dangerous. Not only were the daylight hours drawing out, but polar ice began to drift southwards in February, forcing the convoys to sail closer to the Norwegian shore, only some 250 miles from the heavy German ships at Altafjord. Thus the next eastbound convoy, JW 53, of 28 ships, which sailed from Loch Ewe on 15th February, was very strongly escorted. The 'Through Escort Group', of small ships, consisted of the minesweepers *Jason* (senior officer, Cdr Lewis) and *Halcyon*, the *Hunt* Class destroyers *Pytchley*, *Middleton*, and *Meynell*, the corvettes *Dianella*, *Poppy*, and *Bergamot*, and the anti-submarine trawlers *Lord Middleton* and *Lord Austin*.

To support them was the 'Ocean Escort' waiting at a rendezvous north-east of Iceland, of the anti-aircraft cruiser *Scylla*, the escort carrier *Dasher*, and thirteen destroyers, under Captain I. Campbell in *Milne*, with *Faulknor*, *Boadicea*, *Inglefield*, *Fury*, *Intrepid*, *Impulsive*, *Eclipse*, the Polish *Orkan*, *Orwell*, *Opportune*, *Obedient* and *Obdurate*. The cruiser covering force was commanded by Rear Admiral R.L. Burnett, flying his flag in *Belfast*, with *Sheffield* and *Cumberland* in company. Once again there was a heavy covering force in the deep field.

German air reconnaissance picked up the convoy on 23rd, although the main concentration of U-boats was avoided next day by means of H/F D/F. U.622 did make an attack on two destroyers in the screen, but missed. Ten Junkers Ju, 88s attacked on 25th and damaged the 7,050 ton *Empire Portia*. Attacks by more Ju. 88s and by U.622 on 26th achieved nothing at all.

JW 53's main opponent was the appalling weather. JW 52 had been lucky. Now the Arctic Ocean reverted to normal. The convoy's whole passage was made through a violent gale which damaged *Dasher* so badly she had to leave. *Sheffield*'s fo'c'sle had been so constantly battered by high seas that her turrets were trained on the beam, to try and prevent the blast screens (covering the apertures where the barrels passed through the front turret plates) from being driven in. But one colossal wave smashed against the side of 'A' turret and tore the entire turret roof off. Six merchantmen were scattered in the gale and returned to Iceland, but the remaining 22 were eventually shepherded together by the escorts, formed up in good order and reached Kola Inlet on 27th, some ships going on into the White Sea, where they arrived on 2nd March. The Luftwaffe dive-bombed ships of the convoy in Murmansk. The 7,173 ton *Ocean Freedom* was sunk on 13th March, and the 6,744 ton *Empire Kinsman* damaged.

The return convoy of 30 'empties', RA 53, set out from Kola on 1st March, with the same escort and the same weather. But they met much more determined opposition. U.255 reported the convoy on 2nd and shadowed with only short breaks for several days. U.255 sank the 4,978 ton *Executive* on 5th and torpedoed the 7,191 ton *Richard Bland,* which did not sink. The convoy drove off an attack by twelve Ju.88s later in the day and U.255 lost contact.

By 9th March, the convoy had largely broken up in the gale. One steamer foundered and U.586 sank the straggler *Puerto Rican.* The next day U.255 came up with *Richard Bland* again and sank her. The close escort was fully occupied in rounding up the scattered convoy, and were greatly helped by the radar of the battleship *King George V.* RA 53 reassembled and reached Loch Ewe on 14th March.

By then, there was more news of *Scharnhorst.* Doenitz had arrived at the Wolfsschanze on 25th January 1943, eager to take over the reins of power, and Hitler had presented him almost at once with a directive which seemed to realise all Doenitz's dearest dreams. All construction and conversion of heavy ships was to stop at once. They were all to be paid off, except those which had some use for training. All the resources, of manpower and materials, so released were to be devoted wholly to the U-boat arm.

It must have seemed to Karl Doenitz that the millenium had arrived at last. For years he had been proclaiming the decisive role his U-boats could play if they were only given the proper resources. He had protested over and over again at the low priority given to U-boats and the pitiful amount of support they had received in what, to Doenitz, was their all-important struggle in the Atlantic.

By 2nd February, Doenitz had prepared a detailed plan for carrying out Hitler's directive. All work was to be discontinued on battleships, heavy cruisers, light cruisers, aircraft carriers and troop transports, except the ships allocated for training purposes. Work was also to stop on weapons and equipment, but the rundown of ships and weapons was to be carried out gradually so as to avoid alarming the German public. Every big ship was to be paid off except *Prinz Eugen, Admiral Scheer, Lutzow, Nurnberg* and *Emden,* which were to form a training squadron. *Tirpitz, Lutzow* and *Nurnberg* were to remain operational in Norway until they paid off, *Lutzow* and *Nurnberg* on 1st August 1943, *Tirpitz* later in the autumn.

Scharnhorst and *Prinz Eugen* were to operate in the Baltic, *Prinz Eugen* to pay off and join the training squadron on 1st May. *Scharnhorst* was to pay off on 1st July. The medium armament of *Tirpitz* and *Scharnhorst* was to be removed and set up as coastal batteries ashore. But the removal of the main armament would 'be tantamount to breaking up the ship'; it was thought that the ships would have greater potential as heavy mobile batteries if their main armament was left intact (and, presumably, the ships towed to and fro along the coastline).

At this point, Doenitz appears to have had second thoughts. Or perhaps he was a much more wily manipulator than Hitler ever suspected. Certainly he was a great deal better at 'handling' Hitler than Raeder had ever been. Raeder's professional last will and testament might not have impressed Hitler, but it had a profound effect upon Doenitz. Reading it, and remembering what Raeder had said to him when he turned over his office, Doenitz was convinced that Raeder was right. Hitler might not be able to take Raeder's point about the uses of capital ships, but Doenitz certainly could: as long as the German Navy had heavy capital ships, even if they were up in Norway, the enemy would be forced to keep at least an equal number of capital ships of equal size or greater, just in case of a break-out. The German heavy ships, Raeder had believed, *could* be employed successfully in the Arctic, but if they were, then they must be freed from political restrictions and all the cautions which had bedevilled them so far.

Raeder had written that the lack of aircraft carriers in the German fleet had imposed severe limitations on the ways in which the fleet could be used and had 'acted as a drag on prospects of achieving success'. However, Raeder wrote, 'I must point out that the possibility of scoring a success most certainly still exists, provided that the fleet remains constantly on the alert for every possible contingency and waits for the favourable opportunity. Even without adequate air cover and reconnaissance, opportunities will always occur when, by making full use of favourable weather conditions, we can achieve surprise and strike a worthwhile blow.'

Doenitz became more and more convinced that the big ships should be saved. In mid-February he summoned Schniewind and his Chief of Staff designate, Rear Admiral Heye, to Berlin for a conference. He found them of the same mind. Both said that, even with the enemy's superiority in radar, if there was a favourable opportunity, the big ships could still win a success.

Doenitz also consulted Vice Admiral Kummetz, who had once been in command of the Northern Group. Kummitz said that the Luftwaffe support would have to be increased and the aircraft used directly in support of the ships. There must be a chance of rehearsing the operation before it was undertaken. Above all, there must be no political restrictions. Doenitz agreed and told Kummetz that, as he had experience of those northern waters, he must be prepared to take command of the Northern Group again.

After what he called 'mature reflection', and having given due weight to the opinions of the officers he had consulted, 'who all maintained unequivocally that our big ships could still be usefully employed in war', Doenitz decided to pay off only the ships 'which no longer possessed any fighting value and which could not be used for training purposes, and to retain in commission all those which might still be used in battle or as training ships'.

He decided to pay off the cruisers *Hipper, Leipzig* and *Koln*, and the old battleships *Schlesien* and *Schleswig-Holstein*. He would keep *Tirpitz* and *Scharnhorst, Scheer* and *Lutzow, Prince* and *Nurnberg. Tirpitz* and *Scharnhorst*, with attached destroyers, would form one group, to defend Norway against enemy landings and, as chances occurred, to attack convoys bound for Russia. The rest would stay in the Baltic for training purposes and 'until the need arose to commit them to battle'. That was the plan. It now only remained to put it to Hitler.

To say, as Doenitz did, that Hitler was 'highly astonished and indignant' was one of the understatements of the war. Doenitz broached his new plans, baldly and without any attempt at equivocation, at a meeting with the Fuhrer at the Wolfsschanze on 26th February. Hitler could hardly believe the evidence of his ears. On 8th, a fortnight earlier, his Grand Admiral had been giving him details of scrapping heavy ships, hauling guns ashore, devoting men and repair facilities to U-boats, and so on and so on.

Hitler's rage always had a short fuse. Once again he soared off into a lengthy diatribe on the inadequacies of the Navy: every high hope had been dashed down in the bitterest disappointment; they had brought him nothing but tales of gloom and doom, starting with *Graf Spee* and working up to the present day; not a victory to their name; a story of unremitting disaster and failure; admirals who did not know how to command, ships that did not stay afloat, men who did not know how to fight.

Doenitz replied that it was the necessity to stay afloat which prevented the ships from fighting. No navy could achieve anything if it were not allowed to take any risks. The commanders at sea could not be blamed for political decisions.

Hitler retorted that such political restrictions had not originated from him. All he wanted his fighting ships to do was to fight. This they had failed to do. In any case, it hardly mattered whether the heavy ships were paid off or not; so far they had contributed nothing, and he no longer expected anything of them. The situation on the Eastern Front was very serious and the battle there was growing ever harder. The Russians were being reinforced by these convoys, this last one of twenty-five ships particularly (Hitler was presumably referring to JW 53). It was an insupportable state of affairs and could not continue.

Hitler's exasperation was understandable, if not excusable. After all, he had discussed these matters with Doenitz at a full conference as recently as 13th February. Doenitz had made his proposals then for paying off the big ships, for giving complete priority in every department to the construction, repair and refit, manning and training of the U-boats, and for proper air support from the Luftwaffe. To every item Hitler had given his 'complete and final approval'. Now, here was Raeder's old argument arising all over again.

It may have been Raeder's argument, but it was no longer Raeder putting it. Doenitz was evidently a much better Fuhrer-debater. If the Fuhrer wished to stop the convoys to Russia, Doenitz insisted, his ships must fight. If they were to fight, then they could not be paid off. Eventually, Doenitz's persistence was rewarded. Hitler's 'unalterable resolve' was altered. He accepted Doenitz's proposals, albeit, as Doenitz said, 'reluctantly and with bad grace'. But he could not resist one Parthian shot. When Doenitz said he expected action within three months, Hitler replied that it might be six, and then Doenitz would have to admit that Hitler was right all along.

That might well be, but in the meantime Doenitz wasted no time in issuing a new directive on policy to the commanders of the German surface ships, including a statement of principle on which the battle group in northern Norway was to operate against the convoys: 'The conditions required for successful operations by surface ships against traffic in the Arctic will occur very seldom, since the enemy, to judge from past experience, will deploy for the protection — immediate and indirect — of his convoys, forces of such strength as will undoubtedly be superior to that of our own forces. Nevertheless, there may occur opportunities for attacking unescorted or lightly escorted ships or small groups of ships sailing independently. Whenever such an opportunity occurs it must be seized with determination, but with due observance of tactical principles.

It may sometimes be considered necessary to attack heavily escorted convoys with all available forces; orders to deliver such an attack will be given if the convoy in question is deemed to be of such value that its destruction is of primary importance to the situation as a whole.'

After that, it was no surprise that by the beginning of March 1943 there were strong indications from ULTRA that *Scharnhorst* might be preparing to make another move. On 4th March, aircraft were transferred from bases in north-west Germany to Stavanger and Bergen — normally a sure indicator. Special Intelligence for 3rd and 4th March was being read within three days, so it was known by 7th that *Scharnhorst* had been transmitting and receiving several 'Officer Only' signals to and from the German Admiralty and Gruppe Nord. These signals were made on a Baltic frequency and direction-finding suggested *Scharnhorst* was transmitting from the western end of the Baltic, or even from the Great Belt area.

Tell-tale signs were now coming one after the other from ULTRA. There was an extensive mine-laying operation in the Great Belt during the night of

4-5th March. A Sperrbrecher was ordered to escort 'certain naval units' from the southern end of the Great Belt at 7.30 am on 5th as far as the Skaw. At 8.30 am on 6th the Great Belt was closed to shipping for 24 hours.

Scharnhorst was actually off the Skaw at about 6 pm on 7th March but unfortunately Special Intelligence was not being read currently and her movements had to be reconstructed later. Reconnaissance of Gdynia on 8th revealed that *Scharnhorst* had left but there was still no evidence that she had passed through the Belts and the Kattegat. On the contrary, a signal to *Scharnhorst* at 1 pm on 6th, on a Baltic frequency, informed her that air escort was impracticable before 9th March. Opinion in the Operational Intelligence Centre in the Admiralty was that *Scharnhorst* was still in the Baltic on the evening of 6th March. However, ULTRA showed, on the night of 9th March, that *Scharnhorst* had made a signal at 10 am that day on a frequency which indicated she was then off the coast of Norway. It was also known that the destroyers *Richard Beitzen* and *Erich Steinbrinck* had passed through Fro Havet sound on their way in to Trondheim at 7 am that morning. *Friedrich Ihn* was ordered to Bergen for repairs but was to proceed to Trondheim as soon as possible. The signs were that these destroyers had escorted *Scharnhorst* up the coast.

Meanwhile the news that *Scharnhorst* had vanished from Gdynia was enough to cause furious activity on the Allied side. In the Clyde, the aircraft carriers *Indomitable* and *Furious* came to short notice for steam. Cruisers sailed from Seydisfiord in Iceland to meet the incoming RA 53. The battleship *Anson*, flying Fraser's flag, moved up to Hvalfiord. The C-in-C Mediterranean was requested to make Force H available, in case *Scharnhorst* broke out into the Atlantic. 'Break out' patrols of ships and aircraft were carried out along the Norwegian coast, in the Denmark Strait, and in the Iceland-Faeroes passage.

Scharnhorst was actually well on her way north on 8th March. At 2.15 pm she was in the Norwegian Sea between Bergen and the Shetland Islands. At 7 am on 9th she was south-west of the Lofoten Islands and heading for the great entrance to Vest Fiord. By 2 pm she was in Bogen Bay near Narvik and confirmed her arrival by signalling Commandant Gdynia at 6 pm: 'Send everything to Narvik'.

Scharnhorst left Trondheim on 11th and although air reconnaissance of Narvik on that day showed only the cruiser *Nurnberg* and two torpedo-boats there, *Tirpitz*, *Scharnhorst*, *Lutzow* and destroyers were all in Bogen Bay. The whole force left Narvik on 22nd March and arrived in Alta Fiord on 24th. Reconnaissance revealed only a light cruiser and two destroyers on 6th. But Special Intelligence from ULTRA confirmed that *Tirpitz*, *Scharnhorst* and *Lutzow* were all in Alta Fiord on 5th April.

The known presence of this very powerful force of heavy ships so far north, and so close to the convoy routes, the long and increasing hours of daylight, and the imperative necessity to divert every available convoy escort to meet the crisis in the Atlantic, all meant that convoys to Russia stopped after JW

53. No convoy sailed after RA 53, in March, April or indeed for the rest of that spring and summer.

In the meantime, every movement, actual or suspected, of these monster ships sent tremors along the Allied intelligence lines. The Norwegian shore watchers from their huts in the mountains, the naval attachés in Stockholm, the decoding services providing the stream of ULTRA decrypts, the eternally listening direction-finding receivers, the staff of the Operational Intelligence Centre, all maintained a never-ceasing watch.

Nowhere was greater attention paid to these three ships than at Scapa Flow, where on 8th May 1943 Bruce Fraser relieved his old chief, Sir John Tovey, and became Commander in Chief, Home Fleet, hoisting his flag in the battleship *Duke of York*.

CHAPTER 2

Fraser and the *Duke of York*

Iɴ that summer of 1943, Bruce Austin Fraser was 55 years old and at the peak of his career. He himself would have said that the command of a premier fleet in time of war was the summit of any professional naval officer's hopes. Fraser himself was a man of short stature and stocky build, with an eternally cheerful and open-faced expression, a ruddy healthy complexion, fair hair and blue eyes. He actually looked like a sailor, and had been one ever since he was a 13-year-old lad and went to *Britannia* in 1902 as a naval cadet.

Fraser was one of the most able and lovable admirals the Royal Navy has ever produced. He was always the most easy-going and approachable of men. His philosophy in life, according to his Flag Lieutenant Lieut Vernon Merry, RNVR was 'so very simple: his attitude towards any individual officer or rating, from the highest to the low, or to any Ship's company or fleet, was that they and he had the very good fortune to belong to the finest Service in the world. As he talked to them it was vividly apparent that they and he were absolute equals; the fact that he was an Admiral, and the other was perhaps just a newly-joined Ordinary Seaman, was completely immaterial to him. Bruce Fraser made it abundantly clear that he was sincerely interested and concerned about that man's job in the ship, his action station, his home and welfare, his training and his future. He would discuss these matters at great length with his fellow equal, and even if he could not do this with every shipmate of this fortunate young man, it permeated through to the whole ship's company in no time, and thus they all felt equally honoured, and even more that they had an Admiral who was vitally interested in them. It was Leadership of the highest quality.'

It was a leadership made up of many small acts of thoughtfulness and consideration. When *Belfast* was due to steam down from Scapa Flow to Rosyth to give leave at about the same time as *Duke of York*, *Belfast*'s commanding officer, Captain 'Freddie' Parham, himself a future full admiral, suggested he might go down in company with the flagship. 'That would be very nice indeed,' said Fraser. 'But I don't think it would be fair on the railway company, to expect them to lay on enough special trains for *both* ship's companies to go on leave at the same time.' Parham was amazed that

Fraser should remember such a significant detail, at a time when he had so many cares and responsibilities as Commander-in-Chief.

Bruce Fraser was a master of the endearing gesture and the apt phrase, just when it seemed that he might be getting into difficulties. Much later in the war, when he was Commander-in-Chief of the British Pacific Fleet, he was called upon to receive from the Australian Minister of War a cheque subscribed by the workers in the Ministry of Munitions for the British Centre, set up in Sydney for the benefit of sailors of the fleet. According to Anthony Kimmins, who was there, Fraser 'started off very badly, as he is not good at saying the conventional things which such occasions demand. I began to wriggle uncomfortably in my chair. I felt he was being a flop, but then as always he produced the unexpected ace.

'I noticed,' he said, adopting that benign and innocent expression which he reserves for such occasions, 'that the cheque which was handed over just now was made out for fourteen hundred pounds, eleven shillings and three-pence. If the girl who subscribed the threepence would be good enough to come up on to the platform, I should like to give her a kiss!'

However, Fraser also had a cutting edge. One young officer in *Duke of York*, Lieut. Henry Leach (himself a future First Sea Lord) said Fraser 'never raised his voice but the quiet, cold statement 'That's bad' was reproof enough for most'. He was quite capable of administering what he called a "J.G.S.U." — a Jolly Good Shake Up — to an offending ship, although even then, as Lieut Merry said, 'he was most selective on who was shaken up, being meticulously correct and affable with non-offenders in that ship, but his displeasure struck home most effectively on whomsoever it was merited.' He could be 'ruthless and retribution would be swift and crushing. It did not happen very often, but I have known of an officer being ordered to leave his ship within half an hour, and of ratings of the personal retinue sacked on the spot'.

Fraser was always a 'big ship' man, although not always willingly. The smallest ship he ever served in was the light cruiser *Boadicea*, flying the broad pennant of Commodore Sir Robert Arbuthnot commanding the Harwich Flotilla. It was Arbuthnot (later, as a Rear Admiral, killed in action at Jutland) who recognised Fraser's talents and, though Fraser rather hankered after the destroyer life of small ships, steered him towards gunnery which had always been, was then, and remained for many years, the broadest avenue to promotion.

Fraser had a quick intellect and delighted in his mastery of all the technical details and intricacies of guns and gunnery. He gained five first-class passes in his courses as a sub-lieutenant, and came top in gunnery. In his gunnery course at HMS *Excellent*, Whale Island, he was the best all-round student and went on to Greenwich for the 'dagger' advanced gunnery course. Later he returned to Whale Island on the junior staff.

As a young lieutenant, Fraser was hard-working, lucky, and ingenious. He was clearly a 'coming man'. He had, as they say, God's thumb-print on his forehead. His first appointment as 'G' was the aged cruiser *Minerva*, which began the First World War on convoy duty in the Red Sea and Eastern Mediterranean. In her, Fraser served during the Gallipoli landings, where he once augmented *Minerva*'s fire-power by commandeering an army field gun and mounting it on top of *Minerva*'s fore turret.

The gunnery officer designate of the new 15-inch gun battleship *Resolution* was killed at Jutland and Fraser, though very junior for the appointment, got a 'pierhead jump' to take his place. In *Resolution* Fraser spent the rest of the war, saw the surrender of the German High Seas Fleet and then went out to the Mediterranean, where he was promoted Commander.

In 1920 Fraser led a party of some fifty sailors from *Resolution* ashore at Baku, the oil port on the Caspian Sea, to support anti-Bolshevik forces against the Russian revolution. No sooner were Fraser and his party ashore then Baku declared itself for the Bolsheviks. Fraser and his men were imprisoned for eight months. Fraser kept his little band together, in body and in spirit, maintained their morale by his own example, and their diet by bartering for fresh spring onions and green vegetables. His fellow prisoners recognised what Fraser had done for them and, when they were released, clubbed together to buy him a dress sword (which he presented to the Naval Museum at Portsmouth in 1980).

The post-war Navy of the 1920s was a perilous place for many officers, whose numbers were decimated by the 'Geddes Axe'. But Fraser's progress towards the top was sure and unwavering. He went back to Whale Island as Commander 'G', an absolutely sure-fire promotion appointment, in 1921, and then, a year later, to the Admiralty under the Director of Naval Ordnance and Director of Torpedoes and Mining, thus establishing the pattern of his career: passing from one prestigious Admiralty appointment after another, to seagoing appointments in one flagship after another. In 1924 Fraser was Fleet Gunnery Officer in the Mediterranean Fleet, first under Admiral Sir Osmond de Brock in the battleship *Queen Elizabeth* and then under Admiral Sir Roger Keyes in *Warspite*.

Fraser was promoted Captain on 30th June 1926 and came back to the Admiralty as Head of the Tactical Section of the Naval Staff; his friend and colleague, Dudley Pound, was then Assistant Chief of Naval Staff. In 1929 he went to the East Indies Squadron in command of the cruiser *Effingham* and as Flag Captain to Admirals Sir Bertram Thesiger, Sir Eric Fullerton and Sir Martin Dunbar-Nasmith VC — three Commanders-in-Chief in four years.

In 1933 Fraser became Director of Naval Ordnance and was much concerned in the earlier stages of design, procurement and testing of the new 14″ guns, in quadruple turrets, and the 5.25″ Dual Purpose (High and Low Angle) guns — both to be fitted in his future flagship *Duke of York*. He was therefore one of the very few — perhaps the only admiral — in all naval history who was intimately involved in the production of weapons which he himself was to use with great success in battle.

From the Admiralty Fraser went to sea again, in command of the aircraft carrier *Glorious* in the Mediterranean — a crucial appointment for Fraser and for the Navy. At that time, control of the Fleet Air Arm was still vested in the RAF, as it had been ever since 1918. Regular naval officers (those who ever thought about the air branch at all) tended to look on it as 'not quite the thing', just about equal on the social scale to a job in the motor trade, and certainly not a likely path to flag rank. Aircrew tended to be recruited from the eccentrics, the idiosyncrats, the non-conformers, those impatient of discipline, all those who would never have made gunnery officers, indeed those who generally abhorred Whale Island and all its works.

Fraser was therefore one of the few comparatively senior officers, and one of the even fewer gunnery officers, who had some first-hand knowledge of the problems and potential of naval air power. He did not, as so many officers did (including the great Andrew Cunningham himself) look upon air power as a useful adjunct, as merely a means of slowing down an enemy so that the main guns of the fleet could come up and dispatch him. With intensive exercises, including some of the Navy's first night-flying trials, Fraser in *Glorious* made some of the first important moves towards the concept of air power as a weapon on its own-capable, for instance, of the strike at Taranto. In two ironic quirks of naval history, *Scharnhorst* sank Fraser's old ship, and Fraser sank *Scharnhorst* — but without the aid of air power.

Fraser was promoted Rear Admiral on 11th January 1938 and became Dudley Pound's Chief of Staff in the Mediterranean during the Spanish Civil War — a time of great operational and political difficulty. He came home on 1st March 1939 to become Third Sea Lord and Controller of the Navy, responsible for the Navy's ships and equipment; here again, with the war now clearly approaching, Fraser made a tremendous contribution to the Navy's preparedness, such as it was, and especially the state of the Fleet Air Arm on the outbreak of war (which would have been much worse without him). Promoted Vice Admiral in May 1940, made KBE in 1941, KCB in the Birthday Honours List of 1942, Fraser became Second in Command of the Home Fleet on 28th June 1942.

Brilliant as he was in the Admiralty, with such accomplished expertise in committee, moving with such ease in the corridors of Whitehall, Fraser always seemed conscious that he was not seeing enough action. No sooner had he joined the Home Fleet than he sailed in *Victorious, incognito,* 'just as a passenger', on an Arctic convoy, and in August 1942 he took passage in *Rodney,* in the 'Pedestal' convoy to Malta, again 'just for the experience'.

When he visited a ship's wardroom, with the senior officers prominently ranged in the foreground, Fraser would often make his way through them to the rear, where he would find the junior officers, unaware, and instantly engage them in conversation. Of course, their seniors would have their turn shortly, but Fraser wanted to hear from the 'grass-roots', from the young men, and then compare his impressions with what he later gained from their seniors.

Unmarried himself, and hence with no children of his own, Fraser nevertheless had great sympathy and understanding for young people. When he hoisted his flag in *Anson,* it happened that for some reason he had no flag-lieutenant. He could have had an experienced lieutenant or lieutenant-commander communications specialist, or at least some regular RN officer from the main stream of the Navy. Perhaps none was available, or perhaps Fraser deliberately chose otherwise. Instead, he accepted the personal recommendation of *Anson*'s Commander, George Colville, and chose Vernon Merry, a very young and inexperienced officer, who had left his job on *Lloyd's List* to join the Navy as a 'Hostilities Only' Ordinary Seaman, and had recently joined *Anson* as a Midshipman RNVR. Only barely twenty years old, and with no watchkeeping ticket, Merry had just shipped his first 'wavy' stripe as an Acting Sub-Lieutenant RNVR. But Fraser summed the young man up at a glance and so began a working relationship and a close friendship which were to last until Fraser's death nearly forty years later.

Merry has given an account of his chief's daily routine as Commander-in-Chief. Fraser normally got up at about 8.45, very late indeed for a sea-going routine, and breakfasted at 9.10 alone (having suffered himself as a midshipman, forced to breakfast with his Captain, he vowed he would never inflict such an ordeal on anybody) whilst he read the overnight signals.

After a staff meeting at 9.30 in the Admiral's Cabin, and a brief paper-signing session with his Secretary, Fraser was off in his barge to visit ships, not less than two in a forenoon and sometimes four. They would have been warned by signal the night before that 'If convenient, I would like to visit you informally and walk round your ship at 10.30; normal routine to continue.' Needless to say, it always was convenient.

The visits may have been informal but they were nevertheless very thorough and Fraser attached the greatest importance to them. They were his means of getting to know his ships and his men, and of getting himself known to them; during these visits he unobtrusively summed up individual officers and their efficiency, gauged the temper of ship's companies, and formed his own opinion on equipment and material.

Often Fraser chose one department in a ship and questioned a cross-section of its personnel on everything relating to their jobs. It could be, according to Merry, that 'an Able Seaman radar operator told him his Fire Control set was unserviceable for lack of a simple spare part. He would then question the Radar Officer for confirmation, and then pass on to something else. On return to the flagship or to the shore office, the Flag Lieutenant would inform the Fleet Radar Officer of the incident, which in effect meant that the C-in-C expected the Fleet Radar Officer to get down to that ship immediately and stay there until the set was serviceable again, and then to report personally on what was the root cause of the problem.' His staff knew that Fraser was 'not just niggling over a petty concern' but that it might reveal 'a ghastly blockage in the logistic set-up' which needed a JGSU. It also showed the ships that the staff was there to look after their interests.

Fraser would not tolerate any 'feeling' between ship and staff. He knew, from his own experience in *Effingham,* the debilitating bickering and time-wasting which arose from ship-versus-staff feuds, especially in an over-crowded flagship in time of war. If there was a complaint, the plaintiff was not under any circumstances to 'make a scene'. He was to go in person, to the C-in-C if he was on the staff, to the Flag Captain if a ship's officer. Fraser and his Flag Captain would then deal with the matter. 'The penalty for creating a scene or undue rudeness was to be instant removal from the Flagship'. But in practice that never happened. Fraser himself 'would join no clique and brook no gossip and would never say a bad word about anyone in the Navy, however aggravating some might prove, and would only allow others to criticise constructively'.

Fraser was normally back in the flagship by 12.30 for lunch, but as soon as the meal was over and the signals had been read, he liked to be left alone, undisturbed until 4.30. 'Not for him a chance to "get his head down" but he would sit on the settee in the After Day Cabin, sucking his pipe — sitting there "just thinking".' Nor were his thoughts idle ones. He was constantly turning over in his mind problems of strategy and tactics, examining alternatives, rehearsing his response to every conceivable manoeuvre his likely opponents might make. As Merry said 'he would fight hypothetical fleet actions, rehearsing dispositions, ranges, 'A' arcs, factors of light, wind and weather and enemy capabilities and courses of action' ... his battle against *Scharnhorst* had already been fought out in this way many a time before the real thing.'

Another officer who had frequent chances to observe Fraser at close quarters was his Staff Officer (Intelligence), Lieut. Edward Thomas RNVR: 'Fraser had a wide-ranging mind. He left others to do the paper work and spent a lot of time thinking about how the activities of the Home Fleet fitted into the context of the war as a whole. I would often bring urgent intelligence papers to his cabin and find him sitting back in a huge armchair, puffing an equally huge pipe — and thinking. He received ULTRA signals and summaries not only about home waters but also about other theatres (not the Pacific). A good deal of ULTRA was available about the Russian front. Ever since Kursk (July-August 1943) Fraser had watched closely the progress of the apparently unstoppable Russian march westwards. He used to ask as many questions about this as he did about the simultaneous Allied landings in Sicily and Italy, and the capitulation of the latter (which, because of the surrender of the Italian fleet, affected his calculations). When, from the middle of December 1943, ULTRA told him of *Scharnhorst*'s intensive exercises he became convinced that the German leadership would send out the Battle Group, not only to deny supplies to the Russians, but also to provide the German population with something to take their minds off defeat and aerial bombardment. So he copied the *Scharnhorst* and exercised intensively while outward bound from Akureyri. The exercises were not all good-natured. Their success owed much to the administrations of our dear Chief of Staff, William Rudolf Slayter. After the battle he remarked that "it had gone off just like an exercise — except that nobody grumbled".'

It could thus be said that the action off the North Cape was won, or at least half-won, in the day cabin in *Duke of York*. By comparison with the depth of Fraser's thought, and the range and breadth of the support he received from his staff, his German counterparts appear hastily prepared and ill-served, their philosophy thread-bare and light-weight, their staff-work perfunctory, their commitment shallow and rudimentary. They were like brittle amateurs, pitted against true professionals.

When his tea was brought in at about 4.30, Fraser would throw off his reverie, and be prepared to see his staff again. By 5 pm he would be pacing the quarterdeck, which he did every afternoon for about an hour, while staff or ship's officers joined him for spells, falling into step with their chief as he marched up and down.

At about 6 pm Fraser 'would settle down at his desk to allow the Chief of Staff or Captain of the Fleet to report on what had cropped up during their day, and rather more reluctantly he would allow the Secretary to have his session with the already ruthlessly culled paper-work. He trusted his Secretary Captain (s) implicitly and allowed him an almost complete autonomy, but inevitably there were letters, reports, courts martial, honours and awards, promotion and signatures from which he could not escape. Residual reading, helped by a glass of gin, lasted until it was time for dinner.'

'Bruce Fraser always kept a very good table. I believe Table Money for Commanders-in-Chief at that time was £17.10s.0d. a day, and Bruce Fraser would never have seen any change out of that. Quite apart from the VIPs and the Senior Echelons up from London to Scapa Flow (mainly in the summer) he delighted in (and it was no chore to him) entertaining recently arrived Flag and Commanding officers, the Executive Officers or First Lieutenants, Engineer Officers and when the carriers were there, the Commander (Flying) and Squadron commanders. When the guests comprised Destroyer, Submarine or Carrier Officers, champagne was always served — battleship, cruiser or other big ship officers only got wine. There were at least four courses, and the conversation was always lively and everybody was soon put at his ease. Apart from the personal staff of Secretary and Flag Lieutenant, the other members of the "Cuddy" were the Chief of Staff, Captain of the Fleet, and the Flag Captain.'

Fraser had a good staff, who served him well (they would have been firmly weeded out if they had not). There was a 'flush' of gunnery officers: not only Fraser himself, but his Chief of Staff, Captain Michael Denny; the Captain of the Fleet, and commanding *Duke of York,* Captain A.C. Chapman; the Fleet Gunnery Officer, Cdr G.T. Coney, and his assistant, Lt.Cdr Michael Le Fanu.

Michael Denny was one of the first senior officers to study the means of applying the greatly increased range and accuracy of ships' surface radar to tactics of fighting at sea. Known as 'The Nugget', because 'he was pure gold', Denny addressed himself with tremendous energy to translating theoretical ideas into the actual training of the sailors who operated the sets, maintained the electronics and plotted the results.

Denny was relieved as Chief of Staff shortly before the *Scharnhorst* action by Commodore Slayter, another very able staff officer. Bill Slayter spoke with a slight but characteristic drawl, and had a somewhat sardonic sense of humour. He was a very tall man and very bald, occasionally referring to his head as 'my dome'. He was described by Sub. Lt. Adrian Carey, of the destroyer *Onslaught,* who had once been an ordinary seaman bridge watch-keeper in the cruiser *Liverpool* when Slayter was in command, as having 'a rather red face and very long nose, so that he always seemed to me to resemble a rather ugly bird (do I mean a macaw?). He was a very heavy punisher, always dishing out the maximum for whatever offence — with the result that his defaulters' list was never long.'

'In action he was cool and a great builder of confidence. I can still picture him looking through his binoculars at a wave of attacking aircraft and saying 'I think this is where we turn to starboard, Pilot'. 'Starboard twenty, sir!' Unlike the daredevil destroyer captain whom I was later to serve he always wore his anti-flash gear and tin helmet at action stations and expected others to do the same. When we were under tow after being holed by an aerial torpedo in the Malta convoy of June '42, I remember his squatting behind the bridge superstructure as two bombs fell — and the rest of us were happy to follow his example. He was the first to his feet to see where they had fallen, remarking to nobody in particular, 'I'm not one of those silly buggers who stick their heads up'. It seemed to me that he made friends almost irrespective of age or rank, and that he never forgot them. Certainly I cannot forget him.'

Chapman was also relieved shortly before the North Cape action by Captain The Hon. Guy Russell, described by his old friend Parham as 'a really splendid man, with a very active brain and a brilliant turn of humour and speech, he was everything that the perfect gentleman of a senior captain should be'. Russell had commanded the battleship *Nelson* during the naval support phase of the landings in Sicily and Italy and he knew a great deal about firing big guns at night. He had developed improved methods of blind firing and plotting procedures; he practised his officers and men in such small, but vital, details as proper 'eye-drill' to avoid the temporary loss of vision when the big guns fired. He made sure that *Duke of York* had one final full calibre firing before leaving Scapa. 'His arrival, 'they said of Guy Russell 'played a rich dividend and quickly filled the vacuum which was inevitably created when someone like 'The Nugget' leaves a team'.

Guy Russell was remembered with great affection and respect by all the young officers in *Duke of York*. He 'was a wonderful man,' wrote Henry Leach, 'big in every sense of the word — physically, in leadership, in charm and in his understanding of human nature. He had a well-developed and unique method of registering commendation or reproof to his subordinates, based on his intimate knowledge of London. For the former he would grin and drawl "Bond Street", while a coldly growled "that was pretty Whitechapel" had the opposite effect. His repertoire was extensive and contained much finesse!'

The Fleet Gunnery Officer and his assistant both missed the action. 'I went with the C-in-C as a matter of course' wrote Coney, but 'on this occasion the old man decreed that it was the worst (darkest) run of the winter, and time *Duke of York* had a blow through at sea, and *inferred* that nothing much was likely to happen, so he would leave his (so-called) gunnery and radar advisers behind to help Real Admiral commanding First Cruiser Squadron (CSI).'

Le Fanu was also left behind (actually he went on leave to get married). In fact, Le Fanu, perhaps the ablest naval officer of his generation (and a future First Sea Lord) often stayed ashore, to organise what he called 'Scapa Services' — arranging training programmes, fixing shoots, targets, allotting practice areas and laying on the hundred and one different facilities ships visiting Scapa needed for their training. Le Fanu was the licensed court jester, a practical joker, a very gifted composer of light verse, and a most endearing personality, endowed with 'the common touch' to an unusual degree. But underneath the lightheartedness, there was a tough, ambitious and capable character who, as Coney said, 'was more than good' at his job. With Lt. Cdr. Bill Parry, the Fleet Radar Officer, he ran 'Scapa Services' as a very crisp little outfit.

In some ways, the action off North Cape was a communicator's nightmare, with frequent breaks in communications with the Admiral in north Russia; the need to keep widely spread units of the Home Fleet all in touch with each other; with ULTRA, Scapa W/T, the Admiralty, the convoy escort commander, *and* his commodore, and lurking U-boats, all playing parts at one time or another. In fact, largely due to the expertise of Cdr. Peter Dawnay, the Fleet Wireless Officer, and Lt. Cdr 'Dickie' Courage, the Fleet Signals Officer, and their communications staff, the whole undertaking was, as Merry said, 'a communicator's dream' in the end.

It is always fashionable for ship's officers to jeer at the 'gilded staff'. Staff officers have been figures of popular derision at least since Shakespeare's time. But the Home Fleet staff, especially those who spent some time ashore at Scapa, had a more than usually difficult time. They were confined to desks, with little exercise and almost no leave, for months on end, their existences seemingly ruled by their telephones. It was no wonder they laughed so hysterically at Le Fanu's jokes.

Fraser took over as C-in-C in something of an operational lull for the Home Fleet. The convoys to Russia had been suspended. They had been discussed at a meeting of the Defence Committee (Operations) on 16th March 1943, at which Mr Churchill expressed surprise that the March convoy was not to be sailed because of the threat of surface units. He suggested that the convoy be sailed, 'as bait'. Admiral Pound, the First Sea Lord replied that it would be unlikely that the German ships would accept battle with the Home Fleet unless the Home Fleet had already been mauled by other forms of attack.

Mr Churchill still felt something could be done. He suggested that the convoy could be used as bait, even if it only went as far as the area just west of Bear Island, and then turned back. What, Mr Churchill asked, about an aircraft carrier to go with the convoy? He was sure that such a convoy should sail as arranged on 27th March and be used 'to tease the enemy and keep them in suspense' even if the circumstances did not justify its sailing. Pound drily replied that 'we had run 23 convoys through to Russia in circumstances which had never justified their sailing'. That seemed to conclude the discussion.

Fraser wrote to Pound, semi-officially, on the question of restarting the Russian convoys, on 30th June. In Fraser's view the general situation was still very much the same as it had been when the convoys were stopped in March. Luftwaffe strength in Norway had certainly been reduced, but their reconnaissance had been if anything improved by radar-equipped flying boats. U-boat numbers 'were diminished but sufficient for successful operation in those restricted waters'. The surface ship squadron, of *Tirpitz, Lutzow* and *Scharnhorst,* was more powerful than it had ever been.

Fraser himself did not think that the convoys to Russia were any longer vital to Russia's survival; in his view they should not be resumed unless they were essential to the prosecution of the war on the eastern front, or they would 'enable the German surface forces to be brought successfully to action'. Thus, by a paradox of naval history, the Germans were holding their ships in readiness to attack the convoys, whereas Fraser thought the convoys would be useful only as a means of bringing those German ships to action. What one side looked on as prey, the other thought of as bait. Personally, Fraser did not think it likely the German ships would put to sea unless they fancied a chance to attack a convoy which had no powerful covering forces, or to attack British heavy ships which had, in some way, already suffered damage. If *that* ever happened, then the particular convoy and its escort and any covering ships might be in very serious danger. 'In my view,' said Fraser, 'the effort required is not justified by the results to be expected; but if the decision (i.e. to run the convoys again) is otherwise, it is essential that adequate forces ... should be provided.'

But if there was a temporary shortage of action for the Home Fleet, that did not mean that Scapa Flow was empty or that Fraser's staff and ships were idle. On the contrary, Scapa had never been busier nor 'Scapa Services' more fully stretched. Every large ship, and many of the smaller ships, newly built or refitted and recommissioned came up to Scapa for their 'work-ups'. All the big ships of Force H, the battleships *Nelson, Rodney, Warspite* and *Valiant,* the fleet carrier *Indomitable,* and a score of cruisers and destroyers, arrived in Scapa in June 1943 to prepare for operations in the Mediterranean, including the landings in Sicily and in Italy.

The battleships in particular practised heavy gun-fire in support of troops which had recently landed against opposition. This was to prove invaluable experience for the Allies; at Salerno, the heavy guns of the fleet held the ring at a very critical point, when it seemed not at all unlikely that the expeditionary force might otherwise have been driven back into the sea.

Early in June an operation was mounted to relieve and resupply the Norwegian garrison in Spitzbergen, as well as sending stores and mail to the ships which had been in Kola Inlet since JW 53 arrived there in March, and to bring back two corvettes from Vaenga Bay. The cruisers *Cumberland, Bermuda* and two destroyers sailed from Iceland on 7th June, and arrived at Spitzbergen on 10th to land their stores and personnel, before going on to Kola Inlet.

The heavy ships of the Home Fleet covered this operation after which, at the end of June, *King George V* and *Howe* left to join the Mediterranean Fleet. Fraser now had in the 2nd Battle Squadron, *Duke of York, Anson* and the old, unmodernised, and almost obsolete *Malaya* (who in fact, left in July to be reduced to 'Care and Maintenance', her crew thus being released for other ships). To bring the Home Fleet up to strength, the US Navy sent the two battleships *South Dakota* and *Alabama,* and five destroyers, under Rear Admiral O.M. Hustvedt. Either Admiral Hustvedt's force, or one of Fraser's battleships and two cruisers, were stationed at Hvalfiord to guard against a German 'break-out'.

On 8th July, Fraser led every available ship in his fleet, including the old carrier *Furious,* just about to go to refit, on a 'coat-trailing' expedition, Operation CAMERA, along the coast of Norway. It was intended to simulate a large scale combined operation against southern Norway, thus stimulating Hitler's well known obsession with the likelihood of an Allied invasion of Norway, and also to divert attention from Operation HUSKY, the landings in Sicily, due to take place on 10th July.

Fraser's ships went within 150 miles of the coast, 'inviting the enemy to investigate'. However, the enemy did not seem to take a great deal of notice, and certainly did not deploy any forces to meet this 'threat'. But the lack of response from the Luftwaffe was remarkable. Fraser's ships operated safely, closer to the Norwegian shore than any other British Fleet since 1940. Towards the end of July, the fleet sailed again on Operation GOVERNOR, the carrier this time being the recently refitted and repaired *Illustrious*. The Luftwaffe did react, but five of its shadowing aircraft were shot down by *Illustrious'* American Grumman F4F Martlet fighters or by escorting Beaufighters of Coastal Command.

After GOVERNOR, *Illustrious,* three cruisers and several destroyers from the Home Fleet left to escort the *Queen Mary* to Halifax, taking the Prime Minister and his Chiefs of Staff to the 'Quadrant' Conference at Quebec. *Illustrious's* place was taken by the American carrier *Ranger,* and when Hustvedt's two battleships also left later in the month, bound for the Pacific, they were replaced by the heavy cruisers *Augusta* and *Tuscaloosa*.

Fraser's flagship *Duke of York* was one of five *King George V* Class

battleships, all laid down between January and July 1937, after the ending
on 31st December 1936 of the Washington Treaty which had limited capital
ship building for the previous fifteen years. The five, in order of completion,
were *King George V*, *Prince of Wales*, *Duke of York*, *Anson* and *Howe* (all so
named after some of the customary shuffling and reshuffling of warships'
names which figures in so much of the small print of *Jane's Fighting Ships*:
Duke of York was originally called *Anson*, *Anson* was *Jellicoe* and *Howe*, *Beatty*.)

Duke of York herself was laid down at John Brown's, Clydebank, in May
1937 and launched on 28th February 1940. While she was building there was
a suggestion she might be transferred to the US Navy, in exchange for eight
8″ cruisers, but she survived this proposal and was commissioned in
September 1941, then steaming up to Scapa Flow where the main body of
her ship's company joined her. Her normal complement was close to 1,700
officers and men but in full wartime array, with the admiral's staff and
additional personnel for intelligence duties and for maintenance of electro-
nic equipment, her complement was nearer 1,900 of whom, by 1941, most
were 'Hostilities Only' ratings. When, before passage down the Clyde, the
Commander cleared lower deck and asked all those who had never been to
sea before to show, 'more than 85% of the assembly displayed their
innocence'. It says a great deal for the older, more experienced men, the
Master at Arms, the senior chiefs and petty officers, led by their officers, that
this mass of raw material was transformed into an efficient fighting ship in
under six months.

With their square bilges and heavy side armour, the *King George V* Class
made good, stable gun platforms. They were 745 feet long, 103 feet in the
beam and drew 35 feet, six inches. Their four shafts gave them a maximum
speed of just over 29 knots. *Duke of York* was designed to carry four Walrus
aircraft but by 1943 these had been landed and the starboard hangar had
been converted into a cinema and lecture room.

Fully armed and loaded, *Duke of York* was a bruising opponent. She
displaced 44,450 tons, of which more than 14,000 tons was armour, which
was 16″ thick on the barbettes and on the front faces of the turrets. Her main
armament was ten 14″ guns, mounted in two quadruple and one double
turret. The quadruple turrets themselves weighed 1,550 tons each, and the
double 'B' turret 900 tons. The weight of a full salvo was 15,900 lbs, or more
than 70 tons, and the guns had a designed rate of fire of two rounds per
minute per gun. At 15,000 yards range the shells could penetrate 13 inches of
armour plate. The maximum range was 36,000 yards, or more than 20 miles:
thus *Duke of York* could have berthed alongside HMS *Belfast*, near Tower
Bridge, and comfortably landed her shells, each weighing nearly three-
quarters of a ton, on the runways at Heathrow Airport.

The secondary armament was sixteen 5.25″ guns, mounted in pairs in
eight turrets, four on each side of the upperdeck. The 5.25″ was a Dual
Purpose High Angle/Low Angle gun, an anti-aircraft and an anti-destroyer
weapon, considered heavy enough to stop a destroyer but, at the same time,

it was the heaviest calibre of gun which could be handled rapidly enough to deal with aircraft at long range. The guns were fully automatic, capable of 18 rounds per minute, with a maximum range of 22,500 yards or nearly 13 miles, controlled from directors high in the superstructure. There were also nearly 90 close range anti-aircraft guns, consisting of two-pounder pom-poms, 40 mm. Bofors and 20 mm. Oerlikons.

Duke of York's first captain was Cecil Harcourt, a gunnery specialist, and a senior and very experienced officer. He was a stern martinet who took no pains to endear himself to the sailors who, for their part, took the greatest care not to get 'on the wrong side of the Captain's defaulters' table'. In his first address to the ship's company Captain Harcourt stressed that they 'must be ready to sink the *Tirpitz*'. This was a theme he repeated many times, until the ship's company came to believe he harped too much upon it: 'He's on about the bloody *Tirpitz* again' they used to complain. However, it was significant that, from the earliest days of their first commission, it was impressed on the *Duke of York's* crew that their primary duty would be to deal with the German heavy ships in the north.

In January 1942, *Duke of York* took Mr Churchill, Lord Beaverbrook and other members of the Prime Minister's party across the Atlantic to America for the Arcadia Conference, soon after the United States had entered the war. The weather was foul, many of the distinguished guests on board were sea-sick and *Duke of York* suffered from a design defect of her class. She was very heavy forward and always shipped mountains of green water over the fo'c'sle and as far aft as the forward turrets when going into a head sea in rough weather. Later, the sheet anchor and its cable were removed, which reduced the dead weight forward but *Duke of York* was always a very 'wet ship' when driving into a heavy head sea. Quantities of water always found its way down onto the forward messdecks and even into the shell handling rooms. There was a standing joke, in rough weather, that 'there are seals in 'A' shell-room again'.

After his trip to America, Churchill continued to take an almost proprietary interest in *Duke of York*. At Scapa, during one of his visits to the fleet, he came on board and told the ship's company: 'When I saw my ship, I felt I had to come and see you. I hope that soon you'll be able to have some more leave'. Whereupon, according to Peter Woodhouse, a member of one of the 5.25'' crews, at the back of the crowd, a voice said: "Har har har!" He turned to the Captain to ask the meaning of this, and it was explained to him that we had had no leave since we had been up there — more than a year. "We must see what we can do about that", he said. A couple of days later, we went down to Rosyth and gave ten days leave each watch.'

Duke of York was a 'West-Oh' ship, whose home port and manning barracks was Devonport. The sailors came mostly from the West Country, Wales and the north of England, with some Scots. There was not much love lost between *Duke of York* and *Anson* (manned from Portsmouth), or *Howe* (a Chatham ship). Nor was *Duke of York* herself generally popular with other battleships such as *King George V* (whose ship's company fired broadsides of spuds at *Duke of York* when the two ships were alongside at sea in the Pacific: in those days, much later in the war, the opinion of the British Pacific Fleet was that *Duke of York* might have sunk the *Scharnhorst* but she had done precious little in the Pacific).

Ship's companies always suffer from mild paranoia, if allowed the chance to do so, becoming easily convinced that they have a 'green rub' in the matter of leave, mail, sea time, whereas other ships are unfairly blessed with the life of Riley. Captain Harcourt was promoted rear admiral and left the ship (there was no cheering farewell, no spectators on deck at all, apart from dutymen, when Harcourt went over the side for the last time) and Captain George Creasy became the new captain.

The contrast in personalities could hardly have been greater. George Creasy was enormously popular with the sailors. He took a more sanguine, less stern view of life than Harcourt and the ship's company immediately warmed to him, as the very best type of ship's captain, able to run a big ship with the light touch of a small ship. It was Creasy who defused a potentially dangerous situation when, in Woodhouse's account, *Duke of York* had spent "six weeks languishing in Iceland. *Anson* arrived, bearing Vice Admiral Fraser, and took us north to cover a convoy, afterwards steaming down through the Denmark Straits. Shortly after our return to Hvalfiord came the pipe: "Mail will close at 1800". At once the ship was in uproar (in a muted way, of course!). We had been there for six bloody soul-destroying weeks, and now the *Anson* was going back to the bright lights of Scapa and leaving us here! The stokers held a meeting on their messdeck. Everybody else dripped and grumbled. The news got to the Skipper. When the mail went over to the flagship, Captain Creasy went with it. When he came back, he brought the mail back with him, and we went down to Scapa instead.'

Of all the places in the world visited by the British matelot, Iceland was one of the least liked. It was a bleak place, with the jagged unwelcoming silhouettes of its mountains visible for many miles from the seaward. Nor was the country any more cheerful on closer acquaintance. Far inland there were many more inhospitable-looking peaks, seemingly row upon row of them, surmounted by rolling ranks of dark clouds, which very occasionally broke aside to allow great shafts of sunlight to shine on caps of perpetual snow.

There was snow on Hecla, the active volcano, set in a landscape of massive glaciers. Small fishing boats could be seen chugging along, close in to the shore. In summer and early autumn the Gulf Stream water, surprisingly warm, gave some good trout fishing in the fjords. Small-holders went from patch to patch of vivid green cultivation on the mountain sides, cutting hay and piling it on their boats until the craft looked like floating haystacks.

The fleet normally used three main anchorages: Hvalfjord, some twenty miles northeast of Reykjavik; Seydisfjord, on the east coast, where the cruisers often refuelled; and Akureyri, on the north coast of the island, which was generally used by the battleships. All three, in the opinion of the Home

Fleet, were beautiful, if you liked cold, boring scenery. But all three were exasperating and could be dangerous. The mountain slopes plunged steeply into the water. Even on the calmest days, a violent katabatic squall might come tearing down those slopes and the ships, exhausted by patrols or convoy passages, had to hoist all boats, shorten notice for steam, and keep anchor watches. For the ordinary sailor, it seemed too much to bear that, having endured the weather outside and the enemy, he should be allowed no peace even in harbour.

Ashore, the Icelanders kept their delight at being occupied by the British (and later by the Americans) well in check. Generally, they were as unwelcoming as their scenery. Sometimes two hundred sailors would be taken by the duty destroyer on the two-hour trip to Reykjavik where it was possible to shop for such things as cosmetics, silk stockings, night dresses, lengths of tweed, lavender water, sheepskin coats, and what Captain Parham called 'ridiculous things, called kirby grips, for my wife' none of which were available in British ships. The only drink was a non-alcoholic beverage called Bjr. But in the canteen at Hvalfjord, there was Canadian beer — 'highly explosive stuff which landed many a good man in cells'.

Later, when the Americans came to Hvalfjord, they built a camp, an officers club and an ammunition dump. British officers could use the club, to drink rum and cokes and play 'craps'. But walkers had to take care. Once, wrote R.L. Garnons-Williams, a midshipman in *Belfast,* 'we took a wrong turning and strayed towards the ammo dump and were stopped and scattered into the ditch by a shout of "halt!" followed smartly by the whine of a bullet and the crack of a rifle. We learned later that a sentry had shot his Commanding Officer — who had strayed — a few days earlier! As we were in a group our sentry had probably only fired in our general direction and missed! It certainly taught us not to be casual with Americans in the future.'

Iceland was out of range of the normal BBC broadcasts and the ships had to make their own entertainment. In *Duke of York,* there were films in the hangar, and endless playing of records on the ship's internal S.R.E. (Sound Reproduction Equipment). Some enterprising sailors, such as Woodhouse, wrote their own radio scripts for shows such as the 'Goon's Club'. There were ship's concerts: *Duke of York* had several men who had been professional entertainers in civilian life, including a singer called Robertson Dean, and every warship has amateur talent.

But most sailors for most of the time had to make their own amusements. Captain Creasy himself took up tapestry work. There were dozens of painters, carvers, metal-workers, whittlers, modellers and marquetry workers, knitters and seamsters. One man collected ten thousand match sticks and built a model of *Duke of York.* Another unravelled worn-out woollen clothing and made it up into rugs and mats. A third unpicked the coloured threads from cotton waste and sewed patterns on canvas. There were occasional exhibitions of arts and crafts on board. Many men earned money in their spare time, running 'firms' for tailoring, a 'snob shop' (cobblers), 'dhobeying' (laundry) and barbers. The most popular sport was fishing, with lines over the side. Some did physical training, or judo, or weight-lifting, in the dog watches. The ship had a very good boxing team, with at least three sailors who had been professional pugilists before they joined the Navy.

Compared with Iceland, even the rigorous climate and spartan pleasures of Scapa Flow seemed like the 'bright lights' of the 'Riviera' to the sailors of the Home Fleet. Scapa was at least a return to something approaching a normal life, although not all would agree that Scapa Flow was 'normal'. It was as bare and bleak as Iceland and just as treeless, a sea-scape of space and sky and sea-birds, where the Northern Lights crackled and the Scapa wind blew most days and most nights, sometimes for days and nights on end. An Orkney gale could blow away a barrage balloon with ease, taking its tender and all its ancillary equipment, and clear a fuelling jetty of full fifty-gallon drums as though they were thistledown.

In winter, it was dark at Scapa Flow by three-thirty in the afternoon and it stayed dark until the middle of the forenoon. In summer it was hardly dark at all. A man could read a newspaper on the upper deck comfortably until well after half-past eleven at night. A prolonged stay in Scapa without leave sometimes gave rise to a form of dementia known as 'Scapa Rats'; the sufferer exhibited a large range of clinical symptoms, from a mild obsession with growing a beard to an uncontrollable urge to leap into the Flow and strike out for some mythical shore, shouting 'Good old Gallipoli' in between gulps of incoming water.

Ashore there were many more facilities than there had been for the sailors of the previous war. On Flotta, the island in Hoxa Sound, there was a NAAFI club, a beer canteen, football matches and cricket in season, athletics and, of course, walking. There was a golf course, laid out by the men of the Grand Fleet twenty-five years before, and there were even squash courts across the Flow at Lyness, where a considerable base eventually grew up.

At Scapa there was regular mail, newspapers and BBC broadcasts. Scapa was also well within the operational range of ENSA, with shows and concerts and recitals. There was a Fleet Entertainment Officer, Lt.Cdr 'Kim' Peacock RNVR, who was reputed to have been one of Gertrude Lawrence's leading men. Some of the performers had mixed receptions. Evelyn Laye came on board *Duke of York* one forenoon, to look round the ship. By the time she had finished her tour and been entertained in the wardroom, the sailors were having their dinners.

'Suddenly', said Peter Woodhouse, 'she came over on the SRE saying that she thought we might like to hear her sing to us. Then, accompanied by the First Lieutenant on the wardroom piano, she launched into a rather high-falutin' — and high pitched — song. It was not well received. Tots had been drunk, gibbering was taking place, soup was being slurped, so the only response to her kind effort was 'Switch that bloody row off!'

Best of all were the concerts put on by the ships themselves, such as the grand gala performance for HM The King in August 1943, His Majesty's second visit to Scapa of that year, but his first with Fraser as C-in-C. King George VI, himself a professional sailor, who had been at Jutland as a Sub-Lieutenant, much enjoyed his visits to the fleet, which were as big morale-boosters for the men at Scapa as his father's visits had been in the previous war.

The King should have gone to sea on Friday 13th, but that ill-omened day was changed because of the Fleet's superstitious care for the King's safety. Instead, His Majesty visited *Malaya, London* and the Greek destroyer *Themistocles,* had lunch in *Anson,* and then went to Sutherland Pier to attend a concert in the new theatre built by working parties from the ships and the shore batteries under the general supervision of REME.

There was a Wren choir, and two Petty Officers from *Anson* performed 'The Green Eye of thee Little Yellow God; one reciting, the other standing behind him making 'appropriate gestures'. The Physical Training Instructors of the fleet went through some energetic exercises in unison; 'some were rather pathetic,' noted Midshipman Peter Cree of *Duke of York,* bleakly, in his Journal, 'the sere and yellow was visible under the weather-beaten countenance and singlet and shorts are not the best garb with which to hide the globular advance of age'. Collapse of elderly vaulting horses.

Lt.Cdr Peacock himself 'contributed a very amusing imitation of an ARP warden lecturing on Gas to a service audience'. But the *'piéce de resistance'* was a sketch written by Lt. Vivian Cox RNVR, of *Duke of York,* called 'The Petticoat Battleship', in which what Cree called 'a motley selection of officers' 'designed' a battleship like dress-makers — 'the various shades of grey, the artistic grouping of guns, and the armoured belt (rather indelicate, only to be discussed in private) ... '

Everyone who served in *Duke of York* has his own memories of Scapa: the seemingly interminable journey up there, in the train 'Admiral Jellicoe', and the often fearsome boat trip from Scrabster across the tidal rips and occasionally terrifyingly steep waves of the Pentland Firth; the rat- and cockroach-infested accommodation ship *Dunluce Castle;* the seal who regularly swam around the ship's port after gangway and developed a *penchant* for chocolate; the concerts held in the 12th Century cathedral of St Magnus in Kirkwall; the HMS *Hood* Memorial Chapel, only recently a cow-shed for a local crofter, but rebuilt, reroofed, and decorated with the crests of many ships on its austere walls; the Toc H centre in Kirkwall, which served some 10,000 troops a week in its heyday, with its library, billiard tables and recreation room; and all the legends of Scapa — the basking shark which once swallowed a Master at Arm's alarm clock back in the 1930s and could still be heard tolling its bell as it crossed the bar ... and the snow bunting which once nested on board *Norfolk* and now returned, bearing the ghost of Nelson, whenever the ship went to sea ... and the mermaid who once combed her hair until it shone so bright it guided Prien and U.47 in to sink *Royal Oak* ...

For Peter Cree and some of the other midshipmen there were occasional *banyan* swimming and picnic parties with the C-in-C, giving some pleasant *vignettes* of Fraser in his unbuckled hours. Once they took steak, sausages, and potatoes, tinned peaches 'and the best cheese I have tasted for years' over to Swanbister. 'It was worth a fortune just to see the Commander-in-Chief splashing his flag lieutenant who was chary of entering the chilly water, bouncing a soccer ball on his secretary sleeping in the sun, and stalking a cow for milk, a bunch of tempting grass in one hand and a glass in the other ... '

But the most pleasant memories of all are of the dances: by 1943 there were many hundreds of Service women, Wrens, ATS, Waafs, and nurses from the hospital ships, serving in a score of bases and establishments all over the Orkneys. The first Wrens arrived in Kirkwall in 1940 and were restricted to the employment then considered fit for women: cooks, orderlies, drivers, storekeepers and clerks. But, as the war went on, their responsibilities grew with their numbers, and by 1943 Wrens were working as coders, boarding officers, meteorologists, hydrographers, and doing maintenance work on torpedoes, aircraft and guns.

There was, in fact, nothing the Wrens could not do — except go to sea. Ships were open to Service visitors on Sundays when Wrens, ATS, and Waafs came on board and, as Peter Woodhouse recalls 'gave us the pleasure of their very chaste company for a few hours; this went on until a couple of ATS girls were plied with pusser's rum and met with a fate worse than death before they went ashore. After that, the visits were stopped.'

It was a kindly-meant but misunderstood gesture by Fraser himself, when he invited his own Wren driver to make a trip, alone and unaccompanied by any other Wren, on board one of H.M. Ships, which precipitated a major crisis in the W.R.N.S. Fraser thought it a 'storm in a tea cup' but such was the brouhaha, with dark talk of 'resignations' by senior Wren officers, that Fraser had to ask the Director of WRNS, the 'chief goldcrested wren of them all' to come up to Scapa. Fraser eventually charmed her into stirring the flagship's Christmas puddings, and all was smiles. But it had been a nervous episode.

It was a leading Wren, a signalling wren, who has left the perfect description of Scapa life: 'We had magnificent views of Orkney by day and night — even the blackout was wonderful, with the Northern Lights — and the summer days when the sun was still up at midnight were glorious. Then, it never really got dark, just dusk merging into dawn. We worked watches of four hours on and four hours off for twenty-four hours on end, and then had twenty-four hours off altogether. Those were precious off-duty spells in the course of which we could explore the islands, climb up to those magnificent cliffs around the Old Man of Hoy, see the loveliest wild flowers and drink in the smell of it all, the flowers, the sea, the heather — and the ships' oil and the jetties.

'Our quarters were at Haybrake, where we slept in big huts, twenty-eight in each hut. For those whose taste did not run to cliff walks there was plenty to do off duty. The base cinema at Lyness was free and the Garrison Theatre for the Army, nearer Long Hope, charged 3d., 6d., and 9d. And the films were always the latest. Every Saturday night there was a Base dance; and we had loads of invitations to Fleet dances at Flotta and Army dances at one or other of the Lyness camps.

'Yes, life in the Orkneys was great fun. Or was it just because I was only nineteen that such things stick in the memory more than the unpleasant recollections. Surely I am forgetting how cold, wet and windy it was there for months on end, how awful the food was; and how our bread always arrived soaked from the mainland, bearing mould in all the colours of the Northern Lights!'

On the day after the concert, His Majesty embarked in *Duke of York* who, with *Renown, Anson, Belfast, Phoebe*, and led by the Indian sloop *Godavari*, went to sea for a full day's programme of exercises: the main and secondary armaments carried out reduced charge shoots, the anti-aircraft guns fired at towed drogue targets, aircraft 'strafed' the ships, submarines and 'E-boats' made attacks, and there was an engagement with two 'enemy' cruisers.

The 'King's Day' was, in fact, not so very different from a dozen other day's training in which, as the sailors said, 'Gunnery was the great god'. The guns crews were constantly drilled and exercised. There were frequent sub-calibre shoots (it being too expensive to use full calibre ammunition, and too wearing on guns and barrels). In the Flow, destroyers steamed up and down, acting as moving targets, to give directors and range-takers practise in estimating an enemy's course, speed and inclination. Below decks, there was an elaborate model of an enemy ship at sea, according to Leading Seaman R.O.L. Thomas, one of 'Penzance' director's crew (and incidentally a member of the *Duke of York*'s boxing team), this was 'a contraption fitted with levers which activated imitation 'fall of shot' splashes and we had to call out the necessary spotting corrections.'

Nevertheless, the months went by and *Duke of York* still had no chance to use her gunnery expertise. She went to sea in March 1942 for the Home Fleet's abortive search for *Tirpitz,* returning with the rest, bitterly disappointed at a golden chance missed; she provided distant cover for the Russian convoys PQ.17 in July, and PQ.18 in September. In November she steamed south, to act as Admiral Sir Neville Syfret's flagship for the 'Torch' landings in north Africa. There, *Duke of York* lay off Algiers by day, and swept northwards by night, in the hope of meeting the enemy. But, unlike *Scharnhorst, Duke of York* had still never fired her guns in anger.

Occasionally, on certain rare summer evenings, a magical calm, like a tranquility of the soul as well of the elements, descended upon Scapa Flow. The waters of the Flow spread out as flat as a mirror, in which the silhouettes of the motionless ships at anchor were perfectly reproduced. The air was so still a puff of tobacco smoke hung for what seemed like minutes. Sounds carried for miles: every word of a bosun's mate on the quarterdeck of the ship astern could be clearly heard, and the Royal Marine bugler was audibly clearing his throat in the flagship a quarter of a mile away. When the bugle's notes had floated out over the silent Flow, every ship lowered her jack and ensign, taking her time from the flagship and being careful not to complete the lowering before the flagship.

In the flagship, Fraser's day usually ended with a familiar routine, like a well-loved ritual. The Flag Lieutenant would take in the last batch of signals at some time between eleven and eleven-fifteen. As Fraser sat down to read them, he would say 'Have a night-cap, Flags'. Flags would say 'Thank you, sir' and Fraser would invariably add, 'And pour me a Scotch'. 'He'd read the signals while I got the drinks, then I'd sit on the back of the settee, facing his desk, and he'd say "Right Flags, what are we going to do tomorrow?"'.

The true, the only proper answer to that, lay far in the north, behind the nets and booms and patrol vessels of Alta Fjord.

CHAPTER 3

Bey and the *Scharnhorst*

IN April 1943, shortly after they arrived in Alta Fiord, *Scharnhorst, Tirpitz* and nine destroyers made a short sortie to the area of Bear Island. It was grandiosely called a 'patrol', but according to *Scharnhorst*'s survivors it was not much more than an exercise, and, from their accounts, there was the strong inference that nothing much more than that could have been expected from *Tirpitz*.

Scharnhorst's relations with *Tirpitz,* the flagship, normally secured in her berth further down Kaa Fiord, were far from cordial. All *Scharnhorst*'s survivors spoke slightingly of *Tirpitz*. Discipline in *Tirpitz* was reputed to be much stricter than in *Scharnhorst*. *Tipritz*'s commanding officer, Captain Meyer, was supposed not to be much of a seaman, and was referred to in derogatory terms. *Tirpitz*'s ship's company were generally much younger and much less experienced than *Scharnhorst*'s, who had mostly served together for years and seen action together. According to *Scharnhorst*, *Tirpitz*'s 'boys had a hangdog look about them'. Nothing would have induced a *Scharnhorst* man to transfer voluntarily to *Tirpitz*. When some leading stokers from *Scharnhorst* were drafted to *Tirpitz,* ever afterwards when they met their former ship-mates they bemoaned their fate, and pined for the good old days in *Scharnhorst*.

Morale in *Scharnhorst* was evidently high to the end and even survived the disaster of the sinking. No officer survived. The senior survivor was a petty officer. Only four survivors had action stations above decks, where they had any chance to see what was happening. The rest were largely unable to tell the differences between torpedo hits, shell hits, or the concussion of their own guns firing. Leaderless, and after the shock of the action and *Scharnhorst*'s last dramatic minutes, her survivors could have been expected to be apathetic, demoralised and ready to fall in with almost any suggestion by their captors.

On the contrary, *Scharnhorst*'s survivors together presented what their interrogators were surprised to discover was 'a front of tough, courteous security-consciousness'. Their continuing pride in their ship, and their meagre and limited knowledge of the action, gave their interrogators a very difficult interrogation problem, especially as some of them had been inexpertly examined already and had received enough information from

British sailors about the action to colour their own versions. Their accounts of the action have to be treated with a certain reserve.

But there can be no doubt about their feelings towards their ship, their memories of events and living conditions on board, their view of their officers, and their recollections of life in a foreign occupied country in a hostile climate. They were living an isolated existence for months at a time, hundreds of miles from home, with no regular newspapers and little news of everyday events, apart from the ship's internal broadcast system. They knew little of what was happening on the eastern front, and had no chance to hear first-hand accounts of bombing and its effects upon civilian morale in Germany. They therefore impressed their interrogators with their tendency to have an 'almost colonial mentality', being 'more German than the Germans'.

The climate was particularly trying for men from the plains of northern Europe. The mountain sides, and the ranks of dark trees, like illustrations from childhood books of *Grimm's Fairy Tales,* seemed unchanging and unfriendly, whatever the season. In the winter, ice crept cut from the shore, as though looking for the ships in the fiord, and the cold eventually penetrated into the very depths of the ships. In the spring, when the ice partially melted, the shoreline became a morass of mud and melting ice. In the summer, the sun never set, but it was never really warm; what heat there was bred myriads of biting midges which made trips ashore a misery. At any time of the year, when there was a gale at sea, wild winds would hit the inland side of the mountains and bounce back and forth from side to side, churning the fjord waters into confusion. These torrents of freezing air, known in Norwegian as *Elvegust* poured down from the high mountains and whipped the waters into a surface storm so that massive clouds of icy spray, known as *Havrog*, swept the ships from stem to stern.

On board *Scharnhorst*, the day began when the hands were called at 6 am. to lash up and stow hammocks and have breakfast. At 7.30 hands fell in to clean ship. From 9 until 11 am there was instruction, exercises and work ship. Dinner was from 11.30 to 1.45 pm. In the afternoons from 1.45 to 5 pm. there was more work and exercises. For work, messing, action stations, and welfare, the sailors were in eleven divisions: four for the seamen, two for anti-aircraft weapon personnel, one for the 'daymen' such as cooks and stewards, one for the technical ratings, three for stokers and engine-room personnel, one for electrical ratings and one for communications personnel.

The hands were free from 4 pm. until 7 pm. when the technical divisions fell in to clean their parts of ship. Technical divisions rounds were from 7.50 pm to 8.05. At ten past eight, the seamen cleaned their parts of ships and had their rounds from 8.50 to 9.15. At 9.30 hammocks were slung, at 10 pm. lights out and pipe down.

At the Arctic summer drew on, *Scharnhorst*'s sailors were thrown more and more upon their own resources. There was little to spend their money on and thus a great deal of card-playing, in which large sums of money were won and lost. Strictly speaking, playing cards for money was forbidden, but the officers appear to have 'shut their eyes to it'. The nearest village worth the name was Bossekop, some three miles across the water from *Scharnhorst*'s usual berth just inside a spit of land called Oskarnesset, where the sailors went ashore for skiing (at which some of them became extremely expert) and for football in the summer. Later, two piers were built, named Hansa and Bluecher, south of another village called Sopnes, where liberty boats could land. The sailors used to go ashore after dinner and be back on board by 5.30 pm. Otherwise, there were three cinema projectors on board, with the latest German films, and education and feature 'shorts', attended by divisions, in rotation. There was also a large and well-stocked ship's library, with novels and adventure stories, and 'a very few' books on politics.

In November 1943 there was a rare and exotic arrival in Kaa Fiord. The 'KDF' ship *Emmanuel Rambur*, 2,000 tons, a kind of entertainments ship, arrived for a stay of fourteen days. *Scharnhorst*'s sailors went across to her, by divisions, for either a matinée or an evening performance. On arrival every sailor was presented with a glass of red wine, a packet of biscuits and a pack of ten cigarettes stamped with the slogan 'A present from Terbovn'. The first part of the performance was a singsong by five Red Cross sisters and fifteen Norwegian girls, 'ostensibly travelling as stewardesses'. The second part was 'three ageing night-club performers' accompanied by a six-piece orchestra which used to play in 'one of the lesser Berlin cafes' and now called itself 'The Scharnhorst Sextet'.

After the show, the sailors were always taken straight back on board. They complained that the officers were allowed to stay in the KDF ship, indeed they spent the night on board, or brought some of the girls to spend the night in their cabins in *Scharnhorst*.

Very few sailors went on leave to Germany while *Scharnhorst* was in Norway. Leave was rarely granted except on compassionate grounds, and small batches of sailors went at very irregular intervals. The journey back to Germany was an ordeal in itself. There was first the steamer to Sopenes, then a bus to Alt-Eidet, followed by another steamer down the 500 kilometres to Narvik and an overnight stay before going on to Tromso, Harstadt and Trondheim. From Trondheim there was a 24-hour train journey to Oslo and a third steamer to Copenhagen or Aarhus, followed by another train to Berlin. There were frequent delays and overnight stops, sometimes lasting more than one day. A man's leave did not actually start until he crossed the German frontier, which was just as well; one *Scharnhorst* sailor said it had taken him from 3 am. on 3rd October 1943, until 4 pm. on 16th, to get from Kaa Fiord to Germany. 'Of course,' he said, 'if you're an admiral you get a plane and do the whole thing in two days in style.'

On 14th October, a plane landed on the waters of Alta Fiord, bearing a relief captain for Huffmeier. This event was greeted with huge sighs of satisfaction on board, for 'Poldi''s bad luck had continued. On 14th May, when *Scharnhorst* had been embarking stores and ammunition in Alta Fiord, there was a serious accident. The ship was subdivided into 21 watertight sections, numbered from I to XXI, and had six decks: a 'Batterie' (Battery) Deck, 'Zwischen' (Tween) Deck, 'Panzer' (Armoured) Deck, and three 'Platform' Decks, the 'Oberes' (Upper), 'Mittleres' (Middle) and 'Unteres' (Lower). While stores were being brought on board there was a violent explosion on the 'Tween Deck, in Section III. There was an 'immediate panic' and 'C' Turret magazine was flooded as a precaution. In the area of the explosion there was 'nothing but mass of severed pipes, decapitated bodies and odd limbs'.

Those human remains were gathered up and placed in 18 hammocks. But when a roll call of the ship's company was held, only 17 men were found to be missing. The contents of one of the hammocks was apparently made up of the odd limb or two belonging to the others. This was held, for some reason, to be the fault, not of 'Poldi' but of the Engineer Officer, Korvetten Kapitan (Ing) König. Next of kin were informed that the men 'had fallen in action against the enemy'.

On 6th September 1943, *Tirpitz, Scharnhorst* and ten destroyers sailed from Alta Fiord for Operation ZITRONELLA, a sortie against the Allied shore installations on the island of Spitzbergen. This became a special bone of contention between the ship's companies of the two capital ships. *Scharnhorst* strongly suspected *Tirpitz* of cheating over the matter of the awards of Iron Crosses, Second Class, afterwards.

Spitzbergen, some 600 miles to the north, had a small party of British and Norwegian meteorologists, with a small garrison of Norwegian soldiers. It was hardly a major strategic objective and clearly it had been chosen as a 'soft target' to give the ships some sea time and German propaganda a chance to publish some pictures of German ships in action, ostensibly firing at an enemy. However, this did not fool *Scharnhorst*'s sailors, who called the whole operation 'a somewhat hollow victory'.

The German ships flew British flags, and a wireless message was intercepted from the island, reporting that 'British ships were approaching'. The German ensign was hoisted and the big ships opened fire, while the destroyers, each with a landing party of some 100 soldiers, closed the shore. *Scharnhorst* and six destroyers actually went into the harbour, 'just as though we were a minesweeper' said a *Scharnhorst* sailor aggrievedly, while *Tirpitz* and the other destroyers stayed outside.

Whilst the big ships bombarded (this was the only occasion when *Tirpitz* can really be said to have fired her main armament in anger) the troops landed and looted various supply dumps and stores, bringing large quantities of cocoa, chocolate, butter, cheese and ham back on board the destroyers. The troops were accompanied by cameramen who took pictures of buildings and shore installations being blown up. The W/T and meteorological stations were destroyed, some coal mine shafts flooded, some oil storage tanks set on fire, and some prisoners taken. It was useful target practice for the gunners, although *Scharnhorst*'s sailors said that 'the final shooting-up' of a 'few card-board houses' was, in their view, a 'distinct anti-climax'.

The guns on shore fired back and did an embarrassingly large amount of damage. The destroyers Z.29 and Z.33 were both damaged. Z.33 had to be taken in tow and Z.29 had to shelter in *Tirpitz*'s lee while patches were welded on the shell-holes in her side. The force then withdrew and returned to Alta Fjord. News of their operation was received in London on 8th and the Home Fleet put to sea. But it was obvious that the birds had flown, and the fleet returned. A Catalina flying boat flew in with fresh wireless equipment on 23rd September and communications were restored for the rest of the war.

Afterwards, the ship's company of *Tirpitz* were awarded some 400 Iron Crosses, amidst accusations of having 'rigged' the points required by the sailors of *Scharnhorst*, who received only 160 Crosses between them, and who had, in their view, done all the hard work and been in commission so very much longer. Relations between the two ships sank to their lowest level.

There was one tragic sequel. A leading seaman from one of the destroyers, who was coxswain of a boat taking troops ashore, was absent from his post and was later found hiding in a corner of the ship. He was court-martialled for cowardice in the face of the enemy, found guilty and sentenced to be executed by shooting. The melancholy ceremony was carried out on *Scharnhorst*'s quarterdeck. This, too, caused a great deal of feeling on board. The sailors thought that *Scharnhorst* was being called upon to do *Tirpitz*'s 'dirty work', and risked bringing 'bad joss' upon their own ship.

The three great ships, *Tirpitz, Scharnhorst* and *Lutzow*, might have been out of the Allies' sight, up in Norway, but they were certainly not out of mind. *Tirpitz* in particular was a special 'bogey' ship. For years, she had been lurking far away in the north, hidden equally by clouds of *Havrog* and rumour, crouching in her northern fastness, a creature of powerful myth and menace, like Grendel's mother. As the years passed, she seemed to swell, growing ever more dangerous in the Allies imaginations, the more they thought about her.

Such a monster could never be allowed to lie unmolested. Since the first tentative fly-overs by Hampden bombers, while she was still building in Wilhelmshaven in 1940, there had been many attempts to sink *Tirpitz*, by many Allied arms, from Bomber Command, several times, to the Norwegian Resistance, to the Russian Air Force, to the Fleet Air Arm, at sea in March 1942. All had failed, until September 1943, when six 'X' craft 'midget' submarines set off from Loch Cairnbawn in northern Scotland, to be towed by 'orthodox' submarines to their target release areas.

X5, X6 and X7 were to attack *Tirpitz* in Kaa Fiord, X9 and X10, *Scharnhorst*, off Oskarneset, and X8 was to attack *Lutzow*, then in Lange Fiord, another tributary of Alta Fiord, north of Kaa Fiord. X9 was lost with all hands on passage. X8 was also lost, having to be scuttled. But on 22nd September X5, X6 and X7 all penetrated Kaa Fiord and, although X5 was lost before making her attack, X6 and X7 placed their two two-ton explosive charges underneath or very close to *Tirpitz*. The great ship tried to manoeuvre herself away, and partially succeeded, but the detonations damaged her badly enough to keep her out of the war until the spring of 1944. The Captains of X6 and X7, Lieuts. Donald Cameron and Godfrey Place, both received Victoria Crosses.

Scharnhorst was lucky again. X10 could not make an attack because of defects, and *Scharnhorst* was in any case away from her berth, at sea, doing gunnery exercises, reputedly because of her poor showing at Spitzbergen, (although there had never been any complaints about her gunnery before).

Lutzow also escaped but she had already been making preparations to go back to the Baltic. On 21st September, Special Intelligence revealed that additional heavy fighters were being transferred to Bodo. This was a familiar sign that some movement of heavy ships might be about to take place. Eight heavy fighters from Banak landed at Bodo on 23rd. A Russian aircraft made a reconnaisance of Lange Fjord at 8.45 am. on 23rd and reported that *Lutzow* had moved from her protected berth and was lying in mid-stream. She in fact sailed from Lange Fjord later that day.

Signals from Admiral Commanding Polar Coast were being read concurrently at that time and one sent at 11 am. on 23rd and deciphered very shortly afterwards, said that German naval forces were to be expected in inshore waters on 23rd and 24th. At 5.40 the same day, a signal from the German Admiralty forbade the sending of 'dummy messages' on Kootwijk or Naval Air Operational frequencies up to 27th September inclusive. The ether was being cleared for *Lutzow*.

So, too, was her route, of submarines. An anti-submarine hunt was carried out off Aandaslnes on 24th. Late on 25th a signal repeated to *Lutzow* and the 5th Destroyer Flotilla requested radio beacons to be activated at Skraaven, Maaloey, Landegoode and Buholmraasa (all points on the route southward) in succession from 26th. German air force intentions for that day included patrols from the Lofotens, and continuous 'close escort for formation'. At 2.08 pm. the same day, a 'Secret' signal informed all Home Commands that a 'B2' (agent's report, Second Class reliability) stated that a pocket-battleship, probably *Lutzow*, escorted by five destroyers, had passed Renga, south of Narvik, at 8.10 am. speed 15 knots. *Lutzow* had in fact reached Narvik on 24th and sailed again on 26th.

By now there was more than enough indication that *Lutzow* was at sea, and running. Special Intelligence learned that naval authorities at Molde had told the Admiral Commanding North Norwegian Coast at 1 pm on 25th that unless the weather improved greatly, the 'marker-boats' could not be laid out in the positions previously ordered. They would be ready in Holde the next day. The Admiral replied, referring to an operation by its codeword, that the 'time-table between Aalesund and Haugesund had been advanced by an hour and a half. 'Marker-boats' always prefaced the passage of a big ship. That codeword had already been used in connection with the

Luftwaffe orders for 'close escort' on 26th. The accelerated timetable suggested that the ships might well carry on southward without entering Trondheim. AT 8.30 pm on 26th, *Lutzow* was told that she and her escort would come under the operational control of the German Admiralty as from 9 pm that day. This meant that *Lutzow* was by then approaching latitude 63'30'N (off Kristiansund).

A reconnaissance of the west coast of Norway was made at first light on 27th and at 6.24 am. a pocket battleship and five destroyers were sighted some 13 miles west-south west of Kristiansund. However, the accuracy of the report was doubted. It was very possible that the enemy ships were even further south. *Lutzow* was seen again, at 6 pm, with four destroyers, well south of Bergen, in latitude 59'40''N.

By then, the Fleet Air Arm had made an attempt to catch her. When Admiral Fraser had received news of the agent's sighting report he had considered sending *Ranger* to a position where her aircraft could attack *Lutzow* as she passed Cape Stadtlandet. But it was already too late. Nor could Coastal Command mount an attack. By a sequence of unlucky chances, they did not have the aircraft available. However, there was another possibility. No.832 Squadron, Fleet Air Arm, equipped with American Grumman Avenger torpedo-bombers had just disembarked from *Victorious*.

The Avengers landed at Hatston in the Orkneys on 26th and were quickly rearmed with torpedoes. They flew early next day to the Coastal Command air station at Sumburgh, in the Shetlands. When the reconnaissance report of 6.24 am was received, Fraser wanted to dispatch the Avengers at once. But Coastal Command replied that the air escort was inadequate, the aircraft had never worked together, time was too short to allow a proper plan to be prepared, and there was not enough cloud cover. In the event, even the escort promised was not available. Air Vice Marshall Ellwood therefore cancelled the attack.

Admiral Fraser had then to make the point to the Air Vice Marshal, fairly forcibly, that Fleet Air Arm crews were very highly trained, and that had they been flown from a carrier they would not have had any escort, and would have had to take their chances with the cloud cover. Coastal Command at last yielded to the arguments and the Avengers took off at 12.16 pm, escorted by three Beaufighters. The force made a landfall off the Norwegian coast and, relying on the 6.24 am report position, began to search to the north. Actually, *Lutzow* was about 40 miles to the south at the time.

Another striking force, escorted by Wildcat fighters from *Ranger*, was made ready for the 28th. *Lutzow* had been warned to expect air attacks. She was met by a fighter escort early on 28th and passed safely through the Sound and into the Baltic that day. Two destroyers returned to Kristiansund, two went on to Kiel. Z.38 escorted *Lutzow* through the Sound and then entered Kiel. Preceded by some energetic mine-sweeping, *Lutzow* reached Gdynia on 1st October.

Lutzow in fact never sailed west of the Great Belt again. She supported the seaward flanks of the German Army in 1944. On 21st April 1945 she was bombed by RAF Lancasters while lying in the Kaiserfahrte, south of Swinemunde; she was driven ashore by the damage caused by several near misses. Her wreck was blown up, *in situ,* on 4th May.

But, in 1943, *Lutzow*'s passage down through the Norwegian 'Leads' and back to the Baltic, without a finger being laid on her, caused a great deal of heart-searching at Scapa Flow and in the Admiralty. It was a frustrating time for Fraser. He had put to sea in *Duke of York* when he heard of the Spitzbergen raid, but soon had to call off the operation when he realised the trail was cold. Now, after four years of war, when the fleet and Coastal Command should *surely* have improved their liaison, a major enemy warship had got away scot free. Joint investigation, with Coastal Command, showed the need for improved tactical doctrines, for more air searches, further north, and much earlier; but the implications were still ominous for Fraser: if *Lutzow* could do it, why not *Scharnhorst?*

Scharnhorst was now the only operational major German warship left in the north. Her new commanding officer, Kapitan zur See Fritz Julius Hintze, had been navigating officer of the light cruiser *Emden,* then navigating officer and latterly captain of the heavy cruiser *Admiral Hipper.* He had his idiosyncrasies. He was reputed to stay in his bunk until 10 am most days, after which he took a turn round the quarterdeck for an hour or so. He also enjoyed a 'stretch off the land' in his cabin from 1 pm until 3 pm. His cabin was directly under a 105 mm. gun mounting which was near the bridge. Nobody was allowed to walk near the gun, not even for cleaning or maintenance, whilst the Captain had his siesta. Hintze was an avid film-goer, and regularly attended the ship's film shows. Although the survivors later criticised his handling of the ship, Hintze rapidly restored the good feeling of '*Scharnhorst* Immer Voran' in the ship, and made himself genuinely popular with the sailors in his short time as captain. It is clear that morale on board might have been quite different had 'Poldi' Huffmeier stayed in command.

On 28th September, while *Lutzow* was making good her escape into the Baltic, Fraser was in London attending a meeting of the Defence Committee (Operations). The nights were lengthening. The convoy season had come round again. The crippling of *Tirpitz* and the removal of *Lutzow* had changed the situation in the north to the Allies benefit. There were other events, which affected Fraser personally. If he wanted to, he could end this period of frustration and move on to higher things.

Admiral Sir Dudley Pound, the First Sea Lord, and Fraser's old friend and chief, had gone to Quebec with the Prime Minister for the Quadrant Conference in August 1943. Mr Churchill noticed that Pound played what he called 'a subdued part' in the 'far-ranging naval discussions'. This was unusual enough, but when Churchill heard that Pound had refused an invitation to go fishing after the Conference was over, he became seriously concerned. He knew Dudley Pound adored his fishing; he would get up early in the morning, if there was the least chance of a few hours fishing before returning to the Admiralty. Churchill now feared that all was not well.

These fears were confirmed a few days later, when Pound came to see Churchill and told him he had come to resign. He had suffered a stroke. His right side was largely paralysed. He had thought it would all pass off, but it had got worse everyday. He was no longer fit for duty. Churchill expressed his sympathy, and accepted Pound's resignation. He cabled to the Admiralty, to tell Admiral Syfret, the Vice Chief of Naval Staff, to take charge for the moment.

Pound went home in the battlecruiser *Renown*. Churchill invited him to join him, but Pound said he preferred to stay in his cabin and take his meals with his staff. Once home, Pound suffered another and even more severe stroke, which left him almost completely paralysed, unable to speak or to move most of his body. It seemed that Pound had given his health in the service of the nation. He had literally worked himself into his grave. When Churchill went to see him, he shook Pound's left hand and was surprised by the strength with which Pound gripped him. He had, as Churchill said, been a true comrade. He died on Trafalgar Day, 1943.

Meanwhile, Churchill had faced the problem of Pound's successor. He knew who he wanted. The obvious choice was Admiral Sir Andrew Cunningham, an officer of legendary reputation, especially in the Mediterranean, where he was Commander-in-Chief. Cunningham was proposed by the First Lord, Mr AV Alexander, and he was the man the whole Navy expected to take over.

But Churchill had other ideas. In his version of events, he wondered whether Cunningham could be spared from the Mediterranean 'at a time when so much was going forward and all operations expanding?'. In fact, there was another reason for Churchill's hesitation, which went deeper into the personalities of both men. Andrew Cunningham, 'A.B.C.', was a very strong character indeed. There had been sharpish exchanges of signals between him and Churchill earlier in the war. There is no doubt that Churchill looked round for an alternative before bringing such a tremendous personality to the Admiralty.

The man Churchill himself wanted was, of course, Bruce Fraser, and he offered him the post first — very probably after the Defence Committee meeting on 28th September. Fraser, in Churchill's view, was 'an officer of the highest seagoing reputation'. The two knew each other well, Fraser having been Third Sea Lord when Churchill was First Lord. Cunningham, on the other hand, had hardly served in the Admiralty, except for a few months in 1939 as Vice Chief of Naval Staff before he went out to the Mediterranean. Cunningham himself said that 'the office desk was not my strong suit'.

For Fraser, Churchill's offer was a tremendous compliment and a marvellous professional opportunity. He knew he could do the job. Pound's reputation had suffered somewhat as a result of the events around PQ.17.

Here was Fraser's chance to take up Pound's burden and put all right. But Fraser demurred. He told Churchill that of course he would go wherever he was sent, but he himself recommended Cunningham in the strongest terms. 'I believe that I have the confidence of my own fleet,' Fraser said, 'but Cunningham has the confidence of the whole Navy. I haven't even fought a battle yet. If one day I should sink the *Scharnhorst*, I might feel differently.' According to Churchill, Fraser asked him to 'weigh the matter longer'.

Churchill must have been a little taken aback by Fraser's refusal. Fraser himself said that Churchill 'more or less sat back at that and said 'Thank you very much'.' However, he noted that Fraser's 'attitude was most becoming'. The upshot was that Cunningham went to Chequers on 3rd October, where after a 'heart-to-heart' talk, Cunningham was offered, and accepted, the post as First Sea Lord. The appointment was announced on 4th (the 5th, according to Cunningham). Cunningham was relieved in the Mediterranean by Admiral Sir John Cunningham (no relation) and took over as First Sea Lord on 15th October.

For Fraser, now that he was going to continue in the Home Fleet, the most important subject at the meeting of 28th September was the resumption of Arctic convoys. By that time, it was clear that the tide was turning against the Wehrmacht on the Eastern Front. The disaster to Field Marshal Paulus' Sixth Army at Stalingrad in February had been followed by smashing Red Army successes in the battles of the Kursk salient in July. By September, the German Army was in retreat along the whole of the southern front, from Moscow down to the Black Sea. Smolensk in the north was retaken on 25th September. In the first days of October, the Russians were across the river Dnieper, north of the great provincial capital of Kiev. Nevertheless, on 21st September the Russian Foreign Minister M. Molotov, sent for the British Ambassador in Moscow and asked for the convoys to Russia to be resumed.

The resulting diplomatic episode was a most interesting exhibition of national attitudes. The Russians demanded the resumption of the convoys as of right, whilst at the same time hinting that the convoys were not *really* indispensable. Stalin himself responded to Churchill's proposals in the most offensive manner.

Churchill replied that the convoys were an intention, not a promise. Their resumption depended upon progress in negotiations for improving the lot of the British personnel in north Russia, who were still subjected to constant harassment. The Russians were still being unreasonable in all manner of ways, from mail censorship to the withholding of visas, and from unnecessarily harsh sentences on British offenders in Russian courts, to inadequate care and medical facilities for survivors of merchant ships.

It was eventually decided to restart the convoys by 15th November and to run them once a month until February, four convoys in all, each of thirty-five ships. In his telegram to Stalin of 1st October, announcing this, Churchill stressed that this was not a 'contract or bargain, but rather a declaration of our solemn and earnest resolve'. Stalin's reply was so offensive,

Churchill refused to receive it officially and handed it back to the Soviet Ambassador in London.

However, the convoys were to sail to Russia again, and the first requirement was to get back the merchant ships which had been at Kola since March. Captain Ian Campbell in the destroyer *Milne,* with seven other destroyers, a destroyer escort from Western Approaches Command, two minesweepers and a corvette sailed to collect them and escort them back. The opportunity was taken to sail five Lend-Lease minesweepers, T.111-115, and six submarine-chasers, Bo.201, Bo.204 and Bo.208-211 for Polyarno, to join the Russian Northern Fleet.

Campbell's party arrived at Kola safely on 28th October. Campbell noticed at once a slight improvement in Anglo-Russian relations. For the first time the escorts were allowed to berth alongside the jetties in Polyarno, instead of having to stay at anchor out in Vaenga Bay. Campbell himself did his best to be sociable with his Russian hosts. The usual official visits and calls were made and returned. Campbell and the Russian Commander-in-Chief Admiral Arseni Golovko dined together and exchanged presents. But, as Campbell said, 'it was uphill work. The language difficulty could have been overcome with good will, but all gaiety and light-hearted talk was smothered by the attitude of the dour, unsmiling political commissars who attended every occasion, their mean, suspicious eyes flickering like those of cornered animals'.

The return convoy RA 54A, of 13 ships, sailed on 1st November and arrived at Loch Ewe on 14th, having been completely unmolested. But, as Campbell said, 'it would have been something of a miracle if the Germans had found it at all in the combination of fog, snow and winter gales through which it made its blind, storm-tossed way'. The only event of note was the rare sighting, on 6th November, of Bear Island, which featured so often in tales of Arctic convoys but which so few people had ever actually seen. Although one wag among the escort captains signalled Campbell 'Request permission to land libertymen', Bear Island was not a place to inspire affection. It was, as Campbell said, 'one of those sinister, solitary outcrops of land in the ocean which the seaman views with a shiver of distaste'.

The Admiralty had actually undertaken to send 40 ships a month to Russia but Fraser, like Tovey before him, thought this was too large a number to sail in a single convoy, especially during the winter when gales would scatter the merchantmen and make them easier prey. So the first northbound convoy of the new cycle, JW 54A, of 18 ships, left Loch Ewe on 15th November, escorted by eight destroyers, a minesweeper and two corvettes. The Russian minesweepers, T.116 and 117, and three more submarine chasers, Bo.206, Bo.207 and Bo.212, also went with the convoy. Although detected by the German B — Dienst Intelligence Decoding Service, the convoy reached Kola safely on 24th, whence some of the ships were given a Russian escort onward to Archangel. The second half, JW 54B, of 14 ships, left a week later on 22nd, escorted by nine destroyers, four corvettes and a rescue ship; they were met by four Russian destroyers, and arrived in Kola on 2nd December.

The escort group from JW 54A was ready to take the return convoy RA 54A, but unloading in all Russian ports was very slow indeed. Only eight ships were ready to sail on 26th November, from Archangel. The 'Eisenbart' Group of seven U-boats was deployed in the convoy's path but only U.307 briefly sighted escort vessels on 28th. It was at once counter-attacked and damaged with depth-charges. The convoy reached Loch Ewe without loss on 9th December. Its passage had been covered by a cruiser force, of *Kent*, *Jamaica* and *Bermuda*, under Rear Admiral A.F.E. Palliser. Vice Admiral Sir Henry Moore, in the battleship *Anson*, with the US cruiser *Tuscaloosa* and a destroyer escort, waited in the deep field. British submarines of the 9th Flotilla were in patrol areas off the north-west coast of Norway.

Thus, the new season had got off to a most encouraging start, with 32 loaded ships reaching north Russia and another 21 returning to the United Kingdom, all without loss. The German Naval Staff, realising at last that two convoys had passed entirely unmolested, belatedly began to review the situation.

When the British Admiralty, Fraser and the other admirals of the Home Fleet knew that Doenitz had replaced Raeder as Commander-in-Chief, they all expected a great deal more aggressive activity from the German Navy. In fact, 1943 had been a very quiet year, comparatively, in the Arctic. Certainly, Doenitz had saved the big ships, but so far he had done very little with them. By October 1943 the Northern Battle Group was down to *Scharnhorst* and two destroyer flotillas. On 17th November the 6th Flotilla went south, leaving five destroyers of the 4th Flotilla. But they were all 'Z' Class, and three of them were less than a year old. At some 3,600 tons full load, over 400 feet long, capable of over 38 knots, armed with five 15 cm. guns and eight torpedo tubes, the 'Z' Class were fast, large and formidable warships, much bigger, faster and more heavily armed (though possibly not as sea-worthy) as their British counter-parts. There were also two flotillas of U-boats, twenty submarines in all, based at Bergen and at Trondheim, each with its own depot ship.

On 8th November, the Northern Task Force commander Admiral Kummetz left on an extended leave for reasons of health. He had been a somewhat unlucky admiral, with a clammy touch and a listless handling of affairs. His flagship *Blucher* had been sunk by gun-fire and torpedoes from shore, in circumstances of peculiar incompetence, during the Norwegian campaign. In the New Year's Eve battle against JW 51B in the Barents Sea, Kummetz had flown his flag in *Hipper* and, with the captain of *Lutzow*, had succeeded in fumbling a splendid chance to destroy the convoy.

Kummetz had been in the Arctic since June 1942. He now went home to Germany for lengthy medical treatment. On the recommendation of Admiral Schniewind, Doenitz appointed Rear Admiral Erich Bey, the Rear Admiral (Destroyers) as a temporary replacement. Of Bey, Doenitz wrote

'Like Kummetz, he had grown up in destroyers and had received a comprehensive tactical training in both peace and war. He was an extremely efficient officer of very considerable war experience, and he had done well in all the appointments he had held'.

Of all the different personalities involved in *Scharnhorst*'s last days, Erich Bey, known as 'Achmed' Bey, was one of the most important and yet, at this distance of time, one of the most mysterious. As Doenitz said, 'We do not know what were the grounds which caused (Bey) to act as he did. We do not know whether we would have acted differently or more effectively and therefore we cannot criticise but can only ask questions.'

No doubt there were a good many questions Doenitz would have liked to have asked Bey, but the answers all perished with Bey. Certainly Achmed Bey began the war as a note-worthy destroyer officer, with the rank of Fregatten Kapitan (Commander) leading the 4th Flotilla, and made a minelaying sortie in *Erich Steinbrinck* to the Humber Estuary in November 1939. In February 1940, Bey's Flotilla laid more mines off Cromer Knoll.

Promoted Kapitan zur See, Bey commanded the 4th Flotilla under Commodore Bonte at Narvik in April 1940. When Bonte was killed in action against Warburton-Lee in *Hardy* on 10th, Bey took over command of the destroyers and here displayed the first signs of flaws, either in his judgment or his temperament. After dark on 10th, Bey took the two remaining German destroyers which were fit for sea, *Erich Giese* and *Wolfang Zenker*, and tried to break out of Narvik. But on sighting the cruiser *Penelope,* though he himself had not been detected, Bey turned back. In the event, none of the destroyers got away and Bey's eight surviving destroyers, in various states of seaworthiness, were all briskly sunk by *Warspite,* or scuttled, in a second battle of Narvik, on 13th April.

Oddly, Bey's professional reputation survived these set-backs and he was at sea again, in *Hans Lody,* laying mines in Falmouth Bay in September 1940, in action in the Bristol Channel with British cruisers and destroyers in October, and off Plymouth in November. Promoted Rear Admiral, flying his flag in Z.29, Bey led the destroyers in the 'Channel Dash' of *Scharnhorst, Gneisenau* and *Prinz Eugen* in February 1942.

Bey was described by a fellow German naval officer Korvetten Kapitan Fritz-Otto Busch as 'a man of massive build, an excellent seaman and a born destroyer commander. A soft heart beat behind a rather forbidding exterior. In the course of the war he had, as his own men put it, "wangled some tough jobs" and he had not set foot in a battleship since his time as a young midshipman'.

This remark of Bey's, 'the last time I was aboard a capital ship was as a cadet', is often quoted by German commentators, as though in some way it excused his performance. It might indeed be used in mitigation. But Tovey, Cunningham, Vian and many other most successful admirals, were all destroyer men and their experience in those ships was much to their advantage when they came to command heavy ships (although, perhaps

Kummetz was the exception which very severely tested the rule). *Scharnhorst*'s ship's company, of course, knew of Bey's destroyer background. They said he 'had no business to be commanding the battle group'. But possibly they believed he had been tainted by *Tirpitz*.

However, Kummetz had some sound advice for Bey before he left. He advised him to wait until *Tirpitz* was ready again, so that both capital ships could operate together. On her own, *Scharnhorst* would be vulnerable to enemy destroyers, with their superior radar. He reminded Bey that he could not rely on the Luftwaffe for action against surface ships. The prevailing winds, and the usual progress of the weather, was from west to east which gave the enemy weather forecasters an advantage. In other words, the enemy would also be liable to find *Scharnhorst* more quickly and more accurately than she could find them. Kummetz recommended that Bey should ask for the destroyers to be restored again. In Kummetz's opinion, they were the best means of attacking a convoy. It was all sound advice, and Bey took it as far as he was able. But the destroyers were not sent back when he asked for them.

By 20th November the German Naval Staff had considered the likely course of fleet operations that winter and issued their directive. It was a cautiously-worded document and laid down no hard intentions, in fact the one common factor in all German thinking about *Scharnhorst* was its woolliness. Nobody quite knew what the ship was to be used for, or if she was ever to be used or not. The staff directive stated that the Northern Task Force and the U-boats were to be employed against 'convoy traffic'. But there again, as far as *Scharnhorst* herself was concerned, 'operations must be compatible with our small strength, and the use of *Scharnhorst* during the winter is to be considered'. This directive seems to have confirmed Kummetz in his belief that nothing more than a possible sortie by the destroyers would take place, at least until *Tirpitz* was repaired again.

The directive was not a document to set Bey and his staff agog with anticipation — even if Bey had had a proper staff. The contrast between the staff given to Bey, and Fraser's, could not have been greater. Bey's flag captain Hans Meyer of *Tirpitz* was an able and experienced officer, whom Bey knew well. But, of course, when Bey sailed in *Scharnhorst*, his flag captain was Julius Hintze, whom he also knew but who had himself been up in the Arctic 'only half a dog-watch', as the saying went. Kummetz's highly experienced Staff Officer (Operations) Kapitan Hansjurgen Reinicke, who had once been Schniewind's chief of staff, went back to Germany to rejoin Schniewind, and was not replaced. So, too, did Reinicke's deputy, Korvetten Kapitan Fritz-Gunther Boldemann, also without relief.

Thus Bey was left with a scratch staff, a signals officer, Kapitan-Leutnant Rolf Woytschekowsky-Emden, and the squadron engineer officer, Fregattan-Kapitan (Ing) Karlheinz Kurschat. *Scharnhorst*'s survivors said Bey had a staff of some 36, which obviously included members of the personal retinue, some borrowed from *Tirpitz*, with another fifteen officers on leave.

They said they could remember the names of Reinicke (who had actually left), Fregatten Kapitan Heppe, Woytschekowsky-Emden, Oberleutnant zur See (V) Bekemier, (V for Verwalting, a supply officer) and another engineer officer Kapitan sur Zee (Ing) Kaack. (These names may not be accurate. The officers only joined a few hours before sailing and the wonder is that the survivors recalled any names at all.) But certainly, Bey was not given the staff support necessary for a flag officer who was supposed to carry out major operations against the Allied convoys to Russia.

Despite the short notice and the lack of staff, Bey had by 22nd November prepared his own appreciation of the situation. He had consulted his fellow destroyer officer, Kapitan sur Zee Rolf Johannesson, commanding the 4th Flotilla, who took a very gloomy view of the future. In his eyes, the move of the 6th Flotilla back to Germany was equivalent to giving the initiative to the enemy. In the poor light and terrible weather of a polar winter, Johannesson could see little chance of success against a convoy and he regarded his likely task of having to escort *Scharnhorst* as a most unwelcome assignment.

To this glum accompaniment, Bey contributed his own hesitations and misgivings. In winter, when *Scharnhorst* was so vulnerable, he thought it better to use destroyers alone to attack convoys, possibly with *Scharnhorst* in support of them. But five destroyers were not nearly enough, and *Scharnhorst*, he thought, would not be able to make up the difference in effective strength. Besides, *Scharnhorst* herself would need protection. Bey reckoned on two of the destroyers to escort *Scharnhorst*. Thus, by Bey's reasoning, *Scharnhorst* and two destroyers would be required to support the three attacking destroyers.

Looking back, it is hard to see exactly *who* Bey intended should attack the convoys. *Scharnhorst* seemed more of a liability than an asset; she could hardly be said to be supporting the destroyers if two of their number were required to support *her*. However, Bey did include a more cheerful paragraph. 'Any chance of success' he wrote, 'would depend mainly upon good fortune, or on some failure or major mistake by the enemy. But, 'he concluded, 'despite our weaknesses, we have had many favourable opportunities in this war and experience shows that we can hope that luck is on our side.'

There were not many on the German Naval Staff who would have concurred in that, but Bey's unexpected optimism seems to have encouraged the Naval Staff to say, on 2nd December, that 'it might be expedient to employ *Scharnhorst*, in spite of the experiences of the 31st December 1942' (that is, the debâcle in the Barents Sea).

Bey stipulated that *Scharnhorst* could only attack in 'daylight'. But in the latitudes around Bear Island and north of the North Cape, there was no daylight in the proper sense, only a slight lightening of the darkness, an officially defined 'twilight', when the sun never actually arose above the horizon even for a short time either side of noon. *Scharnhorst* would have to develop and carry out her attack during this twilight period. It was no wonder that all the German deliberations about *Scharnhorst*'s possible operations always insisted on accurate prior knowledge of a convoy's position, course and speed, and of any enemy heavy units in the area, together with a good meteorological briefing, before any action whatsoever could be contemplated.

Admiral Schniewind's own appreciation, of 5th December, was no exception. He was perhaps the most pessimistic of them all. The successive withdrawals from the north of the destroyers, the Luftwaffe strength and some of the U-boats, together with the crippling of *Tirpitz,* seemed to him to leave almost no chance at all of any success against the convoys. The force available, already weak, would be even less effective because it had to try and fight in polar blackness. Schniewind insisted on accurate knowledge of the enemy's position, as an absolute prerequisite. But, as he said, this information was very difficult to get in the winter because of the scarcity of air reconnaissance. Like everybody else, Schniewind demanded accurate information about the enemy, a 'fair assurance of success', and good meteorological data before he would consider any action.

Thus, by mid-December 1943, the C-in-C Fleet, the task force commander, and the destroyer commander in the north, all thought there was little chance of any action having any success. The task force commander had gone on long leave. His understudy had been given no proper staff, merely a set of vague instructions so hedged about with cautions and caveats as to be practically meaningless. Only Doenitz, whose reputation to some extent depended upon the issue, still thought something might be done. Meanwhile, the officers in *Tirpitz* and *Scharnhorst* told each other that their ships 'had been put on ice'. In the circumstances, that seemed a very fair conclusion.

But, while the Germans were deliberating and deciding nothing much could be done, the convoys were still sailing.

CHAPTER 4

Scharnhorst puts to sea

THE barren, snow-covered Murman coast of north Russia was, as anyone who ever saw it agreed, best left to the Murmans — and that was to put it politely. Kola Inlet, said every British serviceman who went there, was the arse-hole of the world, and Murmansk was right up it. Captain Ian Campbell, of *Milne*, who was a veteran of several convoys to Russia, called it 'Destination Dreadful': 'One look at the place,' he said, 'and even the aching, weary crews of the escorts had only one wish — to be on their way out again'. Their combined opinions were well summed up by a black Jamaican steward assigned to look after Rear Admiral M.W.S. Boucher, commodore of JW55B, in the American ship *Will Rogers;* asked for his impressions, he slowly shook his head and said, 'I'd sho' like to go any place else — yes' *any* place 'tall.'

Kola Inlet runs roughly north and south, some 40 miles long, with the port and rail-head of Murmansk almost at its southermost end. On the eastern shore, but nearer the sea, was Vaenga Bay, where the escorts' oiler normally lay, and where the escorts themselves had to anchor for much of the war in deep water and on very poor holding ground. Ashore, there was a hutted camp with only the most rudimentary sanitary and domestic facilities for survivors of torpedoed ships, a small hospital, and a pier large enough to berth two destroyers.

Between Vaenga and Murmansk was Rosta Bay, where the merchantmen anchored after arriving with their convoys, waiting (sometimes for weeks) to go alongside in Murmansk and discharge their cargoes; there was nothing at Rosta except a very small and very ramshackle pier. On the western shore of Kola Inlet was, in fact, an excellent little harbour, the Russian naval base of Polyarno which was, as Campbell said, a very snug harbour, sheltered from every wind, and with an entrance with points of land so overlapping that it could hardly be seen from the outside. But it was not until quite late in the war that the Russians, the most inhospitable and suspicious of any Allies in all military history, allowed the escorts to use Polyarno.

Murmansk itself, especially in winter, was like some ghastly vision of a northern hell. Everybody remarked upon the funereal muffled deadness of the town's streets, and the miserable inhabitants shuffling about in the snow.

'Murmansk was a bombed city,' said Boucher, 'fitted with black ghosts moving in twilight over the snow in deathly silence broken only by tinny music broadcast at regular intervals by the State'. The town had been repeatedly bombed and, for the ships, one of the most fatiguing aspects of Kola was the need to maintain anti-aircraft watches twenty-four hours a day, to guard against bombers flying from airfields over the Norwegian border only a few miles away.

Everywhere there were the remains of houses, desolate brick chimneys, parts of crumbling walls, sticking up through the snow. Nor was the prospect much more cheering in summer, when the snow melted. Campbell wrote 'the charred rubble and iron bedsteads disclosed were even more depressing and the smells were indescribable. All that was left were the big new concrete blocks of offices, flats and warehouses, every window boarded up, all glass having long ago vanished'. It was a dismal life for the crews of the merchantmen, and the minesweepers berthed amongst them to lend extra anti-aircraft protection. Survivors from merchant and warships in the camp ashore had a dull, monotonous diet and almost no amusements of any kind.

Allied officers were constantly amazed and disgusted by the way the Russians treated the stores brought to Murmansk at the cost of so much blood and treasure. Crates containing aircraft were left on the jetty for months, at a time when the Red Army was crying out for air cover. Packages marked 'Delicate' were thrown about or dropped. Boxes marked 'Keep Dry' stood in the driving snow. Meanwhile, 80-ton cranes were used to lift 90-ton loads, convict and slave labour was lashed into pitiful action to move heavy equipment, all in nightmare scenes of constant muddle and congestion which often froze into complete immobility, followed by chaos. Threats from the Ministry of War Transport that no more convoys would sail unless the situation improved would bring about the arrival of what Campbell termed 'a sort of super commissar' who would proceed to 'put the fear of Stalin' into the local officials. But, with his departure, the situation returned to its normal state of confusion.

But, worst of all, was the attitude of the Russians themselves. Their gross incompetence was aggravated by their oriental disregard for pain and human life and their brutal contempt for human dignity. For patients in the hospitals there were horrific rumours of amputations without aneesthetics. The Russians would not allow the establishment of British servicemen in Russia to be increased, or the men who were there to be relieved at the proper time, even when they were told that an increased establishment was necessary to handle efficiently the convoys they themselves needed so desperately. Instead, they withheld or withdrew visas, insisted upon bureaucratic minutiae, piled silly regulation upon obstructive rule, and were persistently uncooperative and intransigent. To achieve anything at all, Allied officers had to employ guile and stratagem, to say nothing of a rock-hard liver: the periodic bouts of ferocious drinking, the *Bolshoi Prazniks*, has to be survived to be believed.

Late in December, Fraser arrived in Kola to see for himself. JW55A, of 19 ships, sailed from Loch Ewe on 12th December, escorted and covered as previous convoys had been. Fraser himself led the distant covering force in *Duke of York*, with the cruiser *Jamaica*, and four destroyers, *Savage, Saumarez, Scorpion* and the Norwegian *Stord* (previously *Success*). Of four U-boats on patrol east of Bear Island, U.636 briefly sighted the escorts of the convoy early on 18th December. There was a flurry of German radio intelligence activity which suggested to Fraser that the convoy had been sighted, very probably by aircraft.

Reasoning that the risk of some sort of intervention by *Scharnhorst* was growing more and more likely, while the danger of air attack was decreasing, Fraser decided to take *Duke of York* all the way through to Kola Inlet, the first time that a capital ship of the Home Fleet had ever done so. Meanwhile, the cruiser *Belfast*, flying the flag of Rear Admiral Burnett, commanding the Tenth Cruiser Squadron, had arrived at Seydesfiord on 13th December, to be joined next day by *Sheffield* and *Norfolk*. All three sailed on 15th, to cover the passage of JW55A.

Fraser's visit was recorded in the diary of his Russian opposite number, Admiral Arseni Golovko, who attributed to it some dark reason and questioned Fraser's motives. All the Russian suspicion, ingratitude and sheer insensitivity are perfectly encapsulated in one extract from Golovko's account. 'What is the idea of this (visit)? Does he (Fraser) really want to make a personal study of the convoy conditions in the North Atlantic? Turmoil reigns in the British naval mission. Its chief, Archer (Rear Admiral Ernest Archer) — an overbearing type unlike his predecessor Fisher — tried to profit by Fraser's forthcoming visit to ask me a host of by no means essential questions. In particular he demanded information about our aviation for a report to his superior, assuming no doubt that at the words 'for the Commander-in-Chief Home Fleet' we should be so flabbergasted we should give him everything on the spot. A very unpleasant person this Archer. I have already asked for him to be removed ... For what purpose can Fraser be coming here?'

The exchange of visits between Golovko and Fraser had several surrealist moments, illustrating the vast gulf between the two Allies' national mentalities; the two only met rarely, by accident and in what might almost be called glancing blows. Golovko set out for *Duke of York*, as he thought, 'already in possession of all the necessary information about Fraser. He is a sea-dog who has knocked about the world a bit and is now one of the pillars of the British Admiralty'.

Golovko may have known Fraser's 'biography', as he called it, but he fell to a piece of blatant leg-pulling by Fraser and Slayter the Chief of Staff. It was established that Fraser had visited Russia before and had been a prisoner of the Bolsheviks. Golovko said triumphantly that he knew all about it. At which, Slayter pounced. Yes, but did the Admiral know that Admiral Fraser was *grateful* to the Bolsheviks for this?

Golovko had to admit himself really astonished and was even more taken aback by the explanation: 'Because Admiral Fraser was badly fed in the prison where he was confined and this enabled him to recover from an ulcer that was plaguing him'. Golovko, evidently by now breathing very hard indeed 'had to own up that I did not know of this detail, indicating, as it did, a *very peculiar* form of appreciation of the Bolsheviks on the part of the British Admiral'.

The atmosphere of unreality about the visit continued with the gift of 'a vast quantity of buns' (which Golovko had tested and admired during his tour of *Duke of York*) — 'the acme of hospitality' Golovko called them. In return Golovko gave Fraser his magnificent black marble desk top, because Fraser had admired it (there were obvious dangers in this; as Fraser said, 'What happens if you come on board *Duke of York* and say you liked her? 'Oh, said Golovko, 'I'd treat it as your wife!') But the suspicions remained; 'All the same,' wrote Golovko, 'I still do not grasp for what purpose the C-in-C of the British Home Fleet should have decided to visit us at the height of the polar night season.'

A few of *Duke of York's* sailors, including Peter Woodhouse, managed to get ashore in Vaenga: 'At every intersection of the small Main Street, was a sentry with rifle and bayonet, who frustrated any attempt to turn off so our explorations were very limited indeed. But the people, officially unfriendly, were unofficially quite the opposite. Most of the people were Koli, who claimed no knowledge of Russian, and there were very few sailors who knew any Russian either. However, the locals were anxious to buy anything we had — they would pull out rolls of roubles and offer them in exchange for cigarettes: wrist watches particularly attracted astronomical offers. But their money was no use to us except as curios. We weren't allowed to exchange money and anyway there was nothing to buy.'

Golovko gave a dinner for Fraser and his staff and afterwards entertained them with the Red Fleet choir. Here, perhaps the two nations came closest together. One song in particular, 'Farewell Stony Hills!' was a favourite of Golovko's. He knew it by heart and it never failed to arouse an echo of emotion in him 'especially at bad moments'. The words, ironically, were appropriate for both navies:

'... but there will be fire enough for the battle.

I know, friends, that there is no life for me without the sea,

Just as the sea is dead without me.'

The choir, known to the sailors in *Duke of York* as 'the Soviet White Sea Glee Party' also gave a concert for the ship's company in the hangar. It was well received, although as R.O.L. Thomas recorded, 'some of the choir members helped themselves to souvenirs from Captain Russell's day cabin whilst their mates were performing.

According to Golovko, 'the visitors were delighted by the choir, and especially by the dances and the few songs sung in English. They even entreated me to let them take the choir to Scapa Flow and Rosyth for a fortnight. All in all we received our British visitors as real allies'.

Certainly, there was a temporary improvement in conditions for British servicemen at Kola while Fraser was there. Mail deliveries, for instance, improved remarkably. But as Fraser said, the moment he left, everything went back to the same as before. Certainly, the suspicions remained. On 19th December, Golovko recorded that Fraser had received 'a radio message of some sort from sea' and left in such a hurry he sent his apologies to the mission 'explaining that he was returning to England. A strange hurry. Where are the British racing off to now? To meet the convoy and support it?'. In fact, as Golovko must have known, *Duke of York* and her escort were on their way back to Akureyri, to refuel and prepare to cover the next convoy. JW55B, the second half, was due to sail on 19th, although bad weather delayed its departure until 20th.

The fast (ten knots) convoy JW55B, the 'bait' which was to bring *Scharnhorst* to sea, sailed from Loch Ewe at 5 pm. The Commodore was Rear Admiral Boucher, in *Fort Kullyspell*, leading the 19 ships at the head of the third column (of six). The Local Escort, which would be relieved in approximately 64°N., consisted of the two corvettes *Borage* and *Wallflower* and the minesweepers *Hound* (Senior Officer of the local escort) and *Hydra*. The Through Escort, all from Western Approaches Command, was the minesweepers *Gleaner* (Senior Officer), the destroyers *Whitehall* and *Wrestler* and the corvettes *Honeysuckle* and *Oxlip*.

JW55B passed through the Minches during the night of 20th/21st and at 8 am the next day formed into its convoy disposition of six columns, increasing speed to $9\frac{1}{2}$ knots. During the day the convoy carried out exercises, practising emergency turns, and firing short range armament. There was air escort for much of the day. Meanwhile, the Fighting Destroyer Escort sailed from Skaalefjord at 11.45 pm that night, to rendezvous with the convoy sometime in the afternoon of the following day. It was led by Captain J.A. ('Bes') McCoy DSO, Captain (D) of the 17th Flotilla, in *Onslow*, with the destroyers *Onslaught, Scourge, Orwell* and *Impulsive*, with three Canadian destroyers *Haida, Huron* and *Iroquois*.

Just as JW55B was sailing, so JW55A was arriving at Kola, preceded by the cruisers *Belfast, Norfolk* and *Sheffield*, who anchored in Vaenga Bay at midnight on 19th. The 'White Sea Glee Party' came on board *Belfast*, to give two concerts, to the wardroom and the ship's company. They had lost none of their acquisitive habits. They used the midshipmen's Gunroom as a 'Green Room'. Nothing was locked, except the gunroom bar cupboard, but when the midshipmen next went to their lockers they found, as Midshipman R.L. Garnons-Williams, wrote 'apart from the books, which were in English, nothing of even the slightest value was left! My proudest possessions were a pair of very light coloured briar pipes my grandmother had given me for Christmas 1942, only one of which I had smoked — both were missing and may well still be being smoked by an aged Russian music hall artist — I hope in Siberia.'

The convoy conference for RA55A was held in *Belfast* on 20th, attended by the Captains of the escorts, the convoy commodore and his staff, the masters of the merchantmen. Such conferences were an essential part of any convoy's life. At their simplest level, they 'gave a face to a name' so that every master had at least met the commodore or the escort captain who was signalling them. Then there was advice about routes and destinations, warnings about straggling, making smoke, dropping too much gash overboard, keeping proper station, showing lights, and answering signals promptly, with details of courses, speeds, zigzags, callsigns, the use of illuminants, all the miscellaneous information which might, in an emergency, make the difference between life and death.

Naturally, there was some discussion about *Scharnhorst*, the remaining Big Bad Wolf in the Arctic. Obviously there was a chance she would come out, but the convoy was to be escorted by 'Scotty' Campbell in *Milne,* with nine more destroyers, *Meteor, Ashanti,* the Canadian *Athabaskan, Musketeer, Opportune, Virago, Matchless, Beagle* and *Westcott,* the corvettes *Dianella, Poppy* and the Norwegian *Acanthus,* with the minesweeper *Seagull.* This was a powerful, numerous and experienced escort, which should be enough to take care of any danger. If not, there was the 10th Cruiser Squadron as a covering force, not too far away.

The principal figure at the convoy conference was the flag officer commanding the Tenth Cruiser Squadron, Vice-Admiral Robert Burnett, DSO. 'Bob' Burnett, or 'Nutty' Burnett as he was known, was then 55 years old, of medium height, but thick-set and burly, with a ruddy complexion and an ever-ready laugh. He was a 'small ship' man, having commanded destroyers in the First World War. In his cabin he had a photograph of himself as a young Lieutenant, standing under the bows of his first command, Torpedo Boat No.26. The caption was 'Alone I Did It': the torpedo boat's bows were high and dry; the ship was hard aground, as a result of an 'overland journey' because of a navigational error.

That self-mocking caption was typical of Bob Burnett (he always preferred the stress on the first syllable of his name: *Burn*-ett) who used to say of himself that he 'was a stupid fellow who had been lucky'. He had commanded destroyers in the Grand Fleet, the Western Approaches and the Dover Patrol, but he had then become a 'springer', specialising in physical and recreational training. He was a first-class referee at rugby, soccer, hockey and water-polo, all games he played well himself. He had been Navy sabre and midweight boxing champion. He was promoted captain in 1931, Rear-Admiral in December 1940, each time 'one more promotion he had neither expected nor merited', he said.

Bob Burnett abhorred 'back seat driving'. Straight dealing in all things was his motto. In a battle he was as steady as a rock. His mere presence on a bridge steadied everybody and had an impressive and calming effect. 'Freddie' Parham knew him very well: 'He was a physical training expert and, as he himself used to say, slapping himself on the stern, 'This is where all my brains are'. He wasn't a clever chap, he'd come bottom of his term, jolly nearly, I think. But he was a tremendous personality and he really was — it sounds smug and silly — but I believe he really was a *fighting* admiral, with a sort of fighting instinct. Of course, he was *immensely* popular. I can remember going to concerts, given in my ship the *Belfast,* which was his flagship and we'd walk in, he'd go in ahead of me and I'd take his coat and I'd follow him in, and as we came in the whole place would burst into cheering! I didn't mind, because I loved him so much myself. He always did the right thing. He was the very last person in the world ever to have done a staff course (nor did I, incidentally). He wasn't really a tactician. But he'd got a fighting instinct.'

From March 1942, when he was appointed Rear Admiral commanding destroyer flotillas of the Home Fleet (very much the same kind of appointment Erich Bey filled in the German fleet), Bob Burnett flew his flag at sea on several occasions which gave him every chance to indulge his fighting instinct. In the anti-aircraft cruiser *Scylla* in September 1942 he had fought through the Arctic convoy PQ.18. With forty ships it was the largest of the convoys to Russia, but three ships were lost to U-boats and another ten to torpedo-bombers in fifteen days of furious action. In December, Burnett flew his flag in the cruiser *Sheffield,* covering JW51A, and went through to Kola Inlet with the convoy. On the way back, with *Jamaica* in company, Burnett was in the right place again to take part in Sherbrooke's action in the Barents Sea. *Sheffield* hit and damaged *Hipper* and reduced the hapless German destroyer *Friedrich Eckholdt* to a burning shambles, after the unsuspecting German had closed them thinking they were friendly. Between them, Burnett and Sherbrooke caught Kummetz and his ships between the British cruisers and destroyers and averted what should have been an overwhelming victory for the German force.

Burnett was awarded a DSO for his services in the Arctic in March 1943, and by December 1943, he was by far the Navy's most experienced cruiser admiral in northern waters. Before leaving Scapa in *Belfast* to cover JW55A, Burnett had addressed the ship's company and told them that this was very probably his last trip. He was not expecting to go to sea again. But he felt that this last trip might well be exciting.

RA55A sailed from Kola on 22nd December. *Belfast,* with *Sheffield* and *Norfolk,* known as Force 1, sailed a day later. Admiral Golovko had held a reception for Burnett and his officers ('we drank vodka and ate stinking fish with the Russian admiral' as Parham succinctly described it). As a farewell present Golovko gave *Belfast* 'Olga', a young female reindeer who, with her bedding, and fodder for the voyage, was installed in the hangar where the Walrus aircraft used to be.

Burnett's flag captain, Captain F.R. Parham, a gunnery specialist, had previously been Deputy Director of the Naval Ordnance Department, and he and his executive officer Cdr. P. Welby-Everard had both been much involved in the application of radar (or RDF, as it was still called in the Royal Navy at that time) to surface fire control. Both had commissioned

Belfast in November 1942 after her lengthy refit and repair at Devonport Dockyard; she had been badly damaged, virtually having her back broken, by a magnetic mine in the Firth of Forth on 21st November 1939. Like every ship in the Home Fleet by that stage in the war, *Belfast* had a 'very green lot of sailors'; most of her ship's company of 900 had never been to sea before and at least four of her junior RNVR officers were on board a ship in officer's uniform for the first time in their lives. However, *Belfast* had already covered several Arctic convoys and had sailed with the rest of the Home Fleet accompanying USS *Ranger* for an air strike on the Norwegian port of Bodo early in October 1943. *Belfast* was known as 'Tiddley B': for the King's visit to Scapa in August, she had been only the ship which had managed to have an overall coat of new paint. Parham and Welby-Everard had worked up their ship and her company almost from scratch and were about to see the results of their labours in action against the enemy.

Sheffield (Captain C.T. Addis) and *Norfolk* (Captain D.K. Bain), the two other cruisers in Force 1, were amongst the busiest ships in the Navy, having been in various actions since the earliest days of the war. *Sheffield*, the 'Shiny Sheff', launched in 1936 and completed in August 1937, was a 9,400 ton cruiser of the *Southampton* class. She could do just over 32 knots, was armed with twelve 6-inch guns and eight 4-inch, and had a complement of over 750 officers and men. When war broke out *Sheffield* was in the 18th Cruiser Squadron at Scapa Flow and she took part in the early patrols of September 1939, when the Home Fleet searched the Norwegian coast for enemy shipping.

Sheffield, with the other Home Fleet ships, spent most of her time searching: for *Gneisenau* and *Koln* in October; for *Scharnhorst* and *Gneisenau* after *Rawalpindi* had been sunk in November; for *Hipper* off Norway in April 1940. She took troops to Aandalsnes on 22nd April and took them off again on 30th. Later, she joined the famous Force H, with *Ark Royal* and the battle-cruiser *Renown*, escorting a troop convoy to Alexandria and taking part in the action with the Italian Fleet off Cape Spartivento in November 1940, escorting a convoy for Malta and Piraeus in January 1941, bombarding Genoa in February and, in May, joining the search for *Bismarck*. On 26th May, when *Sheffield* had been detached to the west of *Ark Royal*, to find and shadow *Bismarck*, she was attacked in error by *Ark*'s Swordfish; *Sheffield* avoided the torpedoes and, with great forbearance, refrained from firing. Later, in June, she found the German tanker *Friedrich Breme* in the Atlantic, which, however, scuttled itself before *Sheffield* could sink her.

In 1942, *Sheffield* was part of the escort for the convoy PQ.18 in September, and in November flew Rear Admiral Cecil Harcourt's flag for the assault on Bougie, in north Africa, during Operation TORCH. In December she wore Burnett's flag whilst escorting JW51B and, with *Jamaica*, took part in the action in the Barents Sea. She had been in commission for over a year and had a comparatively experienced ship's company who were intensely proud of their 'Shiny Sheff'. Her captain Charles Addis, was an able and experienced officer, with a reputation for being unflappable: 'dear old Charles Addis,' said Freddie Parham, 'he was worth a guinea a minute, never ruffled by anything ... '

Norfolk was one of the famous County Class of cruisers, of 10,000 tons, with a speed of over 32 knots, armed with eight 8-inch and eight 4-inch, and a complement of just under 700 officers and men. She too had spent most of her time patrolling: in the Northern Patrol, when she had also searched for *Scharnhorst* and *Gneisenau*, and in the south Atlantic in December 1940 looking for *Admiral Scheer*, covering convoy routes off Sierra Leone early in 1941, and with her sister ship *Suffolk* searching the Denmark Strait for *Bismarck* in May. She sighted *Bismarck* and *Prinz Eugen* on the evening of 23rd at a range of only six miles, was fired on, disengaged under cover of smoke, and sent the first sighting reports to be actually received. She and *Suffolk,* one on the enemy's starboard quarter, the other on the port, shadowed for the next two days.

In 1942 *Norfolk* went to the Arctic, escorting PQ.16, acting as close cover as far as Bear Island for PQ.17, and flying Rear Admiral S.S. Bonham-Carter's flag in the cruiser covering force for PQ.18. Her captain, Donald Bain, known to the sailors as 'Batchy' Bain, had served in northern waters for much of the war and had a personal score to settle; he had commanded the armed merchant cruiser HMS *Andania*, torpedoed and sunk by UA south-east of Iceland on 16th June 1940 (one of three of those vulnerable Northern Patrol armed merchant cruisers sunk that month).

Force 2 returned to Akureyri during the forenoon of 21st December. *Duke of York* led the way and stood upon no ceremony. According to Lt.Cdr Dickie Courage, the Fleet Signal Officer, their entry was 'at full speed in single line ahead up a long inlet in very poor visibility — so poor that it was a job for the destroyers to see their next ahead'. *Duke of York* had the best radar in the fleet (a factor that was to be crucial in the action to come) and everyone on board had the greatest confidence in radar's ability to guide the ship safely up the narrow channel. But 'the ships following astern of us were amazed and somewhat frightened by the speed at which we entered these hazardous waters'.

On securing from sea, Fraser signalled his ships that 'the convoy (i.e. JW55A) has arrived safely' and to *Duke of York* he sent a graceful compliment: 'I wish to thank my flagship for the part they played in making the visit to Kola successful'. Meanwhile there had been news of *Scharnhorst*, whose Battle Group had reverted to longer notice for sea only at 4 pm that day, 21st, after a flurry of activity.

Scharnhorst had arranged on 9th to go to sea for exercises on 14th December. Fraser had been informed of this by ULTRA as early as 11th, and ULTRA continued to give Fraser the details of *Scharnhorst*'s exercises until 19th, when the German Battle Group had come to three hours' notice for sea. Reconnaissance flights from the Lofotens were requested urgently, against a British convoy which was assumed to be approaching. British heavy units were also thought to be at sea. But the reconnaisance for 19th was cancelled, as was further reconnaisance planned for 20th and 21st, all because of bad weather. Finally, at 4.03 pm on 21st, the Battle Group reverted to six hours' notice for sea.

It seemed that the enemy had planned a sortie but called it off because of the weather (it was to blow a full or near gale almost all the time for the next ten days). But Fraser was quite sure that *Scharnhorst* would come out any day from now on. 'With the safe arrival of JW55A,' he wrote in his dispatch, 'I felt very strongly that the *Scharnhorst* would come out and endeavour to attack JW55B. Fortunately my small force had now been in company for nearly a fortnight, we knew each other and had practised night encounter tactics together.'

At 8 am. on 22nd December the Admiralty estimated that JW55B was some 60 miles N.N.E. of the Faeroes. The convoy was steering northwards into reasonable weather, but already having problems with convoy discipline. During the night of 21st/22nd, two ships in the port wing column, *Ocean Valour* and *John Abel,* failed to carry out a course alteration from 002° to 017° and became separated. At first light *Whitehall* was sent to round them up, while the convoy reduced speed to 8 knots to allow them to catch up. The minesweeper *Hydra*, whose sailing had been delayed by an engine defect, also caught the convoy up at 9.20 am.

The air escort was provided by a Sunderland, carrying out anti-submarine patrols ahead of the convoy, which exchanged signals with *Hound* at 10.30, and was given the convoy's estimated position. But at 10.59 another aircraft was sighted by *Gleaner*, stationed on the convoy's starboard quarter, flying on a estimated course of 090, passing astern of the convoy. *Gleaner* identified it as probably a Dornier Do.217 bomber.

It was indeed a Dornier, on a meteorological flight, which sighted the convoy at 10.45, when it was some 400 miles west of Trondheim. The news was signalled by Flieger Fuhrer North (West) at 11.31: 'Aircraft West A5 reports at 1045 in Square 16 West 5410 (63°45'-64°00'N, 5°30'-6°00'W) Convoy of 40 troop transports and protective vessels presumably with aircraft carrier, course 045, speed 10 knots'.

At Kiel, Admiral Schniewind at once jumped to the conclusion that this was an invasion force bound for Norway (an old and familiar obsession of Hitler's). He ordered the U-boats of the 'Eisenbart' Group to concentrate off the entrance to Vest Fjord. The Luftwaffe were to continue to shadow the convoy and report any enemy force within 300 miles of it. Meanwhile, a signal was sent to *Scharnhorst* at 12.25, to bring the Battle Group to three hours notice for sea.

The Battle Group actually reported ready, at three hours readiness, at 1.26 pm. But when the reporting aircraft returned to the Lofotens, the shore staff re-evaluated the significance of what the pilot said he had seen. AT 2.30 another signal said 'Delete troop transports' and insert merchantmen of 2 to 3,000 GRT. Visual recce unreliable owing to poor visibility conditions'.

These signals were decyphered by ULTRA, and an 'Immediate ULTRA' signal at 1.36 am. on 23rd reported the traffic to Fraser, and added that a U-boat had been ordered, at 7.45 pm on 22nd, to operate 'if conditions were favourable'. Direction-finding stations in north Russia had already been reporting U-boat traffic in a position not precisely defined, but somewhere south-east of Bear Island. In fact, when Schniewind decided that the convoy was not a raiding party bound for Norway, the 'Eisenbart' U-boats were ordered back to the vicinity of Bear Island.

By midday on 22nd, JW55B was steering into steadily deteriorating weather. The wind was increasing and the sea rising. The convoy was approaching the rendezvous and at 12.25 the escorting Sunderland flew over McCoy's destroyers and reported the convoy bearing 352°, 24 miles. The Sunderland returned to the convoy and reported McCoy's position to *Hound* at 1.15 pm. Thus guided, McCoy steered north, increasing to 18 knots, with his ships spread out in line abreast, two miles apart. A convoy 'meet' was always an anxious business. Either side's navigation could be at fault. However, safely shepherded by the Sunderland, *Onslaught* sighted the starboard column of JW55B at 2 pm, bearing 027°, and McCoy's destroyers had taken station around the convoy by 3 pm. McCoy then took over as Senior Officer of the escort, while *Hound* and the local escort left for Skaalefjord.

Fraser and Burnett learned of the Battle Group coming to three hours' notice through an ULTRA signal of 10.25am on 24th. But by that time, Force 2 had actually been some hours at sea. All ships had topped up with fuel on 22nd and on the morning of 23rd. The night of 22nd/23rd was bitterly cold, and the sea largely froze over between *Duke of York* and the shore. Fraser and Captain Russell went ashore for a time for some Christmas shopping, 'clothing or something', as Fraser said, the traditional 'rabbits' sailors buy for their families at home. When they got back on board, Fraser said 'all the Icelanders ashore were skating, by light, we were in darkness, of course. I asked the Band to come up on deck and play Christmas carols; and really, it almost brought tears to your eyes'.

In the meantime, at 10.10 am on 23rd a Russian aircraft flying reconnaisance at 8,000 feet over Alta Fjord reported that *Tirpitz* was in Kaa Fjord, with a repair vessel alongside her; *Scharnhorst* and two destroyers were in Lange Fjord, with the usual group of auxiliaries in both anchorages. The weather was clear, with no cloud at all, so there was no doubt *Scharnhorst* was still in harbour. To try and keep her there, on that evening of 23rd Fraser asked Flag Officer Submarines to instruct the submarine *Sirdar,* on patrol off the Norwegian coast, to break W/T silence and make a short message as soon as possible, 'with the object of deterring the enemy ships from leaving harbour'.

At 6 pm that evening Fraser held a final meeting on board *Duke of York* for his captains and his staff, to make sure that everybody knew what he intended to do. He had decided, first, to close the enemy, opening fire with star-shell at a range of about 12,000 yards. This made the assumption, fully justified in the event, that *Scharnhorst* would not have, or would not be using, radar of long enough range to detect *Duke of York* and her escort as they closed. Second, Fraser intended to form his four destroyers into sub-divisions of two, and release them in time to take up positions for torpedo attack. This was an assumption not so easily achieved on the night. Finally, Fraser intended to keep *Jamaica* in 'close support of *Duke of York* but with freedom of action to take drastic avoiding action and open the distance if engaged'.

Fraser 'stressed that every officer and man must be doubly sure he knew his night action duty'. This, as Fraser admitted, should hardly have been necessary to say, but there were many changes of officers and men in the Home Fleet 'and, with constant escort requirements, adequate training is not easy to achieve'. Fraser himself was given absolute control by the Admiralty, who would provide every ounce of intelligence and support they could. After that, it was up to Fraser. He was the man on the spot.

Lt.Cdr. Courage did not attend this briefing. With Fraser's permission, he held a 'lifelike signal exercise' with the other ships of the force on VHF radio/telephone using the actual call signs, signals and codebooks which would be used in the action. For short-term messages, ships used the 'Fleet Code', which was designed, as Courage said, 'only to confuse the enemy for a few minutes and had no real security'.

There was of course a risk that the exercise would be overheard but 'probably no more than the possibility of police radios in the countryside of Sussex being heard in Glasgow. The risk had been considered and accepted'. Sealed orders were opened and the relevant instructions shown to the signalmen. Courage himself felt 'it important that the signal ratings should be familiar with the race card before the actual race took place. The signal exercise seemed to go well 'with people entering into the spirit of the thing and, even more important, they all seemed to have digested the sealed orders'. *Duke of York*'s own internal exercise ended with 'Make to Admiralty — *Scharnhorst* sunk.' 'I was somehow certain,' said Courage, 'we should be making that signal in due course.'

Force 2 sailed at 10 pm GMT on 23rd (ships advanced their clocks by one hour at 1 am the next morning). Minesweepers of the 1st Minesweeping Squadron had prepared the way. The four destroyers, *Savage* (Cdr. M.D.G. Meyrick) and *Saumarez* (Lt.Cdr. E.W. Walmsley) in the 1st Sub-Division, *Scorpion* (Lt. Cdr. W.S. Clouston) and the Norwegian *Stord* (Lt.Cdr.S. Storheil) in the 2nd, led *Duke of York*, with *Jamaica* bringing up the rear. The sailing time had been carefully calculated. The destroyers' fuel endurance did not allow Force 2 to cover the convoy's passage continuously. So Fraser had to sail his ships at the right moment so as to be near the convoy, at its most dangerous time. Fraser planned that at a speed of 15 knots his ships would reach the covering position when the convoy was just east of Bear Island, and would be able to stay for about 30 hours. So Force 2 steamed north-east through the night, in foul weather, keeping radio silence, guns' crews in the third state of readiness, with one pompom and one starshell crew closed up for the night.

Early on 24th, Force 2 held one last exercise. *Scorpion and Stord,* representing a convoy escort, made good a course of 60° at 12 knots, whilst *Jamaica* with *Savage* and *Saumarez* opened out to a distance of 15 miles on a bearing of approximately 150° from the convoy to represent an enemy battle cruiser and two destroyers. *Duke of York* was to act as covering force for the convoy. In an eerily accurate forecast of actual circumstances, the 'enemy base' was assumed to bear 150° from the convoy.

Duke of York was to fire some ten three-gun salvoes, 'throwing short' by 4,000 yards, whilst *Jamaica,* who was between 20,000 and 22,000 yards' range from *Duke of York,* took avoiding action steering within 30° of her mean course. *Jamaica* when her turn came, was to fire 'throw-off' salvoes, to land astern of *Duke of York.* The exercise, like Courage's, went well except that actual firing was cancelled; it was, of course, similar to a dozen other night encounter exercises, but now that the ships were actually on their way towards a very possible meeting with a battle-cruiser, there was an extra edge of realism.

In this exercise, as in action, *Jamaica* was *Duke of York*'s 'Little Sir Echo'. A *Fiji* Class cruiser of some 8,000 tons, compared with *Duke of York*'s bulk, with twelve 6-inch to the flagships 14-inch, and a complement of some 750 officers and men, *Jamaica* and *Duke of York* together made a somewhat 'lop-sided' Force 2. But *Jamaica* lent Fraser another dimension of flexibility. Her presence might distract the enemy at a critical time — and she had six torpedo tubes. She was comparatively new, having been completed in June 1942, but had already seen action with Arctic convoys and had been in the battle of the Barents Sea. Her Captain, John Hughes-Hallett, had won a DSO as the Naval Force Commander for the ill-fated landings at Dieppe in August 1942. He had a reputation as something of a stormy petrel; lower deck rumour was that any ship he commanded was sure of an interesting existence. He was certainly a very stern disciplinarian, known as 'Hughes-Hitler'. He had only joined the ship at the beginning of December but, as one of his officers, Dudley Blunt said, 'only a fortnight later we were in the thick of the action during which our captain handled his unfamiliar ship brilliantly, demonstrating a professionalism in the best traditions of the Navy'.

During the night ULTRA gave Fraser some more information about German reconnaisance flights. A signal of 5.50 am gave Luftwaffe intentions for that day and some details about reconnaisance on the previous day. A Junkers Ju.88 had reported the convoy at 11.25 on 23rd: 20 merchant ships, 12 protective vessels, course 030, speed 10 knots, in position 67 07N, 01 45W. This was amplified further at 12.33 as '17 merchant ships, of up to 10,000 GRT, 3 tankers, proceeding in close order in 7 lines ahead, next to each other, tanker in the centre. Three to four cruisers, 9 destroyers and corvettes. 'Misty weather' the signal concluded.

A signal from Captain (U-boats) Norway was decyphered, with details of yet another sighting, in 68°09′N, 00 01E, this time by a Blohm & Voss Bv.138 flying boat. The aircraft reported one cruiser, five destroyers on a course of 090 degrees; nine miles northwest of them, another 20 ships (estimated) were also located. The signal ended 'It is possible that there is a strong battle group at a distance from the convoy'.

That sighting was at 12.14 pm on 23rd, when the shadowers had been in contact with JW55B for some time and the convoy had even taken retaliatory action. At 11.40 that morning *Orwell*, on the convoy's port bow, sighted two Dornier Do.217s flying in towards the convoy's port side. They skirted the escort, flew down the port side and began to shadow from astern. At 11.45 McCoy signalled to north Russia that he was being shadowed and that *Haida* and *Iroquois* had fired on the shadowers. The Dorniers were thought to have been damaged but obviously not severely, because they stayed with the convoy, sheltering in cloud whenever they were fired on.

Next day, at 7 am, JW55B began to alter course, by easy stages, to 057° in accordance with the convoy plan. Station-keeping was still very poor and daybreak showed the ships scattered over a wide area. At 11.30 speed was reduced to 7 knots, to allow the stragglers to catch up. Up to now the convoy had been doing very well, sometimes making 10 knots over the ground with a following wind, but the best it could now do was $8\frac{1}{2}$ knots.

By noon, when the convoy was only 400 miles from Alta Fjord, the shadowers had caught up again. Bad weather had hindered the Luftwaffe's reconnaissance flights but by midday the convoy had been detected and, in Fraser's words, 'was being continuously shadowed'. *Iroquois* sighted two aircraft shadowing from astern at 12.25 pm, and they were also seen by several other ships in the screen on the convoy's port side. One aircraft reported the convoy at 12.20 pm, 'in 70°27½′N, 03°35′E, 050 degrees, speed 8 knots'. This signal was passed to Fraser by ULTRA at 2.10 am on 25th. Another signal later in the series, at 7.35 pm on 24th, mentioned the convoy's gunfire: 'Twelve merchant ships up to 5,000, three destroyers far apart, nothing further made out owing to bad visibility. Defence by medium and light flak'.

These signals, with others which were not provided by ULTRA, showed that the often-criticised reconnaissance of the Luftwaffe had, in spite of bad weather, established that there was a convoy on its way to Russia, its approximate size and composition, its course and speed, and a fair indication of its position. Fraser was also informed by ULTRA of a signal sent to *Scharnhorst* at 11.24 pm on 23rd reporting that a U-boat was in contact with the convoy bound for north Russia. However, at 10.25 on 24th, (in the same signal revealing that the Battle Group had been ordered to three hours readiness at 1 pm on 22nd,) Fraser was told that, up to 7 am on 24th, there were still no signs that the Battle Group had left Alta Fjord. Nevertheless, it was clear that the Germans must now know that the convoy, probably covered by a strong escort, was heading for the Bear Island area. But they knew nothing of RA55A, westbound for Loch Ewe.

ULTRA had in fact been giving information on U-boat traffic, with details of attacking areas, warnings of intended air reconnaissance and flights, reports of hydrophone contacts, including a mass of information on U-boats' fuel and torpedoes remaining, and weather conditions, for some days. At 00.49 am on 18th December, four U-boats of the 'Arctic' Group, reinforced by three more from the Baltic, were ordered to take up patrol positions along a line 135 miles east of Bear Island. On 19th these seven U-boats were ordered to shift position further westward.

By the morning of 24th, Fraser had decided that JW55B was dangerously exposed. 'Although,' he wrote, 'German surface forces had never before made a sortie to the westward, the convoy which had reached the position 70 40N 03 10E at 1200' (on 24th, confirming how accurate the 12.20 aircraft position had been) 'was entirely unsupported and I was uneasy lest a surface attack should be made'. *Scharnhorst* might, or might not, come out; in the meantime, and always, the first concern of Fraser and of everybody else was the safe and timely arrival of the convoy.

Fraser therefore broke radio silence at 12.01 pm to signal to Rear Admiral (Destroyers) at Scapa Flow, repeating the signal to Admiralty, Burnett and Captain McCoy, in *Onslow*, JW55B's senior escort commander, and to Campbell, RA55A's senior escort commander, in *Milne* asking if, as the situation develops, will you consider diverting RA55A to the northward after passing Bear Island and the transfer of up to four Fleet destroyers from D.3 (Campbell) to D.17 (McCoy) should the opportunity arise.' Fraser then gave his own position, course and speed.

At 1.25 pm Fraser broke silence again to signal to McCoy: 'Reverse your course until 5 pm'. At the same time he increased the speed of Force 2 to 19 knots. 'If the enemy surface forces had searched to the westward, this step would have had little effect in bringing the convoy closer, but it would have prevented the convoy being located by them before dark'.

In fact, the signal had less effect even than Fraser anticipated, because it was, in practice, virtually impossible to carry out. McCoy had had much experience with convoys and their eccentricities. But JW55B was proving to be the most awkward convoy he had ever escorted. Almost all convoys had difficulties with signalling, station-keeping and stragglers. But JW55B was enough to make a saint tear his hair out by the roots.

The convoy was being shadowed, and McCoy could hear, or even see, the shadowers flitting along the horizon in the twilight. But the Luftwaffe was the least of his problems. According to McCoy, JW55B 'had shown that it was incapable of reasonable station-keeping.' One ship, the British *Ocean Gypsy*, in the rear of the fifth column was a persistent straggler; 'with regard to *Ocean Gipsy*, 'McCoy said, 'all that can be said is *concordant nomine facta*'.

The British were not the only offenders. The American *Thomas V. Walter*, in a very important station leading the fourth column, was 'so inefficient at signalling as to be dangerous. Even the simplest morse signal took 30 minutes to pass to her. One message was broadcast by R/T six times, but she did not receive it'.

Added to these problems, there was the weather. There was a huge following sea making it difficult for the merchantmen to steer a proper course. Some of the waves were so enormous that ships disappeared into their hollows for what seemed like minutes at a time. 'It was dark,' said McCoy, 'the convoy was in poor order and coloured lights would present an undesirable display'. He therefore decided, 'I must disobey this order, as to turn such a convoy through 360° and keep it coherent was a manifest impossibility. I therefore took steps to comply with the C-in-C's wishes in spirit if not in letter'. Commodore Boucher suggested a reduction in speed to eight knots (instead of ten) and this was done at 3.40 pm. But the convoy continued on its course (or, at least, as near to it as *Ocean Gypsy* and the rest could manage).

Sirdar, who had been told early on 24th by Flag Officer Submarines to break radio silence, piped up with a weather report, relayed to Fraser at tea-time: wind south-south-west, force 3, visibility 25 miles, sea calm, swell slight, barometric pressure steady. *Sirdar* must have been the only one on either side to experience such balmy weather. There was a gale warning in force for Iceland sea areas, and common factors of everybody's recollections of this day, and following days, in fact of *every* day, were the seemingly perpetual darkness, the never-relenting cold and, above all, the foul weather of gale force winds and mountainous seas.

By the evening of 24th, Fraser was able to review the situation. It was still possible that *Scharnhorst* would attack the convoys, which were now approaching each other on opposite courses, but there was no word yet that she had left Alta Fjord. JW55B had definitely been sighted but there was no indication that RA55A had also been found. It seemed that JW55B was not making its scheduled speed to the east but RA55A was about to pass Bear Island, without being sighted.

There was no proper dawn on Christmas Day, only a lightening of the darkness into a dreary form of twilight. At 7.43 am McCoy signalled across to Boucher: 'Situation today. Enemy will probably attack us today with U-boat and possibly surface craft. Four more Home Fleet destroyers should join us p.m. today. *Duke of York* is about 100 miles astern coming up at 19 knots or more. Three heavy cruisers somewhere ahead. Happy Christmas.'

The four Home Fleet destroyers, *Musketeer* (Cdr.R.L. Fisher), *Opportune* (Cdr.J. Lee-Barber), *Virago* (Lt.Cdr.A.J.R.White) and *Matchless* (Lt. W.D. Shaw) joined at 12.50 pm on Christmas Day, steaming in from the convoy's port bow. The wind was by then Force 8, gale force, from the south-south-east, but the U-boats were still in evidence, with transmissions detected on more than one bearing.

Seven U-boats had been ordered to take up specific attacking positions at 6 pm on 24th, and this group was named 'Eisenbart'. At 9 am on 25th, one of this group U.601 (Kapitan Leutnant Hansen) reported the convoy on a course of 060° in position 72°25′N, 12°30′E. At 10.45 the remaining U-boats of the group were ordered to operate on the basis of Hansen's report. Hansen stayed in hydrophone contact with destroyers and unidentified vessels until 6pm. U.716 (Oberleutnant zur See Dunkelberg) closed the convoy that evening and fired one T-5 acoustic 'Gnat' torpedo at a destroyer, but missed and was driven off by a depth-charge counter-attack. One U-boat returned to Hammerfest with damage and the rest were ordered to take up a new patrol line further to the east.

Now that JW55B's escort had been strengthened, Fraser 'felt confident that, if the *Scharnhorst* attacked the convoy, Force 1 and the escort destroyers would either drive her off or inflict damage which would give me time to close'. That night Force 2 steamed to the eastward at 17 knots. 'There was an unpleasant sea', Fraser wrote, 'and conditions in *Duke of York* were most uncomfortable, few people obtaining any sleep'.

Even fewer people were asleep, at least on Fraser's staff, when the 'Emergency ULTRA' signal was received at 2.16 am.: '*Scharnhorst* probably sailed 6 pm. 25th December'. This was followed at once by a further ULTRA, giving more details and a reconnaissance report from a German aircraft north of the 72nd parallel putting the convoy at 20 miles distant. This was the only sighting made by any of the six aircraft on reconnaissance flights on Christmas Day, but it added to what was now a considerable amount of reconnaissance reporting provided over a period of four days. Hansen, of U.601, also signalled again at 2.20 pm on Christmas Day, with the convoy's position given on the German secret squared chart, course 060°, speed 8 knots.

Access to ULTRA information was always closely restricted, to certain flag officers, and nominated staff officers — the fewer the better (and they were not, incidentally, supposed to place themselves in a position where there was any likelihood of falling into enemy hands). The Admiralty had always to guard against the terrible possibility of compromising the ULTRA source and losing such a priceless asset, by allowing the enemy to suspect its existence. The greatest care had to be taken that ships at sea did not act suspiciously, by turning up at U-boat 'milch cow' rendezvous, for example, too often for luck or coincidence. In this case Fraser and Burnett were both in the ULTRA 'club' and as covering forces could receive and act upon ULTRA normally.

The Admiralty also wanted McCoy to know, so as to avoid him being utterly surprised should he encounter *Scharnhorst*. But McCoy was not privy to ULTRA. It was better for the Admiralty to tell him, rather than Fraser or Burnett, to avoid breaking radio silence. Thus, at 3.19 am on 26th, the Admiralty made another signal, addressed to McCoy, and repeated to Fraser and Burnett; 'Admiralty appreciate *Scharnhorst* is probably at sea'. This was received in the flagship at 3.39 am and has always been given as the time the news arrived. In fact, an ULTRA signal had been received more than an hour earlier.

There was no point in waking everybody up in the middle of the night. The news was broadcast through the ships in the morning, when the watches were changing and the hands were having breakfast. Lieutenant Bryce Ramsden, Royal Marines, in *Jamaica* heard the news at his action station, controlling the port 4-inch H.A. gun director, 'D'you hear there? This is the Commander speaking. We have just received a signal from C-in-C. The *Scharnhorst* is at sea. Hands will be piped to action stations in five minutes' time. That is all.'

'For a second my heart stopped beating, and I tried to digest it,' said Ramsden. 'The *Scharnhorst* is at sea. The *Scharnhorst* is at sea. Then it had happened at last. No one said anything much, except for a momentary exclamation at the news. It was too big a thing, this sudden realisation of weeks, months of sea-time covering convoys, cruisers plodding away near Norway and Bear Island. Russia to Iceland, Iceland to Russia, hours of patient watch-keeping in foul weather and freezing seas, guarding against the possibility of this one thing. And suddenly, in the middle of one such watch, the news had been flung at us. I telephoned down to the control position below to find out if they had heard the pipe. Yes, they had heard it, and that seemed that. A sense of the inevitable came over me. I was embroiled in a great machine of movement and purpose. Something big was going to happen.'

Every ship was buzzing with the news. So the *Scharnhorst* was out after all! Was she as fast and formidable, as powerful and dangerous, as everybody had always said? Well, they would soon know. So the *Scharnhorst* was out. So they would sink her. That was what they had trained so hard to do and that was what they were going to do. This underlying mood of sublime confidence was well expressed by Musician Ernie Heather, one of *Duke of York*'s Royal Marine Band, whose action station was in the Transmitting Station, deep down in the battleship's armoured citadel, where all the information about the target was collated and fed to the guns. Even if *Scharnhorst* did come out, Ernie Heather himself would never see her. But he had no doubt about the outcome. 'We had our confidence in the ship we were sailing in, our confidence in our officers, and — though nobody would ever speak about it — our confidence in each other. So that should we come into contact with that enemy, then we were going to do our utmost and our level best to *annihilate* it ... '

CHAPTER 5

Battle is joined:
Force 1 and *Scharnhorst*

THE *Scharnhorst* had indeed sailed, on the evening of Christmas Day, just as the Admiralty had appreciated. She and her attendant destroyers cleared the last point of land and reached the open sea just before midnight, steering north with a rising gale of wind and a menacing quartering sea from the south-west. To match the weather, *Scharnhorst*'s departure was clouded by the same atmosphere of indecision and uncertainty which had hung over the last few months of her life.

But for Doenitz, *Scharnhorst* would never have sailed. Karl Doenitz had been a brilliant Head of the U-boat Arm, but he was only an indifferently successful Head of the Navy. He was a clever man, and he had a better way with Hitler than his predecessor, but he lacked any long-term strategic vision for the Navy. In any case, the war at sea had begun to turn decisively against Germany by the time Doenitz took over the supreme command and he could offer only palliatives, involving his beloved U-boats in ever more desperate expedients.

However, Doenitz had virtually staked his new reputation upon a successful sortie by heavy ships against a convoy. That would be a splendid *coup* to lay before his Fuhrer. The German armies in the east needed all the support they could get. At a conference with Hitler at the Wolfsschanze on 19th and 20th December, Doenitz told the Fuhrer 'that *Scharnhorst* and the destroyers of the task force *will* attack the next allied convoy headed from England for Russia via the northern route, if a successful operation seems assured. It would pay to reinforce the submarines in the North if the convoys were to travel the northern route regularly. The C-in-C Navy had already ordered additional U-boats to operate in the Arctic Ocean.'

Apart from the cautious little caveat about the 'successful operation', that seemed confident enough, and, as events unfolded later in the month, Doenitz saw 'a splendid chance for the *Scharnhorst*'. The position, as he said, was a 'convoy, carrying war material for Russia and protected by a cruiser escort which was no match for our battleship, was sailing through an area within easy reach of our battle group. Its position, course and speed were known. Because of ice in the vicinity of Bear Island which prevented evasive action and the superior speed of the German ships, it could not hope to avoid our attack.

'Our reconnaissance had not discovered the presence of any heavy enemy formation, though that, of course, did not mean that no such force was at sea. But if it were, it must have been a long way from the convoy, and the *Scharnhorst* seemed to have every chance of delivering a rapid and successful attack'. That was an admirable summary of the position. There is no doubt that *Scharnhorst*, in the circumstances, *should* have brought off a tremendous success against JW55B.

Doenitz could see no disadvantages. If the weather was rough, that surely was to *Scharnhorst*'s advantage. It had been so quiet recently in the north that the British would surely not expect a sortie by *Scharnhorst* (in fact, the very opposite was the case: it was precisely because *Scharnhorst* had been so inactive that Fraser expected her now).

The orders that Doenitz drafted, which he intended *Scharnhorst* to sail to carry out on Christmas Day 1943, were: the enemy was trying to hamper the 'heroic endeavours of our eastern armies by sending valuable convoys of arms and food to the Russians' and the Navy must help; *Scharnhorst* and the destroyers will attack the convoy; any engagement will be broken off at the Task Force commander's discretion (once again, the heavy note of caution); in principle the task force commander was to break off 'on appearance of strong enemy forces'.

The more precise orders which Admiral Schniewind sent to Bey, and which were the basis of the operation codenamed OSTFRONT, were even more cautious: 'group attack on convoy will be delivered by *Scharnhorst* and five destroyers on 26.12. at first light (approx. 1000); concerted attack will only be delivered if conditions are favourable (weather, visibility, accurate information regarding enemy); if conditions do not suit *Scharnhorst* (and here Schniewind seemed to be going in direct contradiction to Doenitz) destroyers will attack alone, battle cruiser to stand off and observe, or, if decided advisable, to be in readiness in outer fjord'. Neither Doenitz's nor Schniewind's signal was a clear-cut clarion call to action. What cumulative effect they had on Bey it is now impossible to say, but Bey should have taken the spirit and not the letter, and attacked with *Scharnhorst*, or the destroyers, or with them all as the occasion arose. A fleet commander of the first calibre would have gone for his opponent's throat, without bothering which hand he should use.

To the ship's company of *Scharnhorst*, and especially the older hands amongst them, it had been obvious for some time that some new operation was brewing. They had begun the fresh programme of exercises on 14th December, returning to Lange Fjord instead of their old berth at Oskarneset in Kaa Fjord. Lange Fjord was much longer and, if anything, even bleaker than Kaa Fjord. Their new berth was near the village of Sopenes, at the head of the fjord, where the buses ran occasionally over the hills to Alt-Eidet, and home leave (for the few who managed it) but otherwise it had not much to recommend it.

But clearly something was about to happen. They went to action stations and manned AA guns for the solitary Russian reconnaissance aircraft droning overhead. The Admiral went back to *Tirpitz* in Kaa Fjord and stayed there, although members of the staff and the ship's officers came and went, as though in obedience to the ebb and flow of rumours — of aircraft sightings, of convoys at sea, of a British heavy group in support. Twice, on 18th December and again on 22nd, they went to reduced notice for sea. By 22nd there could no longer be any doubt that a convoy to Russia was at sea.

The much-maligned Luftwaffe had, in fact, provided a great deal of reconnaissance information about JW55B and its escort over a period of some days. There had been the meteorological aircraft's sighting on the morning of the 22nd. Later the same day, three Focke Wulf Fw 200 Kondors and one Blohm & Voss Bv. 138, all radar-equipped, had flown reconnaissance flights between 3.45 pm and 2 am the next morning from the Norwegian coast out to 9°W, and from the latitude of the Arctic Circle down to Cape Stadtlandet. They had found three vessels, very probably Burnett's Force 1, on the evening of the 22nd and another 'large vessel' unidentified early on the 23rd. 'Results', the signal said, 'are unreliable as sets were partly out of commission'. The German Air Force, like the German Navy, consistently wrote down the effectiveness of its radar.

On 23rd there were more reports, from the Junkers Ju.88 in the morning and from another Bv. 138 in the afternoon, two more sightings on 24th, including one at 7.45 pm of '12 merchant ships, up to 5,000 tons, three destroyers, far apart, Nothing further made out owing to bad visibility. Defence by medium and light flak'. There were six reconnaissance flights on Christmas Day, and one report of the convoy. U-boats also sighted and reported the convoy at various time between the evening of 23rd and Christmas Day. Altogether, a properly kept-up plot should have given a fair picture of JW55B's likely position, course, speed by the time *Scharnhorst* sailed.

The only real uncertainty was whether or not there was a British heavy covering force in support of the convoy (and this, of course, would have a crucial effect on whether and how *Scharnhorst* was deployed). The possibility of such a force being at sea had been realised for some days before *Scharnhorst* sailed. It had been mentioned in Captain (U-boats) Norway's signal of 7.20 pm on 23rd, giving details of the Bv138's convoy sighting just after midday.

Early the next day, staff officers at Narvik and at Kiel had discussed the question over the teleprinter, referring to 'a British unit located yesterday by its transmissions may well be the cover force closing'. There was talk of 'the supposed enemy squadron', of 'complete reconnaissance and security from the enemy ... not guaranteed', of 'the operation of the task force' carrying ' an element of risk', of a decision on 'how far the risk is justified'. The further a staff officer was from *Scharnhorst*, the more in favour he was of her putting to sea and the more sanguine his view of her chances: the authentic voice of the staff officer was echoed by Kapitan zur See Paul Friedrich Duwel at Narvik, who called for 'either an unequivocal Yes, or an equally unequivocal No. I am against any compromise. No one should forget that the *Scharnhorst* is a battleship, not a torpedo boat.' With that the staff officer on the other end of the line in Kiel, Kapitan zur See Hans Marks, on Schniewind's staff, could only agree.

This exchange between Duwel and Marks was reported to have taken place between 5 am and 6.45 am on 24th and it is therefore hard to establish which enemy transmission of the day before they were referring to. Fraser was still at Akureyri and did not sail until 11pm on 23rd. Burnett was at sea, but did not break radio silence.

However, discussion about a possible British heavy force continued on 24th. Late that evening, at 11.45 pm, Fliegerfuhrer Lofotens signalled his reconnaissance intentions for Christmas Day. Two Blohm & Voss Bv. 138 flying boats were to be flown to look for the 'battle group approaching from the south-west' and this heavy group was mentioned again in another signal at 8 am on Christmas Day.

There had been some evidence from direction-finders. Fraser's signals to Rear Admiral (Destroyers) and to McCoy on 24th had been picked up by German direction finders in the Heligoland Bight and at Kirkenes up in the Arctic. The German B-Dienst decoding service actually located a transmission from a British ship at 6.29 pm on 24th (although this was some hours after Fraser's signals had been transmitted from *Duke of York*). The staff at Kiel decided that bearings were inaccurate; all that could be admitted was that the signals appeared to come from a ship some 200 miles astern of JW55B. Schniewind thought there was 'no proof as yet of a cover force being at sea.'

At Narvik, the head quarters of Admiral Northern Waters, von Kluber (who was actually on leave at the time) the signals were assumed to be from the British heavy covering force. Bey, too, who seems to have been growing steadily more alarmed and gloomy about the plans the staff were making for him and the task force, was also inclined to think that a British heavy group was at sea. It seemed to him that the Luftwaffe reconnaissance was still quite inadequate and that none of the conditions he thought essential before *Scharnhorst* could operate were being fulfilled.

The only man who never had any doubts was Doenitz. He demanded much more definite proof that a British heavy covering force was at sea; in his view, all the evidence was negative, that such a force was *not* at sea. Schniewind might have misgivings, envisaging *Scharnhorst* sheltering in the fjords until the time was right, and saying gloomily that 'on the whole the chances of a major success are slender and the stakes high', but Doenitz felt that the convoy could be taken by surprise. Bey might say that he would prefer to attack with destroyers only, leaving *Scharnhorst* in support, but Doenitz countered that a destroyer attack could never succeed, because the convoy was escorted by cruisers. All the meteorologists might point out that the weather was bad and growing worse, that there was no proper daylight and *Scharnhorst* would be at a disadvantage in the gloom. But Doenitz felt that if the weather was bad, so much the better for *Scharnhorst*. In short, Doenitz believed that a great chance had come for a swift 'hit and run' raid by *Scharnhorst*; she could get in close, do untold damage, and get out again, long before Fraser was on the scene. In this, Doenitz was undoubtedly right.

So, with Doenitz adamant that the operation must go ahead, the German Admiralty gave orders, at 2.12 pm on Christmas Day, for the Battle Group to put to sea. Navy Group North signalled the codeword OSTFRONT at 2.15. Admiral Northern Waters at Narvik signalled to the Battle Group at 3.27 'Most Immediate. Ostfront 1700/25/12. (When this signal was broken and arrived in the Operational Intelligence Centre in the British Admiralty, the note was scribbled on it, 'Ostfront will be referred to in English as "Epilepsy").

But by the time 'Ostfront' was received in *Scharnhorst*, Christmas Day had already been irretrievably spoiled for her sailors. Whilst the men of the Home Fleet had been having a memorably miserable Christmas Day at sea (there was a gale warning at 4 am., and Ramsden, in *Jamaica*, said 'I think all of us, while trying to remember Christmas in our homes, were trying to forget it on board') it had begun very well for *Scharnhorst*. In an atmosphere of relaxed discipline, Kapitan Hintze had done informal rounds of the ship, complimenting the men on the decorations of their messes, and where any man had not received his full ration of cigarettes, ordering the amount to be made up to him. The Christmas mail was on board and everybody had their letters and parcels from home. One party of sailors had gone ashore to ski. The shoreline of the fjords was never-changing, but at Christmas time at least, the snow, the fir-trees, the small huts, the smoke rising into the steel-coloured sky, all had a certain appropriate, if bleak, charm. *Stille Nacht, heilige nacht,* sang the ship's choir.

This Christmas peace was shattered at 10.55, by a signal from Bey in *Tirpitz:* 'Battle Group is to be at 1 hours readiness from 1300/25/12. *Scharnhorst* and 4th Z-Flotilla are to acknowledge'. At 1158, the minesweeper R.121, in Kaa Fjord, was ordered 'Proceed to *Scharnhorst* in Lange Fjord. Further orders there.' Johannesson, in Z.29, said later that he had not received the 'Ostfront' signal in his ship until 4.27 pm, only 23 minutes before the prescribed sailing time of 5pm. But he must have been ready in time because *Scharnhorst* signalled at 3.30 'Battle Group ready for sea at 16.30.'

For *Scharnhorst*'s sailors, these sudden orders, in the middle of Christmas Day, were no more than they expected of 'them' on the staff, in fact some of the more cynical of the ship's company believed it was all an exercise specifically designed by 'them' to ruin their Christmas.

At 5.15 pm *Scharnhorst* signalled the patrol vessel V.5903 that she 'would pass outward-bound as from 6 pm.' (This signal, together with that to R.121

to proceed to Lange Fjord, Fliegerfuhrer Lofoten's convoy sighting report of 25th, and the Most Immediate 'Ostfront' signal, were all broken and received in the OIC in the evening of 25th, or early on the morning of 26th, and prompted the Admiralty signal that *Scharnhorst* was at sea).

But *Scharnhorst* did not sail at 5pm as in the Ostfront signal, or at 6 pm as she had told V.5903. Bey and his staff had first to rejoin from *Tirpitz*. Some accounts say that Admiral Bey arrived alongside *Scharnhorst* in R.121 at 5 pm and held a conference on board attended by his staff and the destroyer captains at 5.15. But Leutnant Wilhelm Maclot, Captain of R.56, and Sub.Lt.Werner Hauss, of R.58, who had both been ordered by signal at Hammerfest at 3 pm: Proceed at once to *Scharnhorst* in Lange Fjord, to provide minesweeping escort to 'Point Lucie' (Point Lucie: a navigational reference point west of Soroy Island, marking the north-eastern limit of a German minefield laid off the Norwegian coast) said that they had arrived alongside *Scharnhorst* at 5 pm and R.121, with the admiral on board, had some alongside just before 7 pm. However, there is at least one serious discrepancy in their account: even at their stated full speed of 16 knots, which they could not in any case have achieved in the weather prevailing that afternoon, they could not possibly have left Hammerfest at 3 pm and covered the 50 miles to *Scharnhorst*'s berth at the end of Lange Fjord in two hours.

But the minesweeper captains were unlikely to be wrong in their memory of the weather. According to their account, a very strong south-westerly wind, gusting up to gale force, was blowing along the length of Varg Sund, dead in their teeth. The *Elvegust* was storming down off the mountain slopes on the north side of the fjord and whipping the surface water into a maelstrom of spray and foam. Visibility varied between half a mile at most and a few feet in mist and steady rain. The minesweepers' bows butted into a short but nastily steep sea. Both captains had difficulty in sighting the rows of tiny black buoys marking the net barrier of Lange Fjord. Both Maclot and Hauss had had a great deal of experience of Norwegian coastal waters. It seemed to them very unlikely they would be able to sweep *Scharnhorst* out as far as Point Lucie in weather like this.

Neither of them had been on board *Scharnhorst* before and they were both struck by 'the hectic rush, the feverish activity everywhere. The place was like a disturbed antheap. Every man they met looked as if he was on some vital errand, engaged in a race against time'. The sailor showing them the way 'sped through what seemed a varitable labyrinth of gangways, past doors, companionways, flats, workshops, gun sub-structures, telephones, control posts, then more passages, steep iron stairways, cables and never-ending rows of compartments'.

Maclot and Hauss, slightly ill-at-ease, like all 'small ship' men in the flagship, mentally compared the easy chairs in the cabins, the pictures on the panelled bulkheads, the framed photographs on the desks, with the spartan little cabins and hard bunks of their own ships. They met the signals officer,

Kapitan Leutnant Behr, the Executive Officer Fregatten Kapitan Dominik, and Hintze himself. In Hintze's cabin Hauss noticed a bowl of fruit, nuts and candy, decorated with springs of fir and silver tinsel ribbon and remembered, with a start of surprise, that this was, after all, Christmas Day.

After half an hour on board, Maclot and Hauss went back to their own ships, noting that nobody had even offered them a drink. Hintze asked Hauss to post a letter for him. The mail on board had already closed. This was the last tangible message from *Scharnhorst* to the outside world.

Just before sailing the ship's company mustered aft on the quarterdeck where Dominik spoke to them. One survivor's account said that only the guns crews were there. But a named survivor, Matrosengefreiter (Able Seaman) Günter Sträter, actually a gunnery rating, as loading number on the after 4.1" gun, said it was the Gunnery Officer Korvetten Kapitan Bredenbreuker who addressed them. The men were told that there was a heavily-laden convoy on its way to Russia. *Scharnhorst* was sailing, with five destroyers, to attack the convoy and so to relieve some of the pressure on the Eastern Front.

By all accounts this announcement was greeted with tremendous cheering and one account has it that Dominik was hoisted on to the shoulders of the enthusiastic crowd and carried forward. But there can be no doubt that *Scharnhorst*'s ship's company were in very good heart and welcomed the prospect of action. As one of her officers wrote to a former captain of *Scharnhorst*, 'Despite the polar night and the solitude of this place, the condition of the ship and her crew remains excellent, and we in *Scharnhorst* face the future with pride and confidence.'

The last to come on board was a party of sailors under Oberbootsmannsmaat (Petty Officer) Wilhelm Gödde (the senior survivor, in the end). They had been carrying out a patrol off the surrounding fjord waters, armed with small charges to deter midget submarines or underwater swimmers; this was a protective patrol introduced after the attack on *Tirpitz* three months before.

With Gödde and his party on board, *Scharnhorst* sailed with a total of 1,968 officers and men: 45 ships officers, five staff officers and a second gunnery officer from *Tirpitz* making 51 in all; 379 ships chief and petty officers, and 14 from the staff, making 393; and 1,438 sailors, plus another 14 of the staff, for a total of 1,452. There were also 72 officers under training (five midshipmen, 34 cadets and 33 others). Many of the cadets were members of the Hitler Youth who had joined the Navy under a scheme introduced on 26 July 1943. They had the rating of 'Marine Helfer' and were by that stage in the war the main source of new officers; they would nearly all have been destined for the U-boat arm. They had done a course at the Naval gunnery schools at Swinemunde and further training on the Hitler Youth training ship at Ziegenort, Stettin. They were on board *Scharnhorst* to gain some sea experience.

Scharnhorst had weighed anchor, got under way and cleared the inner boom by 7.55 pm. She was through the outer barrage of Lange Fjord 45 minutes later and steering into the wider Alta Fjord. Johanneson in Z.29 (Korv. Kap. Theodor Von Mutius) took station ahead, with Z.38 (Korv. Kap. Gerfried Brutzer) and Z.34 (Korv.Kap.Karl Hetz) to port and starboard. Outside, they were joined by Z.30 (Korv.Kap.Karl Heinrich Lampe) and Z.33 (Korv.Kap.Erich Holtorf) who had come up from Kaa Fjord. The whole force made a sharp turn to port around the point of Klubbeneset and headed up the long stretch of Stjern Sund at 17 knots.

This speed was, of course, too much for R.56 and R.58 toiling along in the rear. They could make 16 knots, (only 14 with their gear streamed) and that only in good weather. No signal was made to them, and when R.121 tried to raise *Scharnhorst* on the R/T she had a dusty answer; it seemed she had interrupted whilst Bey was speaking to Johanneson and was brusquely told not to intervene whilst deep was thus addressing deep. Nobody took any more notice of the minesweepers and eventually they peeled off to starboard on their own initiative and steered for Hammerfest and home. Astern of them, V.5903 towed the outer barrage net back into position again, to seal off the fjord entrance. To port the shapes of *Scharnhorst* and her escort had already vanished into the blackness.

Meanwhile, at Kiel, Admiral Schniewind had been having second thoughts. He had seen the weather forecast, which did not make cheerful reading: Southerly gale, force 8-9, increasing, sea state 6-7. On 26th, veering to south-westerly, force 6-8, with a heavy south-westerly swell. Overcast with rain showers, visibility 3-4 miles, improving to 10 miles intermittently. Snow-falls in Barents Sea'. This was the weather in the area where *Scharnhorst* and her destroyers were going to have to look for the convoy.

Schniewind had telephoned Doenitz at 8 pm, to reassure the C-in-C that the operation had started well and that he himself had every confidence in the outcome. But Schniewind was already being assailed from all sides by voices advising caution. Kapitan Rudolf Peters, deputising for the absent von Kluber at Narvik, telephoned at 7.15.He too had seen the forecast. In his opinion, he said, the destroyers just could not operate in such weather and he suggested that 'Ostfront' be cancelled. From Lofoten the Luftwaffe reported that the weather was too bad for any reconnaissance flights on the following day.

If the destroyers could not operate with *Scharnhorst*, and there would be no air reconnaissance, two vital parts of the operational plan would be missing. Schniewind's own Chief of Staff, Rear Admiral Hellmuth Heye, urged that 'Ostfront' be called off. At 8.30 Schniewind telephoned Berlin again and spoke to Doenitz' Chief of Staff, Vice Admiral Wilhelm Meizel. Schniewind told him of the weather report from Narvik, of his own misgivings and suggested that 'Ostfront' be cancelled. Meisel said he would pass the message to Doenitz. In a few minutes he rang back. The Grand Admiral could see no reason why 'Ostfront' should be cancelled. The operation was to go ahead. He had already drafted a signal to the task force.

Few admirals in all naval history could have put to sea so bedevilled by doubts and misgivings as Erich Bey. Clearly he did not share the sublime confidence of *Scharnhorst*'s officers and ship's company. He was already setting his doubts down on paper and he passed them to Schniewind in a signal transmitted as *Scharnhorst* was just clearing Stjern Sund and moving out into the open waters of Soroy Sund, at 9.16 pm: 'Reference your proposition figure 6c (this is taken to mean a reference to Schniewind's proposal of the day before that destroyers should operate alone if the situation was unfavourable for *Scharnhorst* herself to attack) in operations zone south-westerly 6-9 expected. Use of destroyer weapons gravely .impaired. (Signed) Task Force'.

This signal must have appeared to Schniewind (who had just heard, at 9 pm. that the Luftwaffe from the Lofotens had lost contact with the convoy) as a despairing cry from a man who wanted to be recalled. But Schniewind could take no action himself. He had read the Grand Admiral's signal which reached the task force just before midnight, and left Bey in no doubt what was required of him and his ships:

"1. Enemy attempting to aggravate the difficulties of our eastern land forces in their heroic struggle by sending an important convoy of provisions and arms for Russians. We must help.

2. Convoy to be attacked by *Scharnhorst* and destroyers.

3. Tactical situation to be exploited skilfully and boldly. Engagement not to be broken off till full success achieved. Every advantage to be pressed. *Scharnhorst*'s superior fire-power crucial. Her deployment therefore urgent. Destroyers to engage as suitable.

4. Disengagement at own discretion, and automatically if heavy forces encountered.

5. Crews to be briefed accordingly. I am confident of your offensive spirit. Heil und Sieg. Doenitz. Grand Admiral."

Hintze passed the Grand Admiral's signal to his ship's company at 3.45 am just as the watches were changing over. Günter Sträter recalled his actual words: 'Message from the Grand Admiral. Attack the convoy wherever you find it. You'll bring relief to the eastern front'.

The Grand Admiral's message was received without much emotion by *Scharnhorst*'s sailors at that hour. *Scharnhorst* had cleared Point Lucie and taken her last fix on a point of land at 11.04 pm. She then steered 010 at 25 knots. The weather was even worse than forecast. At that speed the ships were overtaking a quartering sea but, now and again, even a ship of *Scharnhorst*'s size would seem to slip uneasily sideways into the side of a huge wave, before struggling up and out again, with a most unpleasant motion; there were many sea-sick down below, and not only amongst the raw naval cadets.

As for the destroyers, they were steaming at the limits of their sea-worthiness. Their bows plunged into the great masses of water ahead, and they were being constantly washed down over the whole lengths of their upper deck. Sometimes, a destroyer would rear into the air, showing her forefoot and her keel exposed as far aft as the forward turret. Overhead the gale howled and roared, as though all the devils in an Arctic hell were shouting with fury. For the men on exposed bridges and look-out positions, the bitterly cold wind seemed to slice through to the very bone, and the snow-storms blotted out even the superb German binoculars. There could be no question of fighting in such weather. It was all a man could do to survive.

At sea, *Scharnhorst*'s ship's company were in two watches, four hours on and four hours off. On sailing, the Starboard Watch had gone on watch, while the Port Watch cleared up the ship, stowing away sacks of potatoes and hundreds of boxes and packing cases. The Port Watch relieved the Starboard at midnight, when the night was already bitterly cold and the sea steadily rising. At 4 am the Port Watch were relieved and slung their hammocks for the first time, but as they said 'we were in them just long enough to thaw out a little and then we had to lash them up again'. The Port Watch had breakfast at 6 am., and at 7 went to Action Stations. They were joined at 8 am by the Starboard Watch and both stayed closed up from then until the end. Clearly, most of the Port Watch in *Scharnhorst* were dead-tired long before the action even began.

As the task force headed north, the U-boats were informed that it was at sea, by signal at 12.43 am.: '*Scharnhorst* and five destroyers left Lopp Havet, intention to attack convoy at about 0900/26th'. Bey never had a reply to his signal of 9.16. It was not received in Kiel until 2.19 am and not in Berlin until 3.56 am. (which probably accounts for the suggestions, made for many years after the war, that Bey had betrayed his own ships by transmitting this signal from a position in the open sea; in fact it was sent whilst *Scharnhorst* was still in the fjords, and there was other evidence that she had sailed).

In the meantime, Schniewind had had an answer to his own teleprinter message, recording his misgivings, at about 8 pm the evening before. Doenitz was still adamant that 'Ostfront' go ahead, with *Scharnhorst* if necessary acting alone, 'like an armed raider'. Schniewind therefore signalled to *Scharnhorst*, in a message received on board at about 3 am: 'If destroyers cannot keep sea, possibility of *Scharnhorst* completing task alone using mercantile warfare tactics should be considered. Decision rests with Admiral commanding'.

Bey asked Johannesson in the leading destroyer for his opinion. Evidently an optimist, Rolf Johannesson replied, at about 3.15: 'Following wind and sea. No difficulties so far, but situation remains problematical. Expect weather to improve.'

One of Bey's chief complaints had always been that he was not provided with enough reconnaissance reports. It is true that he did not receive all the Luftwaffe signals, and those he did were late or vague. In that middle watch, two signals were received from Fliegerfuhrer Lofoten, one at 12.38 am. the second at 12.51 am. They were both shadowing reports, by aircraft which had sighted the convoy the previous afternoon, but neither gave the convoy's position or composition. The second, however, by a Blohm & Voss Bv. 138, did mention that there was no covering force within fifty miles of the convoy. But by the time Bey received them, both sightings were nearly twelve hours old.

However, the convoy was still being reported by U-boats. At 3.27 am., Dunkelberg in U.716 reported that he had been forced down by convoy escorts. The grid reference he gave in his signal seemed to chime with *Scharnhorst*'s plot of the convoy's progress. At 4.23 am the task force altered to 030, and at 5 am back to 004. By 7 am, *Scharnhorst*'s Navigating Officer, Korvetten Kapitan Lanz calculated that they were now within 30 miles of the convoy and ahead of it. Bey signalled to Johannesson 'Fourth Destroyer Flotilla to start reconnaissance astride estimated course of 250, speed 12 knots'.

The task force turned on to the new course which was almost dead into wind and weather, with the five destroyers spread out in line abreast, in searching order, and *Scharnhorst* herself some ten miles (a very long way indeed, in the circumstances) astern of them. At 7.55 am Bey signalled a new course to Johanneson: 'Alte to 230'. Although Bey did not seem aware of it, he had now placed his task force almost within 11" gun range of his target. Another forty minutes and the convoy might well have been in sight. With such information as he had, with some luck and maybe some intuition, Bey had very nearly pulled off a brilliant interception. At 8.40 that morning, McCoy estimated that *Scharnhorst* was only 36 miles south-east of JW55B. But, at this very point, things began to go awry.

Scharnhorst had two radar sets, the main gunnery 'Seetakt' set, working on 80 centimetres, fitted high up in the foremast, and the air warning set, very probably a 'Hohentwiel' Luftwaffe ASV set, working on 55 centimetres, fitted lower down on the mainmast. 'Seetakt''s makers, the GEMA Company, had begun development work on the set long before the war (*Graf Spee* had 'Seetakt' at the battle of the River Plate in December 1939). Although it was comparatively low-powered, at only 7 kilowatts, by December 1943 'Seetakt' had been refined to the point where it was a reasonably good gunnery ranging set. Its large characteristically German 'mattress-type' aerial could detect a heavy ship accurately at about eleven miles, a destroyer at about eight and a torpedo-boat at three, but it would not pick up the splashes of falling shell shot. It had reasonable directional qualities, giving bearings accurate to within 0.2 degrees of arc. The 'Hohentwiel', although higher-powered at 30 kilowatts, had nothing like the same tactical capabilities as 'Seetakt'; it could pick up an aircraft at about 24 miles, but surface ships only out to about 4½ miles and its directional powers depended a great deal upon the skill and experience of the operator.

The Germans were always aware that their radar was inferior in performance to the British (this was not in fact *always* so, but the Germans believed it was). Their sets did not have the range, echo definition or reliability of the British sets. The Germans had almost obsessive fears about the dangers of radar transmissions being located and seemed always chary of using radar. Many of their officers tended to discount the efficiency of radar (just as many of the more conservative British captains also did, at least early in the war).

It seems that the standing orders were that radar should never be switched on in German ships without a specific order (the same rule applied, of course, in British warships). But such an order, it seems, was likely to be given only in exceptional circumstances. It is unlikely that *Scharnhorst* was operating her 'Hohentwiel' as she closed JW55B that morning. But, incredibly, it seems possible that she was not operating 'Seetakt' either.

It may possibly have been a fleeting radar contact which caused Bey to turn north at 8.20 am. But he did not inform Johannesson, some miles ahead, and all five destroyers maintained their course to the South-westward. Soon *Scharnhorst* was steaming at right angles to the destroyers. She lost touch with them, and never regained it. In the end, the destroyers played no part whatsoever in the battle.

In the latitude of 73°North, nautical twilight (when the sun is 12° below the horizon, or higher) begins at 8.39 am. There is no civil twilight (the sun 6° less below the horizon) at all. At 9 am, in the first bleak lightening of the gloom, barely worth the name of twilight, Johannesson saw the shape of a destroyer to the north. Z-30 also sighted it and came to the same conclusion: it must be one of the convoy's escorts. Johannesson signalled the enemy report to *Scharnhorst*. But the stranger was Z-38, out of position to the northward. Beyond her, away to the north-east, Johannesson saw a momentary light on the horizon. It was no more than a pale pink glow, like starshell. But German starshell gave a bright white light.

Whether or not Bey had any further plans, whether he received Johannesson's signal and intended to act upon it or not, whatever he might have meant to do, he had no more time. At 9.26 am, on 26 December without any warning from radar or from look-outs, starshell exploded almost overhead, flooding *Scharnhorst* in its cold, terrifying and totally unexpected light.

CHAPTER 6

Scharnhorst and Force 1 turn away

THE *Scharnhorst* might have been surprised, but almost nobody else was. Bey and Hintze might have fancied themselves to be quite alone. In fact, they already had a considerable audience, which was soon to become a worldwide one. In London, in the Operational Intelligence Centre, about a dozen more signals were decrypted in the course of that St Stephen's Day (*not* Boxing Day, it being a Sunday) but no more were passed on after the signal of 3.19 am, to McCoy and all concerned, that *Scharnhorst* was out. ULTRA had played its part. It was up to Fraser now. In the O.I.C., Cdr. Norman Denning, the man who had first set up the Organisation, made a mental calculation on when the British and German forces would encounter one another (he was disappointed to find himself twenty minutes out).

At 4 am on 26th December the convoy JW55B was in approximate formation, but not keeping good station, some fifty miles south of Bear Island and steering about E.N.E. at a nominal 8 knots (but actually nearer 6), whilst the westbound RA55B was well clear, about 220 miles west of Bear Island; although somewhat scattered by gales on 27th and 28th, the convoy reformed with all its ships and reached Loch Ewe unmolested on New Year's Day, 1944.

At 4 am, Force 1 was about 150 miles east of JW55B, and about 145 miles E.S.E. of Bear Island, steering 235° at 18 knots (see map 1) Burnett's intention was to be about 30 miles due east of the convoy's 'furthest-on' position (i.e. the furthest east the convoy could be assumed to have reached by then) by the coming of twilight on the morning of 26th. Force 2 was still 280 miles west of North Cape and about 210 miles south-east of the convoy, steering 084°, at 24 knots. Fraser was still a long way away and needed to make a good deal more easting to be sure of cutting *Scharnhorst* off from her base. However, Fraser was satisfied from the plot in *Duke of York* that the stage was well set.

After he had received the '*Scharnhorst* out' signal, Fraser began to pull the threads together. At 3.44 am he signalled to Force 2 to raise steam for full speed. At 4.01 am he signalled to McCoy to turn the convoy due north (although this order was not actually completed until 6.25 am), and to

Burnett to signal his position, course and speed; in the same signal Fraser gave his own position, course and speed. Once again, he had balanced the risks and decided that it was worth breaking radio silence to keep his widespread forces in touch with him and each other. He also signalled to *Jamaica* and his four accompanying destroyers: 'Message HD 502 (i.e. *Scharnhorst* at sea) concerns you' this was arguably the understatement of the year.

JW55B had known for some time it was being shadowed. There had been High Frequency Direction Finding (H/F D/F) reports of U-boat signals from various sources. Late the previous evening, of Christmas Day, the destroyer *Wrestler* had obtained a 'first class bearing by H/F D/F believed to be enemy submarine transmitting a naval enigma signal', bearing 250 degrees, and considered 'ground wave' i.e. very probably within ten miles. This was almost certainly Dunkelberg in U.716 reporting his convoy sighting and his unsuccessful torpedo attack. At 4.50 am on 26th McCoy signalled to Boucher 'Admiralty considers *Scharnhorst* now at sea'. So now the convoy knew that it was threatened by U-boats and by a powerful surface warship.

Fraser was still putting the finishing touches to his preparations. At 6.28 he signalled to McCoy to turn the convoy to 045° and to Burnett to close the convoy 'for mutual support'. At 6.32 he asked McCoy to give his position, course and speed and, five minutes later, increased the speed of Force 2 to 25 knots. Burnett meanwhile reckoned that he had gone far enough south at 7.12 am when he turned Force 1 to the west. There was a south-westerly gale blowing, with a gigantic sea running from the south-west, and he wanted to approach the convoy from well to the south so as to avoid heading directly into the wind and sea. At 8.15, after Burnett had received JW55B's position, course and speed from McCoy, he altered Force 1's course to 305° and increased speed to 24 knots.

By now, everybody knew everybody else's position, course and speed, and had a shrewd idea of what to expect. As a precaution, at 8.14 am., McCoy positioned the four destroyers of the 36th Division on a line of bearing of 165° from the centre of the convoy, on the starboard, and most threatened side. At 9.25 am. McCoy could see the intermittent glows of star-shell almost in that very direction, approximately on a bearing of south-east. The first stages of the battle had begun.

At 8.40 *Belfast* got a radar contact on her forward Type 273 surface warning set and at 8.44 signalled to the other cruisers: 'Jig' (unidentified radar contact) bearing 295, 16 miles' (actually 35,000 yards). At that time, *Belfast* was steering 325° and Burnett estimated that the convoy bore 287° from *Belfast*, range 48 miles. *Scharnhorst*, if it were *Scharnhorst*, was squarely between Force 1 and the convoy. Bey had pulled it off, and if he could only summon up enough determination, could now go on to win the biggest victory of any German admiral of the war.

Burnett's next move at 9.01 was to form his cruisers on a line of bearing of

180°, or roughly at right angles to the bearing of the enemy contact. This seemed a logical step, but in fact was to lead to tactical difficulties. At 9.06 *Norfolk*'s Type 273 picked up the echo, bearing 261°, range 12 miles and a minute later it was *Sheffield*'s turn: 258°, 10 miles. The bearing was moving left and the range closing. The enemy was steering nearly south. At some time Bey must have decided he was far enough to the north and come round to search to the south.

By 9 am, when the range was shortening rapidly, there was a distraction: *Belfast*'s radar picked up a second contact, bearing 299°, range 24,500 yards. Plotting showed that this echo was keeping on a steady bearing, at a speed of about 8-10 knots. It might have been a straggler, possibly even *Ocean Gypsy*, or it could have been Z.38, straying from Johannesson's flotilla. The echo was held until 9.30, but Burnett ordered it to be disregarded.

The word had been passed round all three cruisers that action was imminent. Many of the sailors had been at their action stations all night. One young ordinary seaman in *Belfast*, on his first trip to sea in wartime, had spent the night in 'A' shell room when 'the order "Stand By" comes down from the gun-house,' he wrote, under the unusual *nom de plume* of 'Banderillero'. 'Everybody gets up, deflates and put on their lifebelts which they have been using as pillows, the shellroom's crew start unshipping the bars which hold the shells in place in the trays. The magazine and handling-room men go down to their respective stations and the hatches are closed on top of them. Everyone is tensed for us to open fire ... '

At 9.15 the main echo bore 250°, range 13,000 yards. Burnett ordered the other two cruisers to form on a line of bearing from him of 160°, but as the bearing of the enemy continued to draw rapidly left, and aft, there was already a possibility that each cruiser might foul the range of any cruiser on the starboard, or disengaged, side of her. Meanwhile, Force 1 was still steering 325°, running past the enemy, towards the convoy.

At 9.21 it was *Sheffield*, the middle cruiser of the three who made the glad, thrilling signal: 'Enemy in sight. Bearing 222°; range 13,000 yards'. Three minutes later *Belfast* opened fire with starshell but failed to spot the enemy. At 9.27 Burnett ordered *Norfolk* to open fire, at the very mount when *Scharnhorst* was altering thirty degrees to port to a course of 150°. Within two minutes Burnett had discovered that *Norfolk* was obscuring *Belfast*'s range and was ordering her to 'drop back, clear my range'. Down below, Banderillero heard 'gunfire to starboard and we can feel our 4-inch guns firing star-shell. We all look at one another and ask, "Why aren't our 6-inch opening up?" or words to this bowdlerised effect. The firing lasts a few minutes and we are all very impatient to know what has happened. Then comes the Commander's voice: "After a few broadsides from the *Norfolk* the enemy, whoever she may be, has turned away and we are now chasing her."

'This is a sign for everyone to relax and ask each other: "Well I wonder what she is. I hope we aren't up against the *Scharnhorst*."

At 9.30 Burnett ordered Force 1 to open fire with main armament and under a minute later *Norfolk* did so, with her main 8″ guns. Despite her lack of flashless cordite for her 8″, so that each salvo nearly blinded everybody above decks, *Norfolk*'s fire was fast and accurate, getting off six full broadsides in ten minutes, before checking fire at 9.40. At about 9.32, Welby-Everard watching from *Belfast's* bridge was 'fairly certain *Norfolk* got a hit with her third salvo as I saw a flash as I watched her salvo fall'.

At 9.30 Burnett had brought Force 1 round to port to a new course of 265° and then at 9.38 (seventeen minutes after the enemy had been sighted) made a very large alternation to port, to a course of 105°. Burnett had now steamed right round the enemy and was now between him and the convoy. But the time that had elapsed before Force 1 turned to port had allowed the enemy's range to open rapidly. By 9.46, when Force 1 altered to 170°, the enemy's range was already 24,000 yards, and still opening. At 9.55 the enemy's speed had gone up to 30 knots, and he had steered further round to port, to northeast.

Perhaps the rapidly increasing range helped to make up Burnett's mind, but he now decided voluntarily to break off contact with the enemy. At 10 am he brought Force 1 back to a course of 305°, and at 10.14 to 325°, heading for the convoy. At 10.20 Force 1 lost contact. The enemy at that time bore 078°, range 36,000 yards, still opening rapidly, and was steering north-east at about 28 knots.

Norfolk had indeed scored two hits. The first 8″ landed in Section IX, between the port Number III 5.9″ gun mounting and the portside tubes, penetrated the upper deck and finished in a technical petty officers' office in a seamen's messdeck, without exploding. The second 8″ hit was crucial, hitting the 'Seetakt' radar high up on the foremost, completely carrying away the 'mattress' aerial. It also put the port High Angle Director out of action, and injured a seaman in the crow's nest. One shell fragment blew the legs off two radar ratings and wounded Leutnant Schramm, the officer in charge of the gunnery rangefinder. According to the account of Günter Sträter, the unexploded shell from *Norfolk* had been measured and found to be 127mm, (5″), which suggested nothing bigger than a destroyer's gun (though actually it must have been an 8″ shell, as *Norfolk* was the only ship to fire her main armament at this time).

Scharnhorst had been taken utterly by surprise. Wilhelm Gödde, at his action station on the port forward searchlight control platform, to one side of the bridge, said he suddenly saw huge columns of water, nine feet in diameter, spurting up out of the darkness about 500 yards on the beam, and clearly visible through the drifting snow. But, according to Gödde, the ship reacted quickly. The forward radar reported the enemy and amidst a confusion of alarm bells, reports, orders and commands, the after 11″ turret 'Caesar' opened fire.

Steursmannsgefreiter (Navigator's Yeoman) Wilhelm Kruse, the only member of the admiral's staff to survive, said that three enemy cruisers were identified. But Gödde, although he said he could see that the enemy's shells

HMS *Duke of York*, as
she left dry dock, 1943
Photo: Imperial War
Museum

HMS *Savage*
Photo: Imperial War
Museum

Favourite pastime:
Sailors of *Duke of York*
fishing from the upper
deck, Iceland, 1943.
(ROL Thomas)
Photo: John Winton

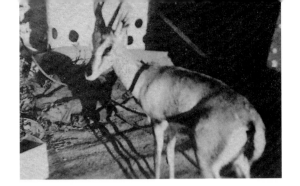

"Olga", the Admiral's
reindeer H.M.S.
Belfast: RIP 26 Dec.
1943 (Welby-Everard)
Photo: John Winton

Some of *Belfast*'s sailors
in what proved to be a
somewhat prophetic
bit of 'mickey-taking'
Photo: Imperial War
Museum

Cdr R.L. Fisher, on
the bridge of *Musketeer*,
1944
Photo: John Winton

Rear Admiral Burnett
Photo: John Winton

Admiral Sir Bruce
Fraser
Photo: Imperial War
Museum

Captain F.R. Parham
on the bridge of *Belfast*,
1943
Photo: John Winton

Admiral Sir Bruce
Fraser shaking hands
with the Russian
Admiral Arseni
Golovko
Photo: John Winton

Kapitän zur See Julius
Hintze, CO
Scharnhorst
Photo: John Winton

Rear Admiral Erich
Bey
Photo: Imperial War
Museum

Scharnhorst, looking
aft. during the
Channel Dash 1942
Photo: Imperial War
Museum

Fo'c'sle of *Scharnhorst* at
high speed in rough
seas
Photo: John Winton

A German destroyer in
northern waters
Photo: Imperial War

Scharnhorst: Starboard
5.9″ gun mounting and
ladder to First Officer's
cabin, in Arctic
weather
Photo: John Winton

Scharnhorst survivors
disembarking
Photo: Imperial War
Museum

HMS *Belfast in*
northern waters
Photo: Imperial War
Museum

'The Happy Return':
Duke of York being
greeted by crews of
drifters, Scapa, 1st
January 1944
Photo: Imperial War
Museum

were fairly heavy calibre, saw only the fiery orange-red flame of the enemy salvoes, with snowflakes dancing in their light, away on *Scharnhorst*'s port quarter, on a bearing of 245°. Shortly after opening fire, *Scharnhorst* altered to 150°, increased to 30 knots and then steered to disengage. According to Gödde, *Scharnhorst*'s main objective was the convoy, somewhere off to the north, and she steered north-east, making smoke as she went. The shell on the messdeck started a fire, which was soon put out. At 9.55 *Scharnhorst* was steering 045°, and signalling to Group North: 'Under Fire from Believed Cruisers With Radar'.

The news that the forward radar was out of action seems to have gone the rounds in *Scharnhorst* very quickly. But Gödde said they were all encouraged by a loud-speaker message: 'Lull in action. We are trying once more to get at the convoy, the destroyers from the south, we in the *Scharnhorst* from the north'.

Bey had already, at 9.45, asked Johannesson to 'Report your situation' and Johannesson had replied at 9.55 'Proceeding according to plan. Square AC4413 (which was nearly 50 miles to the south-west of *Scharnhorst*) course 230, speed 12'. Rolf Johannesson was evidently not the type of dashing destroyer leader to act upon his own initiative; having been told to do something, he went on doing it until told to do something else. Over an hour after he had lost contact with *Scharnhorst*, and had actually seen star-shell to the north-east, he was still searching to the south-west. At 10.27 Bey signalled to Johanneson: 'Proceed on course 070, speed twenty-five'. This was a praise-worthy attempt to draw his destroyers towards him again. But it meant that *Scharnhorst* and her destroyers were all now tending to steam over to the north-east, when there was already some indication that the convoy lay to the north-west.

With hindsight, it is clear that Bey should have tried to force his way past the three cruisers opposing him. They were much smaller, much more lightly-armed, and slower in the sea conditions.

But Bey chose to try and avoid damage, and work his way round towards the convoy. An imaginative and experienced task force commander, or one of his staff, could have deduced much more than Bey and his staff appear to have done, from their opponents' manoeuvres; in other words, by studying the movements of the shepherds, judge the whereabouts of their flock. Bey's opponent had run right past him, and only when he had placed himself between Bey and the convoy, had he then opened fire. In a sense, Burnett's anxiety to protect the convoy had shown in which direction it most probably lay.

It seems that Bey still intended his destroyers to rejoin him, or at least to take part in a joint attack, *Scharnhorst* from the north, the destroyers from the south, because at 1135 he signalled to Johanneson to steer 030°, and gave his own position, course and speed: Square AC4214, north, 27 knots. Bey, like Fraser, was trying to gather the threads together. At some time shortly after this signal to the 4th Flotilla, Bey must have received a sighting report of the convoy from Kapitan Leutnant Lubsen in U.277, transmitted at 1000: Convoy at 0945, Square AB 6365, for at 1158 Bey signalled to the 4th Flotilla to steer so as to operate in that square, AB 6365.

At this point, in the opinion of Doenitz, who was Bey's severest critic, 'Tactical co-ordination between *Scharnhorst* and the 4th Destroyer Flotilla had therefore ceased to exist'. This hardly fits the facts. Bey had been given a (relatively) accurate position for the convoy and had told Johanneson to close it. By that time, *Scharnhorst* had been steaming north, or nearly north, at 27 knots for some two hours. Bey had realised that he was now too far to the north and had turned south-west, for when the next contact was made with her shortly after midday, *Scharnhorst* was steering 230°. So *Scharnhorst* herself was also heading for Square AB 6365. Bey was, in fact, doing his best to concentrate his forces again, after fecklessly allowing his destroyers to lose contact.

But none of this seems to have impressed Doenitz. In his opinion, the three British cruisers had been in an 'extremely dangerous position when they had encountered *Scharnhorst* at 0920. She was 'far superior to them in armour, sea-keeping qualities and, above all, in fire power.' *Scharnhorst* was so much superior that, in Doenitz's view, 'when contact had been established in the morning, the ensuing gun battle should have been fought out to its conclusion.' When the British cruisers had been destroyed, or severely damaged (as Doenitz thought they should have been) then the convoy, protected 'merely by a few destroyers' would have fallen into *Scharnhorst*'s hands 'like ripe fruit'. Clearly, had he survived, Bey would have had an uncomfortable interview with his C-in-C.

Doenitz believed that Burnett's decision, 'when *Scharnhorst* first turned away south and then turned north again, not to follow, but to close the convoy with his three cruisers in order to be able to protect it in the event of further attack by the *Scharnhorst*', was undoubtedly correct. This was ironic, for Burnett, like Bey, was severely criticised, by his own side, for what he had done.

A famous clause of the Fighting Instructions lays down that 'very good reasons should exist before touch with the enemy is relinquished'. In the light of this clause, with its Nelsonian resonances, the Tactical Division of the Admiralty examined Burnett's conduct of this preliminary skirmish. They pointed out that Burnett had had his cruisers deployed on the engaged side, so that *Norfolk* masked the fire from the other two and in fact was the only cruiser to fire her main armament.

Burnett had decided to turn away at 10.14, so losing radar contact with *Scharnhorst* at 10.20. Burnett later defended his decision: 'I was convinced he was trying to work round to the Northward of the convoy, 'he wrote, 'and in view of the limit on my speed imposed by the weather I decided to return to place myself between him and the convoy'. Burnett estimated his maximum speed was some 4-6 knots less than *Scharnhorst*'s. The wind was then south-westerly, force 7-8 (i.e. near gale) with the sea rough.

The tactical experts pointed out that *Scharnhorst* had turned south-east at 9.27, three minutes after *Belfast* opened fire with starshell. But it was not until 9.38 that Force 1 made a large alteration to port, to 105°, which was eleven minutes after *Scharnhorst* came round to south-east and eighteen minutes (a very long time in a naval action at comparatively close ranges) after *Sheffield* had reported 'enemy in sight'.

'I did not immediately alter course to port,' wrote Burnett, 'as I wished to place Force 1 between the enemy and the convoy should he break away to the West and North, further to gain what advantage there was in the light.' But, the tacticians said, Burnett had virtually achieved this object by 9.30 and he could have led round to port without such a delay. At 10.20, when contact was lost, *Belfast* was in fact eighteen miles nearer to the convoy than *Scharnhorst*, and it was mathematically impossible (as demonstrated on the tactical floor) for *Scharnhorst* to have reached the convoy before Burnett could. If *Belfast* had steered due north at 17 knots, she could have shadowed by radar for much longer and still stayed between *Scharnhorst* and the convoy (which, in any case, as the tacticians reminded everybody, still had no less than *ten* destroyers in its escort). It was possible, they suggested, that the way in which the range had opened, and was still opening, partly influenced Burnett to alter to starboard and break off contact. Maybe, they concluded, as soon as it was *certain Scharnhorst* was at sea the cruisers' object should have been changed from convoy defence to shadowing. But, 'faced with a *fait accompli,* Fraser approved Burnett's decision' was the verdict.

At 10.35 Burnett signalled to Fraser, 'Have lost touch with enemy who was steering North. Am closing convoy'. This signal was the start of a very anxious couple of hours for Fraser, the only time in which he ever seemed to have any real doubts about the outcome of the day. He may indeed have later approved Burnett's *fait accompli,* but in the meantime, at 10.58, he signalled to Burnett: 'Unless touch can be regained by some unit, there is no chance of my finding enemy'. Whatever Fraser may or may not have meant by it, this signal precipitated what was nearly an emotional crisis in poor Bob Burnett.

In his distress, Bob Burnett turned to Captain Parham for reassurance. Freddie Parham was the most loyal of flag captains, and personally devoted to Burnett: 'In my humble opinion,' he said, 'It was a *brilliant* decision [to break off and rejoin the convoy]. Our job essentially was to protect the convoy. Almost secondarily our job was to sink the *Scharnhorst* or anybody who came to interfere with the convoy. There is no doubt in my mind that if he had gone off and tried to find the *Scharnhorst* he would have lost her and he would *not* have protected the convoy.

'When he'd taken his decision and settled down to keep with the convoy, he sent for me. He was down in the chart-house one deck below the bridge. He himself worked entirely from the plot. I don't know that he ever came to the bridge at all. There was nothing to be *seen* from the bridge, it was pitch dark all the time. He left all that to me. He sent for me, he said, come down, I want to speak to you. I went down, and he'd cleared the chart-house of everybody else.

'He said to me, Freddie have I done the right thing? I said to him, I'm absolutely *certain* you have. Shortly after that we had a fairly *snorting* signal [of 10.58] from the C-in-C which said, roughly speaking, 'if nobody keeps their eye on the Scharnhorst, how the *hell* do you think I'm going to bring her to action', or words to that effect.

'It was a terrible thing. Poor old Bob, he was a terribly emotional chap, he was jolly nearly in tears about it. I was able to reassure him. And afterwards of course his judgement was proved utterly correct because the *Scharnhorst* turned up again to look for the convoy and ran straight into us. There is no question in my mind that Bob was right, absolutely right.'

In his own report of proceedings sent to Fraser, Burnett defended his decision by saying 'I received your signal 261058 at 1104. Considering my chief object to be the safe and timely arrival of the convoy and being convinced I should shortly make contact again, it would not have been correct tactics to have left the merchant ships during daylight to search for the enemy, nor to have split my force by detaching one or more ships to search, in view of the enemy's high speed and the weather conditions which limited a cruiser to 24 knots. Feeling confident that the enemy would return to the attack from the North or North East, and keeping in mind the object of the operation, I decided to carry out a broad zigzag about ten miles ahead of the convoy. *Musketeer, Matchless, Opportune* and *Virago* were disposed ahead as screen.'

Burnett's decision was given the final imprimatur of approval by the official historian, Captain S.W. Roskill, who wrote, after studying all the reports and track charts, that it was very unlikely the British cruisers could have accomplished the purpose of continuing to shadow the enemy by radar in the circumstances then prevailing. 'Criticism of Admiral Burnett's actions can therefore hardly be sustained.'

The four last-named destroyers joined Burnett during the forenoon. The convoy had turned to the north on Fraser's orders at 9.30 and at 9.37 Fraser ordered McCoy to detach four destroyers to join Force 1, which they did at 10.24. (In fact, McCoy had anticipated the order and asked Burnett at 9.41 if he wanted destroyer reinforcement).

The four destroyers of the 36th Division, led by Cdr. R.L. Fisher in *Musketeer,* had previously joined JW55B from RA55A and, in Fisher's words, felt 'some pride in having found them. We spent a difficult night floundering about in a following sea and snow flurries, trying to keep station on a convoy making good about six knots. I was some five miles astern putting down a shadowing U-boat [almost certainly Lubsen's U.277] when my division was again detached to join Bob Burnett's cruisers after their first brush with the *Scharnhorst* and ran north with him at high speed in appalling weather with the sea astern. The destroyers were almost unmanageable and in danger of broaching. In fact, Johnny Lee-Barber, a much more experienced destroyer Captain than I [in *Opportune*], signalled that it was impossible to go on at that speed. However, we did without serious mishap.

'I had never been in company with Bob Burnett before and was at this time wondering what was to be the form about destroyers attacking, [Cdr. Fisher had previously, before sailing, sought guidance on the tactics 'if we should ever run into surface enemy forces? — 'Does the SO of destroyers dash off on his own initiative and conduct an organised torpedo attack or does he stay in his own station until the Admiral tells him to attack?' — without ever receiving a definite answer'] So I made the signal 'Intend to await your order before leading destroyers to attack'. Carefully worded so that there was no need for him to reply in the event that we met the enemy before he could do so.'

Both Parham and Burnett were baffled by this signal. It was flashed by signalling lamp and received on *Belfast's* bridge: 'Am awaiting your order to attack'. 'I was very puzzled,' said Parham, 'I could just see *Musketeer's* division, and only just — beyond them — the convoy. I reported the signal down the voice-pipe to my Admiral, adding that I could not understand it: I could see no sign of *Scharnhorst*, and, if she were there, surely *Musketeer* would not wait for an order to attack. My Admiral said: 'Signal to him: 'Attack what?' — to which the reply came back: 'Anything that turns up!' Funny afterwards, but not at the time'. It did not seem amusing at the time to Fisher, either: 'He replied 'Attack what?' Exasperated, I jumped on my brass hat and ruined it, replying 'Anything that turns up'.'

The cruisers' radar picked up the outlying ships of the convoy at 10.50, bearing 324°, range 28,000 yards. The convoy was steering 045° again, although with JW55B all courses were approximate: as McCoy reported later, alterations were made in 20 degree swings, but so slowly that more than once JW55B had not achieved its new course before yet another alteration was ordered. Burnett's cruisers took station ahead of the convoy, with the four destroyers a mile ahead, and carried out a broad zigzag.

Convoy and escort steered north-east in a high state of expectation. *Onslaught,* one of the screen, caused a flutter at 11.31 when she reported a radar contact bearing 150° — just conceivably possible for *Scharnhorst*. But Burnett replied four minutes later: '*Onslaught* — J — CS.10' — *Onslaught's* unknown radar contact is me. At 11.37 it was *Norfolk's* turn to set everybody's pulses racing with a fleeting radar contact, but it quickly faded. However, if Burnett had read the situation correctly, *Scharnhorst* should reappear at any time.

Meanwhile, Fraser had been having a frustrating and worrying forenoon. The gentlest of men, he had not meant his signal of 10.58 to cause Burnett such distress, but he was, after all, having the greatest difficulty in keeping track of all the elements present: the convoy and escort, Forces 1 and 2, and the enemy. Burnett had signalled his position at 10.03, giving his course as 305° and speed 24 knots. He had also given the enemy course as 040°, so clearly he was just about to lose touch, even if he had not done so already.

His signal announcing that he had indeed lost content crossed with a somewhat plaintive one from Fraser asking 'Are you still in touch?'. Shortly after 11 am Fraser had to face the fact that *Scharnhorst* had vanished, and nobody knew where she was or what she was doing: At 10.30 he had asked McCoy to bring the convoy back to a course of 045° again and at 11.22 told McCoy to use his own discretion. At 11.55 McCoy began the laborious process of turning JW55B back to steer 125°, to keep Force 1 between the convoy and the expected direction of the enemy.

Part of Fraser's difficulty was the sheer time it took for messages to reach their recipients and be obeyed. Allowances had to be made for delays caused by encoding and decoding, and for poor radio reception. Yet, all the events surrounding the passage of the JW55 convoy, (known as Operation FV), including the actions against *Scharnhorst*, turned on communications. As Courage said, 'it was a communicator's party'.

The main communications burden was borne by *Duke of York*, whose staff kept constant listening watch on three 'Broadcasts', on the Convoy Radio-Telephone frequency of 2410 kc/s, on the North Russian Port Wave of 4172 kc/s, on 18 Group Coastal Command Reconnaissance Wave of 6000/3215 kc/s, and on 500 kc/s (he "SOS" Emergency waveband). Burnett's first 'Jig' radar report was intercepted by *Duke of York* at 8.44 on the Convoy R/T Wave; Burnett addressed this and subsequent enemy reports to Scapa W/T Station at full power. But Scapa W/T was not heard to answer and Cdr Peter Dawnay, the Fleet Wireless Officer in *Duke of York* soon realised that the reports were not being received. He ordered the reports to be retransmitted to Whitehall by 'ship-shore' frequency. (Also, when he saw that enemy reports were going to be broadcast on this frequency Dawnay ordered Force 2 to set watch on Convoy R/T. 'Before doing so,' he said, 'I asked the C-in-C on this point, but I found that he was so engrossed in the tactical situation that this was the only time I did so, and thereafter I took all decisions of this nature myself'.

Because of Dawnay's initiative, *Duke of York*'s signals were soon being broadcast worldwide by the Admiralty, sometimes within *two minutes* of being originated. Dawnay and Courage both had mental visions of staff officers and interested parties all over the world getting out their maps and following the progress of the battle, as it actually took place. Bey and Hintze might at one time have begun to feel themselves alone and beleaguered. Beleaguered they may have been, but they were certainly not alone; in fact, they had never had a bigger audience in all their lives.

As Dawnay said, '... as the minutes went by and contact was not regained it was realised that the situation had taken a bad turn for the worse'. To add to Fraser's concerns, at the time when contact was lost with *Scharnhorst*, the enemy gained contact with Force 2. At 9.11 am that morning three Blohm & Voss Bv. 138 flying boats fitted with Hohentwiel radar had taken off from Tromso. Just after ten o'clock one of the aircraft, piloted by Leutnant Helmut Marx, who had been a naval officer until he was conscripted into the Luftwaffe, saw echoes of several ships on his radar set. He was then about sixty miles north of Point Lucie 1 and the echoes were about twenty miles away.

After four years of war, the German Navy and the Luftwaffe had no equivalent of 18 Group Coastal Command Wave and Marx could not communicate directly with *Scharnhorst*. At 10.12 he signalled to Flieger-fuhrer Lofotens, giving the grid square position and the news 'Several Vessels located'. Marx maintained contact for another hour and a half and had noticed that one of the 'blips' on his screen was very large. At 11.35 he signalled again, 'Contact maintained. Apparently One Large and Several Small Vessels. Believed High Speed Course South' (Force 2 was actually steering 080°, speed 25½ knots).

In the prevailing weather, and with the usual efficiency of German radar sets at that time, this was a masterly piece of flying and shadowing by Marx, as good as any by a maritime pilot on either side in the war. But it was almost entirely wasted. Once again, the Germans wrote down their own radar. Generalleutenant Roth, in the Lofotens, did not transmit the first sighting report until 1.06 pm., after *Scharnhorst* had been in action again, and the second not until later still, and even then, with the vital reference to the 'large vessel' deleted. Even after Marx had landed and been debriefed, Roth did not believe that the Hohentwiel sets could achieve such accuracy.

At Kluber's HQ in Narvik, Marx's 'highly unpleasant' report was received at 1.41 pm. There, the staff were in no doubt that it could only refer to 'an enemy force which intends to cut off the return of our own force'.

Force 2 were well aware they were being shadowed. Three aircraft were picked up by radar and by D/F soon after 10 am., shadowing from the starboard quarter at about 8½ miles range. One of them (obviously Marx) was heard making enemy reports and was in radar contact with *Duke of York* for nearly three hours. It could still be heard transmitting intermittently until about 2 pm, when it seemed to lose touch or return to base.

There were other indications, besides aircraft reconnaissance reports, that a British heavy force was approaching. Scapa W/T might not have received *Belfast*'s signals, but the German B-Dienst decoding service certainly had. Since 9.36 am that morning the B-Dienst Service had monitored a stream of signals on 210 kc/s Fleet Wave from one source with the call-sign J.L.P. (actually CS.10) to Scapa Flow, or to another addressee at sea with the call-sign D.G.O. Many of the signals were in the so-called 'Self-Evident' Code which the B-Dienst Service had broken; but the breaking took about forty minutes, so that 'Self-Evident', a simple and convenient code, still had some value for short-term tactical signals.

According to the German records, B-Dienst picked up the following signal at 9.40, from J.L.P. to Scapa 'Feindsichtung in 222 Grad. (Degrees) 6,5 sm (sea miles)'. This was actually CS10's signal of 9.37 to Scapa, 'Nan 222 — 6½', 'unknown ship in sight bearing 222°, 6½ miles'. The German records show that several other signals were received within minutes of transmission and subsequently broken. The only mystery was the source D.G.O. who was also sending signals, both to J.L.P. and to Scapa. D.G.O.'s signals could not be cracked. For instance, at 9.55 the Germans picked up a signal which they marked 'op-Funkspruch unbek.' ('operational signal, content unknown') from D.G.O. to I.J.V., repeated to J.L.P. This was actually Fraser's signal to D.17 (McCoy), repeated to Burnett, ordering McCoy to send four destroyers to join CS.10.

There were some who suspected the ominous truth of these signals. At 11.13 am the staff at Gruppe Nord/Fleet Command at Kiel recorded in their war diary: 'The reporting from one British unit to another could have been addressed to the convoy from a cruiser, but may equally have been a direction of the supposed heavy cover force towards the target.' If there had been such a supposition, it should surely have been worth signalling to Bey. But it was not, and, incredibly, it seems that *Scharnhorst* had sailed in such haste she had no B-Dienst section of her own on board.

According to Wilhelm Gödde, who certainly was in a good position to see and overhear what was happening, Bey and Hintze did know there was a heavy force approaching. Between 11 am and 11.30, said Gödde, he heard Hintze over the 'artillery telephone': 'From the Captain to all stations: Situation Report. This morning as expected, we ran into the forces covering the convoy — three cruisers of the "town class" type. We have altered course and are now trying to get at the convoy from the other side, that is from the north. We have shaken off the cruisers. An important reconnaissance report has just come in from the Luftwaffe. A British heavy battle group has been sighted 150 miles to the westward; I repeat 150 miles to the westward. That is to say, well out of our way. We are forging on towards the convoy. End of announcement!'

However, Sträter's account gives the time of the announcement as 'about 3.30 pm.' and the content: 'Signal from the Luftwaffe. Reconnaissance plane reports enemy fleet detachment 150 miles west. Keep sharp lookout'. As Roth did not signal until 1.06 pm., and allowing time for transmission and decoding, it seems that Sträter's time was likely to be the more accurate. Probably Bey did know of the heavy force approaching but not until it was almost too late.

As the clock on the flag-bridge moved on towards noon, and there was still no sign of *Scharnhorst*, Fraser became concerned about his destroyer's fuel situation. All the ships in Force 2 reported their fuel state daily at 8 am. That morning *Duke of York* had had nearly 80 per cent fuel remaining, but some of the destroyers were down to 70 per cent and *Scorpion* had only 66 per cent. They had all been steaming at high speed, at or near 25 knots, ever since. Fraser knew that he would soon have to decide whether to turn back or go on to Kola Inlet. If *Scharnhorst* had already turned for home then there was obviously no chance of catching her.

There was another, more appalling, possibility: that *Scharnhorst* had slipped past and was at that very moment heading westwards out into the

Atlantic, while Fraser and his ships were still steaming east. It was true that there had been no previous signs of a break-out, as there had been before *Bismarck*'s escape into the Atlantic, no intelligence about tankers and store-ships being stationed for replenishment. The Allies' control of the Atlantic was much stronger, and long-range air surveillance much more thorough, than they had been in 1941. Nevertheless, *Scharnhorst* was a powerful and fast warship, so fast and powerful that if she were lucky, and she always had been lucky, she might even catch and destroy one of the 'monsters' such as the *Queen Mary*, which were at that moment regularly crossing the Atlantic with 15,000 American troops on board, during the build-up for the D-Day landings in Normandy. These giant liners were only escorted in and out of coastal waters. Far out at sea, they relied upon their speed for defence. *Scharnhorst* was the only weapon the Germans now had which could catch them.

While Fraser himself pondered over these awful responsibilities, the rest of Force 2 seemed possessed by a truly remarkable serenity. Everybody expected a battle. As Lt.Cdr. Rupert Wainwright, *Jamaica*'s gunnery officer, said: 'The C-in-C's appreciation as explained to us at the working level, seemed so clear that most of us were imbued with a feeling from very early on that a battle was inevitable. The general issue of Arctic clothing was, by this stage of the war, quite good, but the extreme cold seeped through exposed bits and combined with the unknown, for those who had not been in action before, to exacerbate anxiety — indeed for those who had! The morale was, however, very high and cheerful'.

The men of Forces 1 and 2 employed the waiting time, very sensibly, in getting something inside their stomachs. In *Belfast*, Cdr. Welby-Everard judged the moment 'ripe for some food so I put our action messing organisation into force and we all got a meal at our action stations — hot soup, meat pies, and a jam tart ...' In *Jamaica*, high up in his director, Bryce Ramsden noticed that 'lunch-time came round and still we were sitting there. Someone passed up an enormous meat sandwich to me, which I devoured, occasionally taking involuntary bites at my anti-flash gear which enveloped my face, leaving just enough room to see and talk.'

Only in the flagship did the action *cuisine* leave much to be desired. Some complained of the toughness of their 'Boxing Day chop'. They were the lucky ones, to get a chop. Lieutenant Henry Leach, a young gunnery officer in charge of 'A' Turret, thought the food supplied was 'one of the most revolting and inappropriate action messing dinners on record (lumps of soggy pork swilling in fannies full of greasy sludge) which had made the most hardened feel queasy in that weather ... ' Up on the admiral's bridge, Vernon Merry also recalled 'the most godawful action messing dinner, a fatty stew, virtually uneatable'.

Fraser thought over his terrible dilemma until midday, when he suddenly made up his mind. At 12.03 pm he signalled by light to Force 2: 'Reverse course to 260.' In the tremendous seas then running, this was a major undertaking for the destroyers, and Fraser told his ships to alter in succession, with *Duke of York* reducing speed to 18 knots to allow the destroyers to complete their turns and catch up.

The last half-hour had been a ghastly period of worry and indecision for Fraser. But now the deed was done, much though it disappointed Fraser to have to do it. If the worst came to the worst and *Scharnhorst* was trying to break out into the Atlantic, then at least Force 2 was on a roughly parallel course, ahead of *Scharnhorst* and to the south. Force 1 would have to deal with any further attacks on the convoy until Force 2 returned.

But Fraser's ships had not settled on their new course into wind and sea when the signal was received from Burnett at 12.05 pm: 'Jig — 075 — 13'. Unknown radar contact, bearing 075, range 13 miles. As Courage said, 'It was an electrifying moment. I was on the admiral's bridge by myself and heads popped out from the plot. 'Turn'em round again!' Anyhow, we were all so pleased that we were about to get back into contact again.'

Sheffield picked up the radar contact at 12.11, bearing 075, 12 miles, *Norfolk* got it at 12.14. The strange contact was closing rapidly and moving right, as *Sheffield*'s radar reports showed: at 1213, 078°, $10\frac{1}{2}$ miles, then 083°, $9\frac{1}{2}$ miles, 094°, $8\frac{1}{2}$ miles, at 12.16.

Burnett had been right, after all. There could be no doubt this was *Scharnhorst*. Bey had wasted three full precious hours. But now he was back. At 12.20 Burnett signalled 'Open Fire' and one minute later, exactly three hours after her first sighting, it was *Sheffield* again who made the great signal: 'Enemy in sight!'

CHAPTER 7

Force and 1 and 2 join up: 'Money for old rope'

I knew now,' said Fraser, writing of his response to the news that the enemy had been detected again on Force 1's radar screens, 'that there was every chance of catching the enemy'. So, too, did everybody else who was in a position to look at a plot and see what was happening. From now on, the proceedings took on an air of inevitability. There were still adventures to come, *Scharnhorst* would steer this way and then that, but the outcome could already be foreseen.

At 12 noon, JW55B was completing its wheeling turns to achieve a course of 125°, while Burnett and Force 1, some nine miles to the north-east, were preparing to fight their second engagement of the day. At 12.23 the destroyers with the convoy could see gun flashes and star-shell on a bearing of 083° and two minutes later McCoy concentrated his fleet destroyers by divisions on the port, or threatened side, of the convoy.

McCoy and his fellow destroyer captains longed to join in the fray. Cdr 'Joe' Selby, in *Onslaught*, was one of those captains, particularly frustrated at not being able to go over the horizon, from where those tantalising glimpses of star-shell and distant thuds of salvoes were coming. The Sub-Lieutenant RNVR, Adrian Carey, whose action station was aft, as officer of the quarters of 'X' Turret, noticed his Captain's 'dudgeon' when he went up to the bridge for the afternoon watch. 'However,' he said, ' "Joe" was a close friend of Bob Burnett and his generosity of spirit took over as we followed the battle with personal sympathy as well as professional interest through a loud-speaker tuned in to the R/T signals from the cruisers which came in loud, clear, and in plain language now that radio silence was broken'.

By then there was a great deal of plain language to listen to. Force 1 had been steering 045° at 18 knots, with *Belfast*, *Sheffield* and *Norfolk*, in that order from north to south, forming on a line of bearing due south from *Belfast*. Burnett had the four destroyers two miles ahead, on a bearing of 090° from him, on his starboard bow. The first enemy bearing therefore came up almost exactly bisecting the angle between the destroyers and *Belfast*'s line of advance. Whatever emotional storms might have assailed Burnett, whatever misgivings he might have felt, whatever criticisms he might later have to endure, his first care was the defence of the convoy and he had placed his ships marvellously well for the purpose: he had his ships neatly disposed across the very course towards the convoy that *Scharnhorst* had chosen (see map 2).

Force 1 altered to 090° at 12.16, and round further to starboard, to 100°, three minutes later. By then radar reports showed the enemy closing on a course of 240°, at 20 knots. The two forces were approaching each other at a combined speed of some 38 knots, well over forty miles an hour, and the range was coming down rapidly, to only 11,000 yards at 12.21, when Force 1 opened fire.

Gödde said *Scharnhorst* suffered no damage in this stage of the battle, but his memory must have been at fault. *Norfolk* was first, with at least one hit and possibly more, at about 12.24; the flash of the hit was not seen in *Norfolk* but it was from *Belfast*, who gave it as a 'probable' to *Norfolk*, because *Belfast* could see nothing at the time to coincide with her own 'fall of shot' hooter. *Sheffield* claimed at least one hit, possibly another, a minute later, seen from *Sheffield* herself.

Belfast had opened with starshell and then with main armament. On the bridge, Parham could at last get a clearer view of his enemy: 'I must say,' he said, 'she looked *extremely* large and *extremely* formidable!' Down below 'A' Turret, Banderillero and his mates were hard at work. '... the "Stand By" is given again. Then there is the most awful crash as our guns go off. I start taking shells from the trays and putting them on the shell ring round the three shell hoists. I repeat this operation every time the guns go off. Conversation starts again. "This is the first time this ship has fired her guns in anger." "I wish they would tell us what we are firing at; anyway I hope it is nothing larger than a destroyer." "It's a pretty feeble enemy, it's not even firing back." From the gunhouse comes a message, "Well done, A and B turrets; now give X and Y a chance." So we are one up on the Marines. The firing lasts about twenty minutes.'

Once again, *Scharnhorst* appeared to be taken aback by her enemy's appearance. At first sighting she seemed to alter slightly to starboard, to the west, and then at 12.25 when the range had come down to as little 4,100 yards, she made a very large alteration to port, to steer south and then settle on a course of about 135°. By then she was under fire from all three cruisers, and from *Musketeer*. One of her survivors reported at least one hit, just forward of 'C' Caesar Turret. The British fire, he said was 'unpleasantly accurate' and a large number of shells burst within 50 metres, filling the air with fragments.

This second engagement was graphically described by Gödde: 'Shortly after 12.30 I and several others sighted three shadows ahead and reported accordingly. The alarm had already been sounded as the result of a previous radar report. But before our guns could open fire the first star shells were bursting over the *Scharnhorst*. The enemy's salvoes were falling pretty close to the ship. The first salvoes from our own heavy guns straddled the target. I myself observed that after three or four salvoes a large fire broke out on one of the cruisers near the after funnel, while another cruiser was burning fiercely fore and aft and was enveloped in thick smoke.

'After further salvoes I saw that the third cruiser had been hit in the bows. For a moment a huge tongue of flame shot up and then went out. From the dense smoke that enveloped her. I presumed the ship was on fire. The enemy's fire then began to become irregular, and when we altered course, the enemy cruisers turned away and disappeared in the rain and snow squalls. During this action the enemy had been ahead and visible on both sides. Our A and B turrets had been firing as had also for a while the two forward 5.9 inch turrets. I did not hear either by telephone or through any other source of any hit received during this phase by the *Scharnhorst*. While the enemy had been scarcely discernible during the first action, this time with the midday twilight we could easily distinguish the cruisers' outlines. The range, too, was much shorter than it had been in the morning.'

Scharnhorst opened fire with all three main 11″ turrets and the starboard side 5.9″ turrets as she turned away to the south and south-east. She did not do quite as well as Gödde observed, but her shooting was a very great deal better than Banderillero and his mates supposed. One early salvo pitched between *Sheffield* and *Norfolk*, close to *Sheffield*'s starboard side and swept her upper deck with a storm of shrapnel pieces 'up to football size', in Burnett's phrase.

Sheffield's Paymaster Commander, Commander Walker, was at his action station as Fire Direction Officer of the 20 mm. pom-pom guns, mounted on the pom-pom deck above the port hangar. One piece of shrapnel, which Walker said was 'about the size of a man's head' penetrated the starboard side, just below and aft of the bridge, severing electric cables and causing a leak in a steam pipe (although the steam heating to exposed positions such as the bridge was shut off at action stations). Nobody was injured, but the starboard bridge look-outs had very narrow escapes. A second shrapnel fragment, '8″ by 8″ and weighing 28 lbs.', came in through the starboard hangar, but again nobody was hurt. By then, *Sheffield*'s upper deck was covered in smoke clouds and acrid cordite fumes. But when the smoke cleared for a moment, Walker could see that *Norfolk* had been hit. There was a 'sickening red column of fire' which hung for about ten seconds over 'X' Turret before subsiding.

From the start, *Norfolk* seems to have been *Scharnhorst*'s main target. She had no flashless cordite for her main 8″ guns and the brilliant flash of her salvoes gave *Scharnhorst* the perfect aiming point. At about 12.33 *Scharnhorst* scored a straddle on *Norfolk*. One 11″ shell hit the barbette of 'X' Turret and put the turret out of action. The magazine below was flooded as a precaution.

A second shell (which may have been one of the salvo which straddled *Sheffield*) hit *Norfolk* amidships on the starboard side, penetrating to the main deck and exploding there, near the ship's secondary damage control head-quarters. Warrant Mechanician Charles Parini was killed, with five other engine-room ratings and a petty officer. A chief stoker and an able seaman later died of their wounds. Two stokers and a marine were very seriously wounded.

Stoker Moth was one of the damage control party, near the explosion. '*Crash!* came the shell about midships starboard side exploding in a compartment adjacent to my own. In the next two or three minutes there was inevitable confusion. Lights went out, and one of my mess-mates standing with his back to the communicating door was thrown across the deck by the blast from the explosion.

'The door was then opened. All was dark. Clouds of steam and smoke came issuing from within, along with cries for help, while a mixture of water and oil was rising slowly in the compartment below.

'I at once informed damage control headquarters: 'Shell inboard — starboard side, exploding in the office flat'. The engine-room forward repair parties, along with shipwrights and torpedomen and damage control parties, were soon on the job, while the medical parties worked feverishly with our ill-fated casualties. Part of the shell exploded down the starboard engine-room hatch, causing a further two casualties.

'Things were now getting pretty much back to normal again and even though both our engine-rooms were full with smoke fumes and acrid fumes from the explosion our engines maintained their topmost speed ...

The message was passed to *Norfolk*'s bridge that the fires above the engine-room were out of control and (erroneously, as it turned out) they would threaten the ship unless speed was reduced. However, as 'Batchy' Bain himself said, 'The men in the engine-room continued to give *Norfolk* more knots than she had ever had before and, instead of dropping back, we were there in the final phase of the action'.

Many of *Norfolk*'s engine-room department, as in all ships at that stage of the war, were 'Hostilities Only' ratings, who behaved magnificently under fire. 'They did not bat an eyelid,' said Engineer Lieut-Cdr. R.H.C. Reed RNR. 'One of the 'hositilies only' ratings, who was formerly farming in the north of England, is only 19. Although we were half-suffocated by the fumes, and even put on our gas-masks to breathe, he just leaned on the rail in front of the indicator dials and recorded every movement for hours as if nothing had happened or was happening.'

In fact a great deal was happening. 'I was standing in the middle of the compartment by the dials,' said Chief Engine Room Artificer Cardey, 'when there was a vivid flash and bits of metal rained down. One hit an engine-room rating, who was just beside me in the leg. Another piece of metal tore off the tops of two fingers of a man who had his hand on a lever. He did not know it had happened until a quarter of an hour later. Water began to pour down through the engine-room hatches. Some fuel oil came with it and I saw one fellow looking like a polished ebony statue because he had been covered from head to foot with the black oil. He was carrying on as if nothing had happened. I went across to the dials and found that the pressure was not affected. Some of the lights had gone out and there was a good deal of smoke, and we knew by the smell that fire was raging somewhere. They were too busy to come and tell us what had happened. Every man in the engine-room had his work to do, so we carried on, and only heard odd bits of information when they brought us down sandwiches and so on. We kept the engines going at full speed for six hours after the ship was hit. There was about 3 feet of water swishing about in the bilges below the engine-room and the lower footplates were covered.'

'We knew what we were up against,' said another Chief ERA, Davies, from Newport, Monmouthshire, 'and set our minds on the engines so that we became quite unconscious of the passing of time. When the *Scharnhorst*'s shell tore in through the side of the ship and ripped up the deck just above us as if it were cardboard, we felt a terrific blast across the engine-room. There was a thick pall of smoke from one corner of the engine-room and a strong smell of burning; but we had 80,000 horse power to control and we had not much time to think of other things. Our ears were keyed for any strange noise in the engines which might give us a first indication of trouble. Most of the men in the engine-room were "hostilities only" ratings. As an old R.N. man I can tell you they were something to be proud of. Not one faltered, and I suppose we were all, at the back of our minds, expecting something to happen any minute.'

The men of *Norfolk*'s engine-room branch as a whole displayed a truly phenomenal departmental *sang froid*. 'My action station was in the after boiler-room', said Chief E.R.A. Cansfield, of Devonport. 'We had been closed up and in action for some time, and I was going to the forward boiler-room when I saw a vivid green flame shoot across the ship, and the next minute one of the flats above the engine-room was burning fiercely. I knew that the fire-fighting parties would deal with that, and went down to my action station again. The 'buzz' went round that we had been hit by another 11-inch shell, but I did not really know anything about that until it was all over and the *Scharnhorst* had been sunk.'

The destroyers led by Fisher in *Musketeer* had been enjoying a hectic period. *Musketeer* had two radar sets, a Type 271 surface warning and a Type 291 aircraft warning set. In Fisher's words they were 'primitive' but at 12.12 *Musketeer*'s 271 picked up a contact, bearing 090°, range 9 miles. At 12.16 when Burnett's force altered to 090°, *Musketeer* was about two miles ahead of *Belfast*, with the 36th Division in line ahead 'snaking' about the mean course of 090°. Four minutes later, *Scharnhorst* was sighted dead ahead, range 11,000 yards, steering head on towards the destroyers.

At 12.22 Burnett signalled to the destroyers to attack with torpedoes, but no attack took place. 'I was anxiously awaiting the signal,' said Fisher, 'which would release me to split into two sub-divisions and attack with torpedoes from both her bows, but it never reached me. It came to light ... that the signal NS ('Destroyers attack with torpedoes') had in fact been received but never passed to the bridge by my harrassed and tired signal staff who had otherwise done splendidly during the past two days'.

In his report, Fisher later wrote that *Scharnhorst* 'did not present a useful torpedo target'. The range was never less than 4,000 yards. However, at 12.22 *Musketeer* opened fire with her four forward 4.7″ guns, range 7,000 yards. *Musketeer* had dual enclosed turrets, unlike most destroyers of the day which had single guns served and fired in the open behind a simple shield. *Musketeer* continued firing until 12.36 and got off no less than 52 rounds. At one stage she was near enough, at 4,500 yards, to see hits on *Scharnhorst* (although not necessarily claimed as her own).

At 12.31 the destroyers increased speed to 26 knots and four minutes later Fisher led round to a course of 135°. By then *Scharnhorst*'s speed had gone up to 28 knots and she was slipping away from Force 1. At 12.31 *Scharnhorst* was steering 110° at 28 knots and the range had increased to 12,400 yards, and still opening; at 12.50 *Scharnhorst*'s range and bearing was 13,400 yards, 138°. Burnett's ships had ceased fire at 12.41. Burnett decided to shadow the enemy with Force 1, until Force 2 could come up.

The whole engagement had lasted about twenty minutes. In that time *Sheffield* had fired 97 rounds of 6″, in 26 salvoes, all fired visually, because her Type 284 6″ gunnery control was unserviceable. Her Type 273 was used to hold the target, while her Type 285 4″ gunnery control set swept all round. *Sheffield* was in fact the only ship at this stage to get some indication of fall of shot using her 273 set.

Norfolk's Type 273 was put out of action by *Scharnhorst*'s fire and her Type 284 8″ gunnery control set was damaged. But it was repaired and in fact *Norfolk* fired 31 broadsides by radar control, firing 161 rounds of 8″ (during the whole day). *Belfast* had Type 273, Type 284 6″ gunnery control and Type 285 ″ gunnery control. In the end she fired 38 broadsides, 14 of them visually directed, expending 316 rounds of 6″. She also fired 77 rounds of 4″.

As *Scharnhorst* began to draw away to the south-east, the destroyers settled down to chase her. 'At two miles *Scharnhorst* turned south,' said Fisher, 'and I, cutting the corner, followed her at extreme range'. (Eventually the destroyers' range from *Scharnhorst* opened to about 20,000 yards, and slightly to the west of her, and stayed at that.) 'It seemed a long time before the cruisers came up astern and eventually overtook us and it was, and is, my impression that they wasted time somehow'.

The cruisers took up station on *Scharnhorst*'s eastward, or port quarter, at about 7½ miles, just out of visibility image and there they stayed. Burnett signalled a speed of 28 knots at 12.41, and at 12.52 ordered his cruisers to form on a line of bearing of 220° — at about right angles to *Scharnhorst*'s course. At 12.56 Burnett sent out to Fraser the first of many shadowing reports: Enemy course and speed, 115, 28 knots, Am shadowing enemy. My position and speed … '

Burnett did not try to engage again. 'Realising that he [the enemy] had been up-to-date, most obliging,' Burnett later reported to Fraser, 'and that if he continued to act as he was doing he would walk into you, I decided to withhold fire until you had engaged in order to avoid scaring him into drastic alterations of course and not to disturb you by various echoes'.

The Tactical Division in the Admiralty criticised the handling of the destroyers in this second engagement. In their opinion, the destroyers *could* have made a torpedo attack at 12.25 (clearly they did not know of the mislaid signal in *Musketeer*). They conceded that Fisher had 'faced a very difficult torpedo problem'. *Scharnhorst* was approaching him head on, and might turn either way. Had the destroyers been disposed in divisions *abeam,* instead of in line, any time after 12.16 (when the whole force had altered to 090°) they should have been able to attack 'regardless of the direction of *Scharnhorst*'s turn', and they stressed the absolute priority of 'getting in *close*'. However, Fisher was at least correct in supposing that Burnett's ships had taken a wide cast out, to the north-east which had delayed their turn back to follow *Scharnhorst*. Force 1 *had* altered to 040° at 12.22, before coming back to 090° again at 12.26.

The Admiralty's comments on the 36th Division were as nothing compared to Doenitz's later strictures on Bey. According to Captain Urbeeks (Norway), who passed it on, at 12.40 pm. Bey signalled 'Engaged by Several Enemy', giving his grid square reference, 'Radar Directed Fire from Heavy Units'. Doenitz's own instructions to Bey had been to break off if he encountered superior force and this is what Bey had evidently decided to do at 1 pm., when *Scharnhorst* altered to 155°, speed still 28 knots. This was a course that would take *Scharnhorst* comfortably back to the Norwegian coast.

But at the same time it was, as Fraser and Doenitz both realised, a course which Force 1 could also comfortably take, with wind and sea roughly on the beam. If Bey had only steered a more westerly course, into wind and sea, *Scharnhorst* would have escaped, for nothing could have lived with her in those sea conditions. She might also, incidentally, have come across the convoy again. She might even have had a chance of rejoining the 4th Destroyer Flotilla.

Possibly Bey feared to steer to the south-west, where he thought a heavy covering force might be approaching. Certainly he made no moves to summon back his destroyers. On the contrary, at 1.43 he signalled to Johanneson to break off, and at 2.20 to return to base. The 4th Flotilla, lacking Z.33 who was a straggler, steered for Point Lucie. At about 6.40 pm, Z.29 picked up a mutilated signal which suggested that *Scharnhorst* was in action. Another signal mentioned an 'Enemy firing with radar control at a range of more than 19,500 yards'. The 4th Flotilla and the 'Eisenbart' U-boats were ordered to concentrate in the area where *Scharnhorst* had been in action, but the destroyers had barely altered to a course to do so and gone up to 27 knots when, at 8.13 pm, they were ordered to break off immediately, avoid contact with the enemy and steer for the Scharen Islands. They arrived at 1.50 am the following morning, and anchored back in Kaa Fjord at 10 am. Z.33 wandered in a little later. Like Rosencrantz and Guildenstern, Rolf

Johanneson and his destroyer captains had heard the thuds and groans and proclaimings of a tragic struggle fought to the death, and had taken no useful part of any kind whatsoever.

As Doenitz saw it, 'this time the *Scharnhorst* was tactically in a much more favourable position, and it was the enemy who were silhouetted against the brighter south-western horizon, while *Scharnhorst* had the dark, northern sector behind her. The correct thing to have done now would have been to continue the fight and finish off the weaker British forces, particularly as it was plain that they had already been hard hit. Had this been done, an excellent opportunity would, of course, have been created for a successful attack on the convoy'.

This was all true enough. But another, and much crueller supplementary interpretation was that Bey, his officers and the ship's company collectively were tired out. Most of them had spent most of the previous night awake and, by that time, they were all dog-weary. They had made two decent stabs at the convoy. On the second approach, Bey must have believed he had a good chance. But there were the enemy cruisers, *exactly* in his path, as though they had known where and when he was coming.

But surely that was enough for one day's work? They were some 240 miles from Alta Fjord. At 28 knots, and allowing time for picking up an escort, and reduced speeds in pilotage waters, say, ETA just after midnight, and then all night in. It was a pleasant thought. Many of *Scharnhorst*'s sailors did indeed take advantage of the present lull to get their heads down and catch up on their lost sleep, no doubt hoping profoundly that the excitements were over for the day. It does seem that a certain afternoon lassitude crept up upon *Scharnhorst* and her people, as she rolled and swung in a beam swell, southwards to Alta Fjord. During the afternoon the sailors were informed over the broadcast that the operation against the convoy had been broken off and the ship was returning to harbour. Later at 3.25 pm. Bey signalled his position, course and speed and his ETA (Estimated Time of Arrival). The Germans themselves have a word for such a state of mind — 'unwarwary'.

Meanwhile, from Fraser's point of view, the tactical situation could hardly have been developing more satisfactorily. Fraser recognised that if *Scharnhorst* broke away to the south-west, there would be nothing he could do. *Duke of York* and the destroyers could not have caught up with her. But *Scharnhorst* was proceeding, almost meekly, on what Fraser called the most 'advantageous' course for her enemies. There were three cruisers just out of sight on her port quarter, and four destroyers ten miles away on her starboard. A battleship with an escort was steadily approaching from wide on her starboard bow. Fraser could not have positioned his assets better had he been able to shuffle them around as pieces on a tactical floor. As Courage said, looking at the plot in *Duke of York*: 'Money for old rope.' As they all said, 'From here on, it was an execution job'.

As the figure of Erich Bey dwindled with every hour that passed, his influence on events steadily diminishing, until his only contribution could be a few, last defiant signals, so the stature of his opponent seemed to increase; Bruce Fraser's personality had expanded, to excite and inspire every man in his flagship, every ship in Force 1 and Force 2, the convoy and its escort, and, beyond the horizon, all those eager men and women all over the world who were busy getting out their charts and dividers and parallel rulers, to follow the battle.

The Admiral's Bridge and the officers closest to Fraser on this afternoon have been well described by Lieut.Cdr.Michael Ogden: 'The Admiral himself stood at the admiral's voice-position in the port forward corner of his bridge ... At the Admiral's elbow, with instructions to remain at the voice-pipe whenever the Commander-in-Chief left the position for one of his periodic visits to the Plot, was his Flag Lieutenant, Vernon Merry. A senior member of his Staff, Commander Maunsell [Fleet Torpedo Officer], stood in the centre of the bridge. In the starboard after corner, where there was an array of voice-pipes including those to the Bridge Wireless Office and flag-deck, Commander (Lt.Cdr) 'Dickie' Courage, the Fleet Signals Officer, was in position to supervise and control the vital work of his Communications Staff. Also in this latter position was the T.B.S. (Talk Between Ships) Radio Telephone set, rarely used in open waters because of the likelihood of radio conversations between ships being overheard by enemy ears.

'Behind double black-out curtains, arranged to ensure that the inner and brightly-lit compartment did not shed a single betraying gleam out onto the darkened bridge, was the Plot, presided over by the tall figure of Commodore Bill Slayter, the Chief of Staff. On the port side within the Plot was one of the new secret centimetric radar screens giving an actual 'picture' of the surface all around *Duke of York* so that the range and bearing of even a U-boat's conning-tower could have been registered at the same time as the P.P.I. [Plan Position Indicator] (as it was called) identified the target as such. A few feet away from the glowing face of the P.P.I. was the Admiralty Range and Location (A.R.L.) Table on which the Tactical Plot would be kept by Instructor-Commander Fleming and his assistant, Lieutenant Vivian Cox RNVR. Inset in the after bulkhead of the compartment was a 'trap' through which messages could be received and passed from the Bridge Wireless Office.'

Vivian Cox served on Fraser's personal staff from April 1942 until January 1946. 'The Admiral', he says, 'used to spend long hours in my map room, puffing his pipe and confiding (God knows why!) in me ... ' He remembered that afternoon as 'really the time when the Commander-in-Chief, Admiral Fraser, was simply dominating the whole ship. He wore no naval uniform, as such, he just wore old trousers and a polo neck shirt — polo neck sweater — and a rather battered Admiral's hat and with his pipe belching sparks and flame he moved amongst us all being extremely confident and quiet and delightful. And I particularly remember we had two young midshipmen, only about teenagers, who had both been to sea for a very few weeks and were very frightened — as we all were — and it was wonderful the way Admiral

Fraser, realising how these two lads were pretty nervous, found time and the humanity to give them all little nameless, useless tasks to do to keep them busy. And at the same time realising that we knew how he felt, winking slightly to us to realise that we also were nervous. It was a real triumph of a single personality dominating a ship's company'.

At 1 pm., Fraser signalled his position course and speed to Burnett and added: 'One shadower'. One aircraft, very possibly Helmut Marx's, was still in contact. 'It was a Blohm & Voss,' said Courage. 'I can remember seeing the brute, lurking about in the mist, circling round, not out of range. We didn't fire at it, because what was the sense? We probably wouldn't have hit it, and maybe the *Scharnhorst* would have seen the flashes, and people would have got alarmed. So Bruce Fraser just sat there, smoking his pipe, and said, let it go round and round. I must say I thought of having a bash at it. It looked to me so *cheeky*. It reported back to the German Air Force, but they made a nonsense of passing the message on. It didn't get to *Scharnhorst* until too late. It shows that the Germans hadn't got the sort of chap at their head office as we had in the Admiralty'.

Courage was, if anything, being too charitable. Although the German Air Force had a shadower in direct contact with Force 2 as late as 1 pm, and very probably for longer than that, it did *Scharnhorst* no good. Bey probably received the first edited signal from Fliegerfuhrer Lofotens at about 3.30 pm., when he had already turned for home, and the second amplifying signal was never received at all. But there had been no need to wait for the aircraft report. The listeners in the direction-finding stations, the decoders in the B-Dienst Service, the staffs at Narvik and Kiel, and in Berlin, already had a mass of signalled intelligence material to show that *Scharnhorst* was under threat.

The Germans could hear 'DGO' chatting to 'JLP', clearly exchanging operational information. After a short wait, they could even read what had been said. 'DGO' went on hobbing and nobbing with 'JLP', like a conspirator talking to his mate, nodding now and again to 'Scapa' and to 'IJV'. As the bearings slowly drew together, their import became unmistakeable. The Germans knew that all this signal traffic vitally concerned the lives of men in their own service. They knew they were overhearing two parties planning to kill their fellow-countrymen. One wonders why nobody in Germany or in Norway had the nerve or the authority to send out one top-priority 'flash' emergency signal, in plain language if need be at that last desperate moment, to warn *Scharnhorst* of what was coming. But the Germans did nothing; they were like school-children standing aghast on the river bank, hands in their mouths, helplessly watching their father's model yacht sail down stream and over the weir.

As the minutes passed, DGO and JLP continued to exchange titbits of information. At 1.01 pm, the enemy's course altered to due south and a few minutes later Burnett ordered his cruisers to form on a line of bearing of 245°. At 1.12 pm he reported the enemy course and speed again. For the next three hours, in a stream of signals, at 1.12, 1.28, 1.50, 2.25, 2.45, 3 pm., 3.20, 3.40, virtually a signal every fifteen, or twenty minutes, Burnett kept Fraser informed of his own position course and speed, and *Scharnhorst*'s range, course and speed. Fraser called it an 'exemplary' piece of shadowing and so it was — one of the very best in all naval history.

Later, Admiral Tovey summed it all up in a letter to Captain Parham: 'I was following your intercepts on the chart, and I knew that you and your fine ship flying Bob Burnett's flag would never let go of the brute unless the weather made it absolutely impossible for you to keep up. The combination of the gallant attack you and other cruisers made on the *Scharnhorst*, coupled with your magnificent shadowing, is as fine an example of cruiser work as has ever been seen.'

There was still just a possibility that *Scharnhorst* had some destroyers in her vicinity, although nobody had seen or heard of any. At 1.18 pm Fraser asked Burnett: 'Report composition of enemy'. Five minutes later Burnett replied: 'One heavy ship'. That removed the last doubts. ('We couldn't actually *read* the name *Scharnhorst* on its side,' said Courage, 'we had to *guess* that!')

There was more good news for Fraser. At 1.47 pm *Norfolk* reported that she had her Type 273 radar set working again. She had kept up well with the rest of Force 1, in spite of her damage. Her signal arrived at a time of a little by-play on *Duke of York*'s flag-bridge. 'We wondered,' said Fraser, 'whether we should have the battle before tea, or after tea. We decided we should have it *after* tea.' So, at 2.16 pm Fraser had the signal flashed by light to all the ships in Force 2: 'If enemy maintains present course and speed, action should be joined at 16.30.'

Courage watched the signal being acknowledged by the ships in company, all flashing their R.R.R.s. 'This was a *nice* little signal,' he said. 'There was the C-in-C puffing away at his pipe, though he was still outside, still on the outer bridge. He did go in out of the darkness and cold later. Here he was, telling the world in general what was happening, saying he hoped to be there at 16.30. Mark you, that was a couple of hours to go. We were having a happy time in *Duke of York*'.

Although U-boats played no part in the action to come, their signals were intercepted from time to time. Just after 2 pm., *Scorpion*'s H/F D/F picked up a U-boat transmission to the westward — very possibly Lubsen, in U.277, reporting the convoy. Earlier, *Scorpion*'s H/F D/F, evidently in very good nick, had detected an transmission from a surface ship, away to the north-east, which caused more flutterings in the staff dovecote. It could have been *Scharnhorst*, or *Belfast*. It could have been anybody.

It was one more problem for Cdr. Dawnay, the Fleet Wireless Officer, who had been having a somewhat harrassing day, a great deal due to the inconvenient position of his Radio Control Office. 'For to get to the Plot from the R.C.O., to talk to the Admiral, he wrote, 'I had to go out on to the bitter and dark wings of the bridge, where I was of course blinded, and then in through the Admiral's bridge to the Plot, going through five doors in all. A wicked experience when in a hurry and doing it frequently. Afterwards I had the trap hatch between the R.C.O. and Plot enlarged so that I could just climb through it, rather than risk a repetition of that obstacle race.'

Dawnay had his suspicions about the accuracy of *Duke of York*'s D/F set. 'At the start, owing to a jammed ring on the D/F set, the bearings taken were clearly hopelessly at fault, and I cursed myself for not having tried out the set in the forenoon. However, after a few minutes, the defect was bowled out and thereafter excellent bearings were obtained. I also had to make a signal to C.S.10 [actually at 1.44 pm] to make more frequent use of Fleet Wave for his reports to ensure a good bearing plot.' But, in the end, the plot was a model.

At 2.35 Fraser asked Burnett whether he still had destroyers in company. The reply, seven minutes later, was: 'No they are following.' *Musketeer* and the other destroyers were out of sight of *Belfast*, some miles to the west and astern of her, but they were still in radar touch with *Scharnhorst*. 'All this time we were doing about 30 knots into a heavy sea,' wrote Fisher. 'Earlier I had told Rear Admiral (Destroyers) that my ship, though splendidly armed with three double turrets and powerful machinery, was useless into a head sea as she was like a silk stocking full of tins of bully beef and one couldn't use her without breaking her up. However on this occasion a few cracked oil tanks would not have been a court martial offence and we slammed into it regardless and found that once one had passed a critical speed of perhaps 18 knots she sailed over it like a speed-boat zip-zipping and leaving no time for falling into the holes. I suppose that is what the constructors had designed her to do, bless them. But the spray was fiercely stinging.'

Having never been in company before, Fisher and Burnett were still slightly at odds. Fisher had wanted to make ground to the eastward, so as to be ahead of *Scharnhorst* should she turn east on meeting *Duke of York* and he 'accordingly edged that way.' But Burnett signalled 'not to stray that way. I remember being a bit annoyed by this as by now I was feeling free to pursue my own tactics.' In fact, at 3.59 pm Fraser actually told Burnett to keep his destroyers to the *westward* in case of a westerly deployment. This was, as Fraser said in his Dispatch, 'to guard against *Scharnhorst* turning in that direction and breaking back to the convoy or to Alta Fjord. Had this happened neither *Duke of York* nor my destroyers could have kept up against the head sea'.

McCoy was evidently still having station-keeping problems with JW55B. Speeding south-east after *Scharnhorst*, *Musketeer* suddenly saw a darkened ship close on the starboard bow crossing from right to left. Fisher thought this might be one of the German destroyers and made the challenge. 'The reply came, rather slowly made, '*Empire* ... ?' and we sped close across her bows. It was one of McCoy's convoy which had missed a signal for a convoy turn and was making her own way alone to Murmansk. Lucky for her she didn't meet the *Scharnhorst* which had passed that spot half an hour earlier!'

The Plot in *Duke of York* now showed that *Scharnhorst* was apparently committed to a course of about 170°, though zigzagging around it, and a speed of about 27 knots. By 3.15 pm Fraser was able to signal to Force 2 that the estimated bearing and distance of the enemy was 025°, 56 miles.

This news, when it percolated around the ships, caused hearts to thump and mouths to go dry. At present closing rates, action was only about three quarters of an hour away. At 3.42, Fraser made the traditional signal, often made by an admiral to his captains before an impending battle: 'Observe very attentively Admiral's motions as he will probably alter his course or speed, either with or without signal, as may be most convenient.'

Norfolk had kept her place very well up to now, but at 3.45 Bain had to signal to Burnett that he had a fire in a wing compartment over an oil fuel tank which could not be controlled unless he could stop the ship rolling. This meant he had to alter to a steadier course and lose bearing. *Nofolk* managed to put out the fire and rejoined Force 1 at about 5 pm.

No sooner had *Norfolk*'s signal been received, than it was noticed from *Belfast*'s bridge that *Sheffield* was also dropping back and at 4.11 pm Burnett signalled to her 'Come *on*!' In fact this crossed another from *Sheffield,* with the news that her port inner shaft was out of action and her speed was only 8 knots.

It was the most wretched luck for *Sheffield.* At continued high speeds, the port inner set of main turbine gearing had failed at 4.10. The shaft had to be stopped and locked, to prevent excessive vibration. By 4.20 she was able to signal to Burnett that she was once again following, with a maximum speed of 23 knots. But the delay, and the reduction in speed, meant that *Sheffield* did not rejoin Force 1 until 9 pm that evening. As Fraser's Dispatch said, 'for the rest of the action she remained some 10 miles astern conforming to the general movement of the battle'. It was a bitter blow for Addis and especially for his engine-room department. But, as Addis himself wrote, it was 'no blame to the Engineer Officer or his staff who must have felt their position acutely.'

Thus Burnett's next report, giving the enemy course as 150°, 27 knots, bearing 160°, 9 miles from *Belfast,* had the significant postscript: 'By myself'. This was not quite fair to *Musketeer* and the other destroyers, who were still there and still be contact, but it did illustrate *Belfast*'s isolation at that stage.

Belfast's main machinery had performed splendidly. Although she was 14 months out of refit, she made 28, 29 and even 30 knots for extended periods. But *Belfast*'s very efficiency had placed her in very great danger, for she was now the only major warship close up to *Scharnhorst* and in an isolated position. It seems that *Scharnhorst*'s after radar set was still working during the run to the south, and she must have had some indication of her pursuers. According to Gödde, Bey and Hintze were certainly aware that they were being shadowed by ships, which they had already identified as cruisers. Yet *Scharnhorst* took no action to dispose of them.

Belfast's amazing immunity was a constant source of wonder (as well as profound relief) to Parham, who could not understand why *Scharnhorst* did not turn and attack, especially when her radar must have disclosed that *Belfast* was alone. 'The *Norfolk* had damage,' said Parham, 'and *Sheffield*'s engines had gone funny. We were alone, shadowing that great ship. She was a *much* bigger ship than us. She'd only got to turn round for ten minutes and she could have blown us *clean* out of the water!'

Force 2 was steering 080° at 25 knots, with the huge following sea, making it difficult for the destroyers to keep up with *Duke of York* and even she was plunging under the waves, looking like a giant submarine just breaking surface. A number of close-range 20 mm. and 40 mm. anti-aircraft guns had been fitted on the fo'c'sle. As the great battleship drove forward into gigantic waves and shipped hundreds of tons of green water over her foredeck and upperdeck, as far aft as the quarterdeck, these guns, with their mountings, fittings and ready-use ammunition lockers were all torn away, together with several ventilation cowlings and other ship's fittings. Water poured down through the empty rivet-holes and open ventilation trunkings, making life very difficult and unpleasant down below.

Meanwhile, in the superstructure above, the men manning the directors and the radar sets were dry, though cold; they had all had their tea, and they were now waiting for the enemy to appear. If all the calculations were correct, the first 'blip' should appear on the radar screen a minute or so either side of 4.15 pm.

At that time, *Duke of York* had the best and most comprehensive array of radar aerials and displays anywhere, and the equipment was maintained and operated in action by a most able staff, of whom almost all the officers were RNVR, with the initials (Sp) after their ranks, and all the ratings were 'Hostilities Only' The flagship, had, in fact, no less than a dozen sets. There was a Type 273QR surface warning set, working on 3000 Mc/s, with a range of over 20 miles, mounted on top of the forward control tower; the aerials were housed in a perspex casin, like a light house-lantern; the 'Q' denoted that *Duke of York*'s set had the latest refinements: roll-stabilised aerial array, and a cylindrical perspex dome around the aerial, an improvement on the previous panelled perspex dome which often gave annoying side-echoes.

For aircraft detection and stand-by surface detection, there was the Type 281 with a range of about 12 miles. Its transmitter was on the foremast and its receiver on the mainmast. There was a subsidiary Type 243 set, working in conjunction, to detect enemy aircraft transmissions. For gunnery there were two Type 284M3 14″ gunnery control sets, one forward on top of the 14″ director, the other aft; for the 5.25′″s there were four Type 285M3 sets, one mounted on each of the four 5.25″ directors — two to Starboard, "Saltash" and "Stonehouse", and two to Port, "Penzance" and "Paignton" *(Duke of York* being, of course, a West Country ship). There were also Type 253, for detecting aircraft Identification Friend or Foe (IFF) transmissions, a Type 91, and a Type FV1 to detect enemy radar transmissions. Although, as *Duke of York's* Radar Officer Lieut (Sp) H.R.K. Bates RNVR said, the radar equipment in 1943 was not much better than quantity-produced laboratory equipment', *Duke of York*'s radar worked very well on the night.

At 4.17 pm., almost exactly on the expected minute, *Duke of York*'s Type

273 picked up its first echo of the enemy: bearing 020°, range 45,500 yards, or nearly 23 miles. It was *Scharnhorst* at last, detected at marvellously long range. Fraser and his staff were jubilant. Their enemy was about to be delivered into their hand. For what we are about to receive, may the Lord make us truly thankful.

While the enemy's bearing remained almost steady (a sure indication, by the rules of ship-handling, that a collision was virtually certain sooner or later) the range came down rapidly: 20 miles at 4.23, 13 miles at 4.36, 8 miles at 4.43. Guy Russell, standing next to Fraser, kept saying eagerly, like a very large labrador hoping for a walk, 'You know you can open fire any time you like now, sir?' Fraser still puffing at his pipe, kept on replying 'No, no. No, no. We'll wait. While the enemy doesn't know we're there, the closer we get, the more certain we'll be'.

Fraser's intention, once he had confirmed from Burnett that only one heavy enemy unit was present, was to engage on a similar course, with *Jamaica* in support, opening fire at about 13,000 yards, or 6½ miles, at the same time detaching the destroyers to make a torpedo attack. Fraser was, in a sense, taking some risk in not standing off and shelling *Scharnhorst* at or near maximum range. For such heavy calibre guns, this was to be a close-range "shoot-out". It was not at all impossible that *Scharnhorst* might be almost as quick on the draw and score a crucial hit on *Duke of York* early on.

However, Fraser pressed in closer imperturbably. He had his destroyers disposed ahead, the 1st Sub Division of *Savage* and *Saumarez* to port, the 2nd of *Scorpion* and *Stord* to starboard. At 4.37 Fraser signalled to them: 'Take up most advantageous position for firing torpedoes but do not attack until ordered' — a signal whose consequences he later regretted.

Jamaica meanwhile, acting as 'Little Sir Echo', as her people self-depre-catingly called themselves, was in station astern of *Duke of York*. They too had had their tea, according to the diary of the Supply Officer Cdr. Hitchens, which laconically recorded one man and his ship's preparation for battle. "1.30. News that *Scharnhorst* was definitely closing about 120 miles off. Arranged tea issue, bread and butter and tea from galley, cake and jam from issue room. Supper pies started. 2.30. Decided that tea must be issued by 2.45. Supper converted into layer pie. 3pm. Saw tubs and baths filled (water was cut off at 3.30) and oil fuel out of officers galley. 4pm. Played bridge in cypher office for about a quarter of an hour. 4.25. *Duke of York* picked up *Scharnhorst* on radar. Went up on signal deck. Blew up lifebelt'.

At first impression, from the gunnery spotting positions in *Duke of York*, *Scharnhorst* 'appeared of enormous length and silver grey in colour'. Lt.Cdr. James Crawford, *Duke of York's* gunnery officer, staring through high-powered binoculars, had the best view of all: "To see this incredible sight about seven or eight miles away, like a great silver ghost coming at you ... It was a gunnery officer's dream come true."

Also making his mental preparations was Bryce Ramsden, in his director high in *Jamaica's* superstructure. '... at about four o'clock, the order came through — "Look out bearing Red Five O". As I gave the order to start the motor and told the control position below to stand by, my heart beat faster. Ten minutes before, the Gunnery Officer had called me on to the bridge and said in a cheery sort of way that he would try and let my 4-inch have a crack at her, and so "Stand by for your low angle procedure." My God! that means about three or four thousand yards from the *Scharnhorst*. I digested this with difficulty, but I hope, with an outward show of calm and happy anticipation.

'The director was now trained into the biting wind, and our bows were dipping into the seas. I strained my eyes through the binocular sight, and saw nothing save a black empty horizon. I settled my tin hat more firmly on top, my camera inside the open front of my wet oilskin out of the spray. My brain was working overtime on singularly dramatic thoughts. Seconds lengthened into an age.'

At 4.37 *Belfast*'s radar picked up *Duke of York*, bearing 176°, range 40,000 yards, another excellent contact. The two plots could now be married in both ships. At 4.45 Fraser told *Belfast* to 'open fire with starshell' while ordering Force 2 to increase to 27 knots. 'When we got the order,' said Parham, 'Illuminate the enemy with starshell! This was simply *terrific!*' 'This was greeted by cheers in Belfast', said Welby-Everard. 'I didn't tell them that during the last hour or so we were by ourselves and if she turned round it would be a hot corner for us!'

Belfast opened with starshell, range about 19,000 yards, at 4.47 but did not illuminate the target, or at least, it was not seen in the flagship. Shortly before, at 4.42 the enemy appeared to have altered course to port. At 4.44 Force 2 altered to starboard onto a course of 080°, to open 'A' arcs — i.e. to open the bearing so that all the main armament, both forward and aft, could bear on the target.

At 4.47 *Duke of York* opened in starshell, with a salvo of four, controlled from the bridge by Lieut. K. Wintle RNVR, fired from P2 and P3 portside 5.25″ turrets. Wintle, whose action station was 'probably the coldest in the ship' saw the four star-shell burst perfectly behind the target and hang there, lighting up *Scharnhorst* as though on a recognition slide.

There she was, a most beautiful ship, sliding through the tremendous waves, a majestic and an awesome sight. Ramsden could see her on the horizon as a 'black silhouette against the flickering candle-glow. Even at that distance the sheer of her bows was perfectly noticeable and she stood out clearly for an instant as if removed bodily from her page in *Jane's Fighting Ships*.' From *Duke of York*'s flag bridge, Vivian Cox saw 'the most incredible sight; the *Scharnhorst* looking like a marvellous fish, like a huge salmon — coming dead towards us'. As the first of the reports came in: Enemy in sight! (from *Savage* on *Duke of York*'s port bow) Fraser himself could see her: 'Four starshell, and there she was ... It was *terrific* — I can still see that illumination now.'

But Fraser, Merry, and Cox on *Duke of York*'s flag bridge, Crawford from his high director tower, Henry Leach peering through the periscope of 'A' turret, Parham over in *Belfast* and Ramsden astern in *Jamaica*, every eye-witness who saw *Scharnhorst* at that moment, was struck by the same astonishing thought: 'Good *Lord*! She's still got her turrets trained fore and aft!'

CHAPTER 8

The Big Guns open fire:
'Plain as a bloody pikestaff'

FOR the third — and last — time that day, *Scharnhorst* had been caught napping. Watchers in *Duke of York* saw, after the first star-shells burst above and beyond, *Scharnhorst* turning hard to port, to steer north and then north-east, as though instinctively recoiling away from this new, just realised menace to the south-west. The men in the destroyers were nearest and had the best view of all. 'When the starshell first illuminated *Scharnhorst*,' said Sub.Lieut. A.G.F. Ditcham RNR, watching through binoculars in *Scorpion*'s Director Control Tower, 'I could see her so clearly that I could see her turrets were fore-and-aft (and what a lovely sight she was at full speed). She was almost at once obliterated by a wall of water from the *Duke*'s first salvo — quite like the spotting table! When she reappeared her turrets wore a different aspect!'

As *Duke of York*'s first broadside thundered out, two 'battle ensigns', the two biggest White Ensigns in the ship, were broken out at each masthead. This had the practical purpose of aiding identification of friend and foe in the heat and smoke of battle but as Dickie Courage said 'it was an inspiring sight when illuminated by the flash of our own guns. This practice goes back to days well before Trafalgar and had been remembered by the Signal Boatswain Harold Kelly'.

For *Duke of York*'s 14″ gun crews, the waiting was over. Now was the time to go to work. 'Then came the long-awaited order "All positions stand-to!",' wrote Henry Leach, in charge of 'A' Turret. 'In an instant tiredness, cold and seasickness were shed and all hands became poised for their individual tasks. "Follow Director!" and the huge turret swung round in line with the director control tower. "All guns load with armour-piercing and full charge load, *load*, LOAD!"; the clatter of the hoists as they brought up the shells and cordite charges from the magazines, the rattle of the rammers as they drove them into the chambers of the guns and the slam of the breeches as they closed were music to all. Then a great stillness for seemingly endless minutes, disturbed only by the squelch of the hydraulics as layers and trainers followed the pointers in their receivers from the director. "Broadsides!" and the interceptors, completing the firing circuits right up to the director layer's trigger, were closed; a glance at the range receiver whose counters were steadily, inexorably ticking down until ... 12,000 yards ... the fire gong rang and crash, all guns fired and the Battle of North Cape had started.'

Duke of York's first ten-gun 14″ broadside was timed at 4.51 pm, at a true range of 11,950 yards. It was very well aimed and completely straddled *Scharnhorst*, hitting her low down on the hull and well forward. A line of greenish sparks was seen shooting along her waterline. The third salvo also straddled, with one certain hit on the starboard side, amidships.

From *Duke of York*'s Director Control Tower, a hundred feet above the water-line, the Gunnery Officer, Lt.Cdr. J.H. Crawford was looking for signs of hits. *Scharnhorst* had first appeared to him as 'an enormous silver-grey shape in the white light of the star-shells. She was 12,000 yards off and showed up well, the first impression being her huge length. The chief thing that remains in my mind was the red glow of the 'gun ready' lamps. Suddenly there was a yell of 'Target!' and someone shouted 'There she is — plain as a bloody pikestaff!'

'The Captain said 'Open fire' and I ordered 'Shoot!' Ding-dong went the firegongs and then there was the agonising wait of three seconds and then the crash as our ten 14-inch gun broadside thundered out.'

'We counted to fifteen and down they came. The splashes completely obliterated *Scharnhorst*, and then there followed a greenish glow along her waterline where she had been hit.'

From astern in *Jamaica*, Ramsden also saw *Duke of York*'s first broadside depart on its ear-shattering journey: 'Even to us, now a thousand yards astern, the noise and concussion was colossal, and the vivid spirt of flame lighted up the whole ship for an instant, leaving a great drift of cordite smoke hanging in the air. Her tracers rose quickly, and, in a bunch, sailed up to the highest point of their trajectory, and then curved down, down towards the target.'

By now *Jamaica* was also in action: 'Almost as soon as *Scharnhorst* could be seen, there was a deafening crack and a spirt of flame as we fired our first full broadside of 6-inch. The concussion momentarily deafened me, and my vision was blurred by the shaking of the director and the sudden flash out of the gloom. We could see the tracer shells coursing away like a swarm of bees bunched together, and could follow them as they curved gently down towards the target. Before they landed the guns spoke again, and the sea was lighted for a brief second by the livid flash'.

Watching intently from the Admiral's bridge, Fraser himself nearly became the ship's first casualty. On the bulkhead was a 'large kitchen-type' clock, used for timing changes of courses whilst zigzagging. It was normally unshipped before full calibre shoots but it had been forgotten. 'With the first salvo it fell with a loud crash between the Commander-in-Chief and me,' wrote Courage. 'That was our most dangerous moment and also the only time either the Commander-in-Chief or I saw the *Scharnhorst*. The Commander-in-Chief then had to take up residence in the Plot to handle the co-ordination of the attacks. I remained outside in the darkness getting rather bored, and could see nothing except the splashing of *Scharnhorst*'s shells which seemed to be much too close for comfort.'

By now *Belfast* was also firing from the north, joined at 5 pm by *Norfolk*, whose arrival was unnoticed on *Belfast* bridge. The sound and the specta-cular pyrotechnic effects of *Norfolk*'s first 'full-flash' salvoes took everybody by surprise. *Duke of York*'s 4.25″ turrets also opened fire, using semi-armour piercing (SAP), with two turrets each side firing star-shell. The 5.25″s lacked flashless cordite in every turret and after a time they began to provide *Scharnhorst* with a point of aim.

For a ship which had been taken by surprise, *Scharnhorst* reacted quickly, her first return salvo being timed at 4.46 pm, only five minutes after *Duke of York* opened. She began with star-shell from a starboard side 5.9″ turret and followed almost at once with a main 11″ broadside, lacking 'A' Anton Turret which was put out of action by *Duke of York*'s first salvoes.

Having watched his own side's shells on their way, Ramsden now had to wait for the enemy's reply. '... the star-shells burst, two or three together, with intense white flares which hung in the air above us. In their light the sea was lit up as by the moon very brightly, and I remember thinking that we must have been visible for miles. I felt as if I had been stripped stark naked, and had to resist the natural urge to hide behind something away from the light, as if it would have mattered! After what seemed like an age her star-shell dimmed and guttered out in a shower of bright sparks, which fell down to the sea for all the world like stubbing out a cigarette or knocking out a pipe at night.'

Scharnhorst opened some 2,500 yards short with her main armament, but quickly picked up the range and soon began to straddle *Duke of York* with disconcerting regularity. As the flagship's gunnery report admitted, this was 'the most testing time of all, for no visible results of our own firing but large orange enemy flashes on the horizon, which appeared extremely menacing. He could hit at any time'.

Anything 'over' pitched close to *Jamaica*, with equally alarming effects, as Ramsden said: 'Just as we had again been plunged into the comforting gloom I saw the angry white wink of her first 11-inch broadside, and said to myself, "She's fired" — not very comforting to those below, and not much better for me. Thank God we couldn't see her shells coming as we could see ours going. The waiting for their arrival was bad enough, but to see them coming all the way would have been far more grim. There was a vague flash off the port bow which I caught in the corner of my eye as I gazed through the binoculars, and then — crack, crack, crack, sharp like a giant whip, and the drone and whine of splinters passing somewhere near.'

Although the science of spotting shell splashes by radar was still in its infancy, *Scharnhorst*'s return fire could actually be detected on the screens in *Jamaica*, 'Our radar operators and their colleagues in the main armament control centre were *distinctly* perturbed, 'wrote Lt.Cdr.Rupert Wainright, *Jamaica*'s Gunnery Officer, 'when, on this their first experience, they saw on the radar tube the enemy shells coming towards *us* with every appearance of accuracy! Fortunately we were not hit, but the whole ship shook and those on the bridge were drenched from a *very* near miss.'

It seemed that the battle was not going quite as Fraser had hoped. At 5.02 he signalled Burnett 'Any more news?', obviously hoping for more hits, and was somewhat disappointed by the negative response. *Scharnhorst* had recovered well from her surprise and was proving a more than able opponent. It had been possible that she had fired torpedoes during her first turn away to port and Force 2 had altered to 060° to 'comb' the possible tracks. When *Scharnhorst* turned to 055° and then to the south-east, roughly to 110°, *Duke of York* matched her. *Scharnhorst*'s mean course was east, but she was not content merely to retreat. While 'C' Caesar Turret kept up a rapid and accurate fire at the pursuers, which it did for most of the action, *Scharnhorst* swung from time to time to the south, so as to open the firing arc for 'B' Bruno Turret, which would then fire salvoes, until *Scharnhorst* returned again to the east.

It was a most effective tactic. The great white flashes of the two 11″ turrets, firing ripple salvoes, supported by the rapid orange-red sparks from the 5.9″ with streams of tracer overhead together made a most daunting sight. Leading Seaman Bob Thomas was 'rate officer' in the port forward "Penzance" 5.25″ director. His job 'in surface firings was to estimate the enemy's speed and the changes in range, "Opening" or "closing", passing the information to the plot in the Transmitting Station down below the armoured deck.' When the action began, 'the darkness soon filled with indescribable noise, the stench of cordite and flash. But more than anything else it was the approach of the red and yellow tracer that made me so very frightened. Fear was so mounting that if I could have escaped from the scene I would have bolted like a rabbit.' Thomas stuck to his duty, but according to his account there were some lapses in self-control, with men shouting at each other in hysteria, and arguing amongst themselves.

At 5.13 Fraser signalled to the destroyers to 'close and attack with torpedoes'. But it was, for the time being, too late for that. As the Admiralty's Tactical Division later discovered, and Fraser himself suspected at the time, a great opportunity for a destroyer attack had already passed. When Cdr. Michael Meyrick had made his 'enemy in sight' signal at 4.50 pm., he had been so close to *Scharnhorst* that *Duke of York*'s starshell had illuminated *Savage* as brightly as it had the enemy, and he was at that time in a good position for a torpedo attack.

But Fraser had already signalled 'do not attack until ordered' a decision he defended years later on the grounds that the single enemy ship had complete freedom of manoeuvre and if she turned away as *Duke of York* opened fire, all the destroyers' torpedoes would be wasted; Fraser felt that he himself was the best man to decide when he had his enemy pinned down, and that would largely depend upon the position Burnett managed to achieve on the opposite quarter of the enemy. But, as the official historian remarked, that 'order given to the destroyers resulted in *Savage* and *Saumarez* losing a favourable opportunity, which was not to recur until one-and-a-half hours later.'

In fact, the enemy's range was reducing so rapidly at about 5.10pm., when still no order had been received to fire torpedoes, that Meyrick was actually forced to reduce speed in *Savage* and retire for a while to the southward, at one point turning through 360°. More than one of Fraser's staff officers must have suspected, as Courage did, that Fraser 'privately rather hoped somebody would disobey his order'.

It was almost inevitable that *Scharnhorst* would hit *Duke of York* sooner or later, and it was very fortunate for the flagship that the damage was not greater. A very interested onlooker on board that day was Wing Cdr. Robin Compston, the RAF liaison officer attached to Fraser's staff: 'Waiting to go over the top will convey the feeling that I personally experienced on the Admiral's bridge between 4.30 and 4.50 pm. when the flagship's first shattering broadside thundered on its way. We hadn't long to wait before the enemy's reply came, the shots short at first and then suddenly the most perfect straddle of our forecastle. Had one of those eleven inch shells scored a lucky hit inboard, how different might have been the outcome of the battle. Shortly after the straddle a salvo pitched in the sea just ahead of us and the *Duke of York*'s stem ran through the swirl some seven seconds after the spurts of water had subsided.'

'On our port bow we saw the flashes from the guns of the cruiser *Belfast* as she engaged the enemy yet again that day, while the brilliant flash of the *Scharnhorst*'s guns, firing broadsides at the flagship enabled us to mark her position in the darkness. During this amazing fireworks display the officers on the bridge were calmly going about their duties, sending vital signals and even finding time in between our broadsides and those of the enemy to give their men a running commentary on events over the loudspeaker. Star shells from both sides lit up the scene continuously. It is curious how naked one feels when a very bright light descends in one's vicinity — "now we shall catch it" is the feeling.'

'A sudden rattle of bits and pieces falling proved, on examination after the battle, that an eleven inch shell had severed rope and steel stays on the foremast just abaft the bridge.'

Courage called down the voice-pipe to Dawnay that he thought some of his aerials had been shot away (the aerial leads for jamming enemy transmission on 80 cm. were indeed severed) but Dawnay replied cheerfully 'Maybe: but we are still on the blower to the Admiralty and everyone else!'

In fact the damage was to the radar aerials and especially the long range Type 273 surface warning set. An eleven inch shell passed right through the foremast (which, *pace* the Wingco, was a steel tripod mast), only feet below the shoes of Lieut. H.R.K. Bates and the boots of Able Seamen Badkin and Whitton, who occupied the 273 office, two-thirds of the way up the mast, at action stations. As Bates said, 'the shock was terrific and the three occupants collapsed in a heap on the very small deck. To their amazement, they were not injured at all and moreover the radar set appeared to be working. But there was no echo now from the *Scharnhorst* and of a sudden the 'mushy' echoes from the huge sea waves had gone.

'I switched off the "office" lights and climbed up into the aerial compartment. By feeling about and aided by letting a pocket torch peep between my fingers, I found the aerials pointing to the sky. By operating the appropriate controls, I got the aerials horizontal and stabilised again by their gyroscope and the sea echoes and echo of *Scharnhorst* were restored. So it was the horrific shock of the German eleven inch shell passing through the mast that had made the aerials topple over. Fortunately all the electrical wires to the set passed along the fore front of the mast and so did not get damaged'.

However, to most of the staff and ship's officers, and to almost all the ship's company, radar was a complete mystery, and the restoration of the echo of *Scharnhorst* seemed like black magic. Bates was popularly supposed to have climbed the mast and personally restored the radar service by holding together the severed ends of the aerials. Hard though Bates himself tried to discount the story, and to explain the truth, the sailors were convinced, and soon gave him the immortal nickname of 'Barehand' Bates. The fact that Bates was a very tall and a very strong man, standing well over six foot, gave extra currency to the sailors' belief that he had held the radar leads together by main force.

The legend was given official encouragement at home. Radar was still secret and the story was put about that Bates had repaired *Wireless* leads, thus restoring to the Commander-in-Chief vital communication with other ships in his force. Many versions perpetrated this misinformation: for instance, C.S. Forester, writing in the *Saturday Evening Post*: 'Had the *Duke of York* remained unable to give orders to the destroyers, the *Scharnhorst* might possibly have survived. But Lt. H.R.J. (sic) Bates effected a temporary repair in the quickest possible way. He climbed the mast — in the dark, with the wind whipping round him and the ship lurching fantastically over the waves — and he held the ends of the aerial together for the orders to pass'.

In another straddle a second eleven-inch shell by coincidence damaged the main mast, carrying away some two-thirds of the port strut of the tripod and some of the mast itself. The after receiver aerial of the Type 281 air warning set was put out of action, and this was not repaired until the ship reached Kola Inlet. A 5.9″ shell hit the Admiral's barge and reduced it to 'a keel and a couple of engines'. But by that time, Fraser had a great deal more to concern him than the loss of his barge. It seemed that *Scharnhorst*, despite everything, was going to get away.

At 5.08 pm. *Scharnhorst* had settled on an easterly course, with short diversions to the south to allow 'B' Turret to engage, and from then onwards she steadily pulled away from her pursuers. By 5.20, Burnett had had to signal that he had lost touch. *Duke of York* continued to fire, first at 'fleeting targets' and then, as the range opened, in blind fire by radar control. As Crawford said, 'We had fleeting glimpses of her through the smoke and the range remained constant. We fired eight more broadsides at the 'bits' we could see through the smoke. We fired more broadsides with the range slowly opening. We could see the enemy's gun flashes — great bursts of orange-coloured flame. We scored three more hits, but even this did not seem to check her'.

At 5.17 pm., when *Duke of York* began firing by radar, the range was 13,400 yards. *Duke of York* went on firing steadily in blind control for another 44 broadsides, 25 of them judged to be straddles, 16 of them as close as 200 yards from the target or less. At least three hits were seen, one of them starting a 'fairly considerable fire on the after superstructure', giving a useful point of aim until it disappeared 'to the intense disappointment of the layer and trainer'.

Jamaica had been dodging about behind *Duke of York*, moving from one quarter to the other and firing whenever she saw a chance. She had opened fire at 4.52 pm., range 13,000 yards, and by 5.42 when the range had opened to 18,000 yards, Hughes-Hallett decided that his blind fire was of 'doubtful value' and liable to confuse the flagship's radar spotting. *Jamaica* ceased fire, having fired 19 broadsides of 6″, and claimed at least one hit.

When *Jamaica* ceased fire, as Ramsden said, 'we could follow the battle more closely. It was a slogging match between giants, appalling in their might and fury. Every time the *Duke of York* fired there came the vivid flicker of the *Scharnhorst*'s reply, the lazy flight of the 14-inch tracer followed by the crack, crack of the 11-inch reply in the sea, and the drone of splinters.'

By 6 pm the range had opened so much, to almost nine miles, that Fraser signalled to the destroyers, at eight minutes past, asking if they could report his fall of shot. At 6.13 *Scorpion* replied 'Your last salvo 200 yards short' (very good shooting at that range) and at 6.16 'Can only see occasional splashes due to smoke'. At 6.20 *Scharnhorst* ceased fire, with the range at 20,000 yards and four minutes later Gunnery Type 284 radar developed a defect and the flagship also checked fire with the range at 21,400 yards.

There was 'a distinct atmosphere of gloom and disappointment' in the Director Control Tower at the order to check fire. It 'appeared that, despite undoubted hits, the enemy would escape with her superior speed.' *Scharnhorst* really did seem to have the luck of the devil. In spite of everybody's efforts, it seemed that she was going to show them all a clean pair of heels. Nobody could catch her now. The destroyers, now over ten miles from *Duke of York*, were still 12,000 yards from *Scharnhorst* and hardly gaining any ground.

On the bridge of *Duke of York*, there was a feeling of bitter frustration and disappointment. They had had their chance and not made the most of it. At 6.40 pm., Fraser made the sad little signal to Burnett: 'I see little hope of catching *Scharnhorst* and am proceeding to support convoy'. This message, though it made very cheerful reading for the convoy and escort, was a painful admission of failure for Fraser.

Years later Fraser admitted 'I *did* give up hope then, for the moment. Of course, I can see now that I shouldn't have sent that signal — Admiral Burnett was furious — but what else could I think? We'd tried everything, and it wasn't enough'. Fraser also reproached himself for not releasing the destroyers to attack early on, when there had been a great chance of success. He tried not to blame his destroyer captains for not showing a little more of the 'Nelsonian blind eye' and disobeying their orders to wait.

Leach spoke for everybody, not just in *Duke of York,* but in all the ships present as 'steadily, gallingly the range counters clicked up as the enemy drew away. I cannot adequately describe the growing frustration of those few who were in a position to realise what was happening; to have achieved surprise, got so close, apparently done so well, and all for nothing as the enemy outpaced us into the night. Quite rightly (to conserve ammunition) fire was ordered to be checked when the range ceased to be effective on an ahead bearing where the ship's movement generated the greatest (cross-level) fire control errors. The resultant despondency was profound.'

But then, Leach wrote, 'suddenly the range steadied, then started to close. Had we done it after all?' Meyrick, on *Savage's* bridge, also noticed the range seemed to be steady. 'We only had a little speed in excess of the *Scharnhorst* and to catch up was going to be quite a business. After a time I had a shout from the officer in the plot who said he was sure we were getting much nearer the *Scharnhorst,* followed almost immediately by another shout and he said he thought she had altered course ... '

Duke of York had only checked fire because her Type 284 Blind Fire Control Radar set for the 14″ guns had developed a fault, and the 14″ Director could therefore no longer 'see' the target. When the 284 returned, *Duke of York* would be able to resume 14″ firing out to ranges of another 15,000 yards. However, by the time the 284 was repaired, the situation had greatly changed. Fraser had also noticed that the destroyers were beginning to gain bearing upon *Scharnhorst.* He had 'already decided to turn towards the Norwegian coast, hoping the enemy [would notice presumably by radar and] 'would also lead round and so give my destroyers a chance to attack. When, however, I saw the speed reduction I turned in straight at the *Scharnhorst'.*

In *Scharnhorst,* they were still reasonably confident of being able to return to Norway. Apart from 'A' Anton Turret, the ship's main armament was still intact, and she still had her speed and seaworthiness: (indeed, more than one of the men who ultimately survived said he was amazed at having to abandon ship; they had had no idea that matters had reached such a pass).

However, there had been ominous portents ever since 4.17pm., when Bey signalled 'Am being followed by a hostile ship'. The question of how much Bey knew about his opponent will probably never now be resolved. It is not even absolutely clear that he knew he was being followed. If he did, and believed his pursuer was a heavy ship, then he was right to do as he was ordered, to break off and make his best speed away (although he might have wondered why his supposedly heavier opponent did not open fire on him). If he believed his shadower was a cruiser, then it hard to see why he did not turn and attack her, exactly as Parham expected he would.

Nor is it clear whether *Scharnhorst* was operating her after radar set. More than 27 years after the event, on a visit to Wilhelmshaven, Henry Leach, by then a Captain, 'had a long, friendly and objective talk on the action with a retired Federal German Navy Captain who had been the Executive Officer of the Scharnhorst until a few months before her end. (Kapitan zur See Helmuth Giessler). In his view his Captain and Admiral were obsessed by the risk of RDF transmissions being intercepted by Direction Finding equipment with which the British were known to be equipped. Although they had considerable faith in the effectiveness of their RDF they preferred not to use it for this reason. This seems a plausible explanation.'

However, Gödde's account refers more than once to a shadower, which could only have been detected by radar. Günter Sträter heard a loudspeaker announcement, which must have been broadcast at about tea-time, warning the ship's company that they were not yet safe, calling for an even keener look-out, and referring to a shadowing ship which had been following since noon and which *Scharnhorst* had not been able to shake off [*Scharnhorst* had not actually made any attempt to shake her pursuers off]. According to Sträter, the announcement specifically referred to radar targets to starboard (i.e. on *Duke of York*'s bearing). The speaker ended by urging the men to be prepared and to keep on the alert, for 'it may be any moment now'.

It seems strange that, if such a broadcast was made, the command did not at least take the precaution of training the main 11″ turrets on the threatened bearing. All eye-witness are unanimous that *Scharnhorst* had her turrets still fore and aft when she was first illuminated. It must be remembered that some of *Scharnhorst*'s survivors' accounts were, as their interrogators found out, coloured by what they had already heard from their captors.

Many of *Scharnhorst*'s men had been catching up on their sleep and the sudden sounding of the alarm at about 4 pm was an unpleasant shock. Even more of a shock was the report that there was a 'heavy unit' in the offing. The *Scharnhorst* had been led to believe that they only had a cruiser to face. The unmistakeable sound and the confirming report of 'Schweres Mundungsfeuer' ('Heavy gun flashes') came as a rude awakening. There had been 'relative calm on board'. That was gone for ever, and the order to 'Load with armour-piercing shell' was the final confirmation that there was now a new opponent.

Such German accounts as there are confirm that *Duke of York*'s shooting made a fast, confident and accurate start. Gödde said he could see gigantic columns of water, from what must have been shells of the heaviest calibre, only 100 to 150 metres on the port side. Other survivors said that *Scharnhorst* was 'ringed with star-shell, which dazzled the range-takers and made their work extremely difficult.' They would not agree with Ramsden's view of their own star-shell which, they said, was 'illuminating only bare expanses of water'.

At 4.56pm., Bey made the 'Most Immediate' signal to Group North which they had half-dreaded, half-expected, giving his grid square reference' AC 4677 (72°39N., 26° 10E.) and adding 'Heavy battleship. Am in action.' By then, Gödde said, 'they were coming fast and furious. The crew was kept on the move to meet one emergency after another. 'General quarters' had sounded. A few minutes later the first star shells were exploding above the ship. The enemy was to our starboard. Then the first heavy calibre shells screeched by, falling uncomfortably close. Soon our own heavy turret guns were answering. As we opened fire, the enemy guns became less accurate, and we could see the splashes further from the ship.'

'On our port side, seek as I might, I could make out no enemy. At about 16.45 a shell struck us in our forward starboard turret A. I was thrown to the deck, and for a moment the heavy smoke cut off the air from me. The Captain came out of the battle station to find out just what had happened. The lookout glasses in the command station were useless. He helped me up and asked me if I was done for. When I answered negatively he said to me: 'Stay here at your post. It is very important that they do not surprise us from this side.' Shortly thereafter we took another direct hit amidships.

'After the heavy hit, Turret A remained motionless, the guns pointing out to starboard. Later I learned, since I now had the ship's telephone, that Turret A was not answering, and nobody could get into the turret on account of the fire and smoke.

'Towards 17.00 the ship took a staggering blow which seemed to throw her off course. I assumed a torpedo hit amidships, although nothing came through on the phone to this effect. Shortly thereafter came the word: 'Starboard Number One 15 cm. gun knocked out'.

According to survivors, a shell from one of *Duke of York*'s first salvoes penetrated the battery deck and exploded on the Tween Deck, on Section XIII starboard side, blowing a hole half a yard in diameter in the ship's side, only about two feet above the waterline. The hole was patched by the damage control parties who welded a metal sheet in place.

The shell which hit 'A' Anton Turret put it completely out of action. The turret was fixed at the limit of its traverse to port (one would have expected it to have been trained to starboard) with all three barrels jammed at about 30° of elevation. The elevating and training gear were both wrecked. The flash of the explosion ignited charges in 'A' magazine and the fire spread to part of 'B' Bruno Magazine. Both magazines were partly flooded. None of 'A' Turret's gun or handling crew survived, but a survivor from 'B' Turret, Matrosengefreiter (Able Seaman) Rudi Birke, described his gun's crew floundering in ice-cold water up to their waists, to recover still usable ammunition, and continuing to serve the guns. A major explosion was averted and the water in Bruno was pumped out as soon as possible.

Soon after the action began, the order 'Flak in Deckung' (AA guns take cover) was given, so that only a skeleton crew, enough to take messages, stayed at the 105 mm. gun mountings while the rest took shelter. Some survivors were bitterly critical of this order (which in the event was never countermanded) and of the generally inept and muddled handling of the secondary armament. Survivors said they heard the Second Waffenoffizier (Gunnery Officer) Kapitan Leutnant Wieting (described by the sailors as 'a cosmopolitan gentleman' whom messdeck gossip said had been a spy in Hawaii) order the port 105 mm. mountings to load with star-shell, while the Gunnery Officer, Korvetten Kapitan Walter Bredenbreuker, counter-manded the order, told them to unload, and reload with armour-piercing. Whatever the precise truth, it does seem that the secondary armament in *Scharnhorst* was not fought as crisply and decisively as it should have been.

The listeners ashore were still receiving scraps of news. At 5.32 Admiral Northern Waters heard *Scharnhorst* reporting: 'Surrounded by heavy units'. At 6.19 *Scharnhorst* made one of her last signals, to Group North: 'Opponent is firing by radar location at more than 18,000 yards. My position AC 4965 (72 09°N, 28 30°E). Course 110 degrees, speed 26 knots.'

Scharnhorst appears to have ceased firing with her 11″ at about 6.20, when the range was some nine miles. She must presumably have been firing by some form of radar control, using her after set, until that time; *Duke of York*'s 5.25″, which had been giving *Scharnhorst* a point of aim, were still firing, although nearing their maximum range, but it seems hardly likely that *Scharnhorst* could still see the flashes at such a distance on a night of such poor visibility.

But at about 6.20 pm, ironically just about sixty seconds after *Scharnhorst*'s signal gave her speed as 26 knots, *Duke of York* scored one long-range, and crucial, hit which penetrated to *Scharnhorst*'s starboard side machinery spaces and put the starboard boiler-room out of action. One survivor, Matrosenobergefreiter Hubert Witte, a messenger on the Admiral's bridge, said that at 6.20 he saw a speed recorder on the bulkhead in front of him dropping from 29 to 22 knots, after a 'shell hit aft'. Other accounts, such as Strater's, said the message over the broadcast was 'Torpedo hit in boiler room Number One. Speed 8 knots'.

While the exact reduction in *Scharnhorst*'s speed is not certain, at one point, the Engineer Officer Korvetten Kapitan (Ing) König was heard on the broadcast, reporting to the Captain, 'I can maintain 22 knots, we will make it even yet' to which Hintze replied, 'Bravo, keep it up'. Clearly, König and his department carried out some admirably efficient damage control, isolating the damaged boiler-room and cross-connecting the remaining machinery, so that *Scharnhorst* soon picked up again, to about 22 knots.

But it was not enough. *Scharnhorst*'s vital superiority in speed was gone. By 6.30, one survivor said, 'Shadows were reported on either beam.' Breden-breuker was said to have retorted that 'he couldn't fire on shadows, he required targets'. As that survivor said, 'Those 'shadows' were tangible enough to pump us full of torpedoes.'

By 6.40 pm the four destroyers led by Cdr. M.D.G. Meyrick in *Savage* had split into two sub-divisions and were some distance apart. The 1st Sub-Division, of *Savage* and *Saumarez*, was about 10,000 yards astern of *Scharnhorst*, following in her wake but steering out towards her starboard side. At 6.43 Meyrick signalled to Lt.Cdr E.W. Walmsley DSC in *Saumarez*, 'Close and attack with torpedoes as soon as possible', 'Open fire with torpedoes' a minute later and at 6.47 'Train tubes to port'. Meyrick could see that he was at last gaining bearing on *Scharnhorst* and a supreme moment for him and his crew was approaching.

Michael Meyrick was a very experienced destroyer officer, from a most distinguished naval family. His father and grandfather were admirals. His brother was killed on the bridge of the ex-US Coast Guard cutter *Walney*, crashing the harbour boom at Oran in November 1942, in an action when the Senior Officer, Captain F.T. Peters, won a Victoria Cross. But Meyrick's crew were mostly Hostilities-Only; only forty per cent of them had ever been to sea before in their lives when *Savage* first commissioned in June 1943. *Savage* herself had a new and experimental armament, with a twin 4.5″ Mk.II mounting in 'A' position, instead of the normal single 'A' and 'B' mountings forward, and single 4.5″ Mk.V mountings in 'X' and 'Y' positions, (to preserve uniformity of ammunition).

Savage and *Saumarez* were sighted from *Scharnhorst* at a range of about 8,000 yards, when survivors said the 'shadows materialised into destroyers'. The 105mm. gun crews were still under cover, obeying the previous order which was never countermanded and *Scharnhorst* lacked proper anti-destroyer gunfire at a critical time. Her survivors 'never ceased to bewail this error and utter violent threats as to how they would deal with the Gunnery Officers if they were only able to lay hands on them. They ascribed the ultimate loss of *Scharnhorst* to this order'. There is something in that opinion.

With a heavy sea running, it was very difficult to spot the destroyers and as *Savage* and *Saumarez* opened fire with main armament and star-shell at a range of 7000 yards hey were answered by 37mm. and 20mm. firing tracers to indicate the target, followed by 5.9″ and even some rounds of main 11″ from 'C' Turret.

For the men in the destroyers it was the most exciting moment of their lives. 'For one and a half hours it was a stern chase, 'said Lt. Dennis, in *Savage*. 'The engines were steaming faster than they had ever done on trial. The heavy seas were very troublesome, and gave the crews of the guns and torpedo tubes a hard time, for they were continually being swept by big waves which went right over them.

'Fortunately the weather had improved a bit since the forenoon, and we were just able to maintain full speed. As we closed *Scharnhorst* she did her best to drive us off with gunfire, but thanks to the captain's manoeuvring no one was hit on the way in, although there were plenty of shells flying about. As we got closer, the remarks heard on the telephone got more and more to the point. Ours were mostly unprintable.'

Scharnhorst's return fire was rapid but sometimes erratic. Meyrick said some of their shells burst up to 1,000 feet overhead, showering the bridge and superstructure and upper deck with metal shrapnel shards — 'one man's life was undoubtedly saved by his steel helmet'.

The man whose professional competence was most at stake was Mr Berner, *Savage*'s Torpedo Gunner. Because of the very heavy seas, washing down the upper deck, he had ordered the tubes crews 'to wedge themselves in between tubes to prevent their being washed overboard. We kept checking communications with the control, and periodically I managed to communicate with the Action Information Room and get information of the range of the *Scharnhorst* which was slowly closing. During the final stages of the attack we were getting close range fire coming across the ship and as the range was closing, from 7,000 yards down to 5,000 and below, I was wondering how much closer we were going to get before firing our torpedoes.'

The same question was very much occupying the minds of the torpedo tubes crews in *Scorpion* and *Stord*, who were also about 10,000 yards from *Scharnhorst* but well over on her starboard side, forward of her beam and gaining position for a good attack. *Stord*, the Norwegian-manned destroyer, had a special debt to pay off. Norwegian warships were normally given a small Royal Navy communications staff, to help with language difficulties. Leading Telegraphist Catlow, in *Stord*, said that the Norwegians 'had a few outstanding debts to settle, as some of them had parents and other relations who had been tortured and shot by the Gestapo. There were others amongst the crew who had themselves suffered before escaping to England.

'As we followed *Scorpion* into the torpedo attack, I for one did not expect to come out of it. As I passed the order to attack up the voice-pipe, I remember thinking sadly of the silk stockings I had bought in Iceland: my girl friend was going to be disappointed. One of the aerial party was sitting in a corner of the office eating a large ham which he had pilfered from the galley, he said if he were going to die, he'd do it on a full stomach.

'We were bracing ourselves now for the turn as we fired our torpedoes, and the expected sound of tearing metal as the *Scharnhorst* opened fire on us, but neither came. I shouted up the voice-pipe to the Leading Signalman to find out what was happening. His comforting answer was "the Captain thinks she's a U-boat, he's going in to ram. At the moment I'm trying to squeeze myself into this voice-pipe, and pull my tin hat over my shoulders".

'Eventually we commenced to heel over as we turned to fire and the *Scharnhorst* who must have been distracted by the attack of the destroyers on her other flank opened fire on us. How she failed to hit us was a miracle, but shells fell all round us and in our wake, but we were lucky.'

Not only the RN ratings in *Stord*, but the watchers from *Scorpion*'s bridge thought that, 'quite frankly, Storheil intended to ram *Scharnhorst*'. Lt.Cdr.

Clouston, commanding *Scorpion,* later said as much to Cdr. Maunsell, the Fleet Torpedo Officer: 'He said that *he* went in pretty close, but that he thought the *Stord* was going to ram the *Scharnhorst,* she went into about four or five hundreds yards, and, mind you, all the *Scharnhorst*'s [secondary] armament was functioning at the time.'

Midshipman Peter Cree, of *Duke of York,* went down to visit *Stord*'s wardroom a month later and two of her midshipmen, Lafiord and Mofstedt, told him 'they had got within 800 yards, but were covered with shame because only one or two of their eight torpedoes had hit'. *Stord* had completed her attack at 6.52, at a range which Cdr. Storheil said was 1,800 yards, and he claimed one hit.

As *Scorpion* attacked, star-shell from *Savage* and *Saumarez* beyond fell between her and *Scharnhorst.* This, as Sub. Lt.A.G.F. Ditcham RNR, in *Scorpion*'s Director Control Tower, later said, had the effect of 'hiding *Scharnhorst* from *Scorpion* and Co. who, by now approaching *Scharnhorst* on a converging course at some 55 knots, were obliged to press on to a very close range in order to sight their target. Obviously it blinded *Scharnhorst* also, or probably I would not be sitting scribbling this ... *Scharnhorst* was inter-mittently silhouetted against her own gunfire but never presented a clear target to assess inclination: when *Scorpion*'s Captain gave the 'stand by' order to the Torpedo Control Officer, he promptly replied that he could not see the target clearly and *Scorpion* held on.

'When at last *Scorpion* and *Stord* began to turn to fire, at something like 2,400 yards, *Scharnhorst* suddenly got a clear view of them and flung her wheel over hard to starboard. This suddenly presented the Torpedo Control Officer (Lt. Stephen Beresford) with a 'beam-on' target on an opposite course, and with a snap calculation of deflection which he quite brilliantly improvised'.

On the way in, Clouston noticed a fire on *Scharnhorst*'s quarterdeck which died down after about three minutes. Meanwhile Beresford, using *Scharn-horst*'s bow as a point of aim, fired a full salvo of eight torpedoes, when the range by the Type 291 radar was 2,100 yards, simultaneously with *Stord* at 6.52.

'All this time,' said Ditcham, 'I was sitting holding my peace in the D.C.T., forbidden to open fire and present *Scharnhorst* with an aiming point. Nothing lay between *Scharnhorst* and the Norwegian Fjords but *Scorpion* and *Stord. Duke of York* and the other two destroyers were astern of her and at that time not an immediate menace. My Captain contended that had *Scharnhorst* held on her course she might have run down *Scorpion* and plastered *Stord* as she went by half a cable away. Whether she could have escaped *Duke of York* coming up astern is immaterial to this contention — that *Scharnhorst*'s Captain panicked and put his wheel over and an onrushing target at a fine inclination became a sitting bird.'

After *Scorpion* had fired, Ditcham said 'my Range-finder's crew followed the target through the stern, and all quite clearly saw the target embraced by our eight tracks and three explosions along the ship's side.'

'As G.C.O. in such an action I was only a passenger, even if I had been allowed to open fire, and thus had time to record these vivid impressions; so had my director's crew, who observed "Get out wires and ... fenders, we're going alongside the ... " I might be forgiven if I mention that at the last moment when beam to beam on opposite courses' [when *Scorpion* did open fire with her 4.7" guns, and got off three salvoes] 'our first broadside landed at the base of the funnel, but the range was then 1,850 yards! By then she was over-lapping the field of view in my binoculars and I put them down.'

From *Scorpion*'s bridge, Yeoman of Signals Mills had *Scharnhorst* 'well in sight like some huge black shadow which threw out spasmodic gun flashes. The ship was dead silent as we closed and as we turned to fire a young Ordinary Seaman manning the oerlikon gun under the bridge suddenly yelled out "Out wires and fenders, port side!".'

Scharnhorst's violent turn to starboard changed the situation dramatically for *Savage* and *Saumarez*. Instead of a stern chase, they now found their target rapidly approaching them on a near-converging course. Meyrick heard a shout from the plot that 'we were getting much nearer the *Scharnhorst*, followed almost immediately by another shout and he said he thought she had altered course. I could now see the *Scharnhorst* in my glasses and realised that this in fact had happened; that she had turned round and was steering between the two groups of destroyers, so giving us the most perfect target.'

As *Scorpion* and *Stord* hauled off to the north, their job done, *Savage* and *Saumarez* hurriedly trained their torpedo tubes round to starboard, to meet the new situation. At 6.53, almost simultaneously with *Scorpion,* indicating that it was a brilliantly synchronised destroyer attack, *Savage* signalled that her attack was completed. 'When the first torpedo was fired,' said Mr Berner, 'although I was ready for it, the flash scared me into thinking we had been hit, but the second flash made me more settled.'

Savage fired her full salvo of eight torpedoes at a range of 3,500 yards and Meyrick claimed three hits, on *Scharnhorst*'s port side. 'Having seen all eight torpedoes safely on their way', said Mr Berner, 'I dispersed the tubes crews forward and aft to stand by to help repair parties, and then proceeded to the bridge where I had the satisfaction of being told that the tracks of our torpedoes had been followed through binoculars and that we had scored two and possibly three hits.

Saumarez made no report of an attack completed, and only fired four torpedoes, but even those were a superb effort. On her approach *Saumarez* was hit by an 11" shell which passed through her Director Control Tower without exploding. But Ditcham's counterpart in *Saumarez*, Sub.Lt. S.J. Thorpe was killed outright, together with another nine men. An eleventh man died before the ship reached harbour and the last man died later in hospital. Eleven men were wounded. The Director Layer was the only survivor of the men in the D.C.T.

Just before *Saumarez*'s torpedoes were fired, an 11″ shell exploded in the water close on her starboard hand and sprayed the whole starboard ship's side and upper deck with a storm of shrapnel. Several splinters penetrated the ship's side and damaged the forced lubrication system for the starboard main engines. The shaft had to be stopped and *Saumarez* could only limp onwards on her port shaft, at about eight knots. However, four torpedoes got away at a range of only 1,800 yards.

'This gallant attack' by the destroyers, in Fraser's words, 'practically unsupported', as he said, turned the battle. Three very heavy underwater explosions were heard in *Duke of York* at this time, and *Belfast* heard six. It seems certain that *Scorpion* and *Stord* between them got at least one hit on *Scharnhorst*'s starboard and *Savage* and *Saumarez* at least three on her port side. *Savage* also fired eight salvoes, a total of 16 4.5″ shells, from 'A' Turret, whilst *Saumarez* fired no less than 48 rounds of 4.7″ from 'A', 'B' and 'X' mountings ('Y' would not bear) as well as some 80 rounds of bofors 40mm. in the latter stages.

Scharnhorst's survivors said that their ship's company was 'generally aghast at the relentless attack by what turned out to be four destroyers', who came within 1,800 metres or less to fire full salvoes of torpedoes. *Scharnhorst*'s hydrophones actually picked up the propellor noises of the torpedoes as they approached, but there were too many of them to dodge and, according to survivors, the ship was hit at least three times.

One torpedo seems to have hit *Scharnhorst* in a boiler-room (this could, possibly, have been when König made his reassuring broadcast to the bridge), a second hit aft and a third forward. But it is impossible to be exact, because many of the survivors could not possibly have been in a position to see or hear what was happening. Günther Sträter said he heard the message 'Torpedo hit in boiler-room I, speed 8 knots' at about this time, and then the very welcoming news that the ship was making 22 knots again. However, as the German accounts say, this was the very last piece of good news for *Scharnhorst*'s people. If there had been any doubt about her fate before, there was none now.

CHAPTER 9

'We shall fight to the last shell': *Scharnhorst's* End

IN *Jamaica*, the news that the destroyers were going in to attack was greeted with surprise, and relief, and excitement. 'I confess to having completely forgotten about them up till then,' wrote Bryce Ramsden, 'but now I blessed their presence. There was a strange lull in the gun-fire. Everyone was on tip-toe, straining to catch the first signs of their attack. The familiar flash of 11-inch again split the darkness, and a minute or so later an incredible and terrifying noise made me momentarily crouch down again. A whole salvo had passed clean over our heads, like the tearing of a huge corrugated cardboard box — an indescribable, devilish sound. "Come on, Adolf, no more of that," I prayed. Again the flicker in the distance, and again we waited for it to arrive. Nothing came. Again the flash, but followed this time by star-shell illuminating the horizon. Thank God, the destroyers must be in. We remained silent and sat back more comfortably.'

Meanwhile the Type 284 14″ blind fire control radar set in *Duke of York* had been repaired after its temporary break. The range was closing quickly and tracking by 284 started again at a range of 22,000 yards, at 6.42 pm. 'For the next eighteen minutes, until 1900,' read *Duke of York*'s Gunnery Report, 'frequent changes were made from Blind to Visual Control without difficulty, as a glow in the smoke and the flashes of enemy gunfire afforded fleeting points of aim. The destroyers were now in full cry and the enemy appeared as a dark source at the centre of a veritable mass of diverging and converging tracer and gunfire.'

Everyone there was conscious that he was witnessing an extraordinary and awe-inspiring scene. 'I felt at times I was witnessing one of Hollywood's gigantic productions,' said Paymaster Lieut. T.B. Homan, standing on the wing of the Admiral's bridge. He was in charge of the light anti-aircraft armament there, which was not manned, so he 'was able to watch the whole action from what might be termed a ring-side seat. It seemed impossible that this was the real thing — a night action at sea.'

Duke of York turned to port, to head for the enemy, and *Jamaica* followed. Watching through his binoculars, Ramsden could see the spectacular signs of a furious destroyer engagement. 'Star-shell flared high, guns flashed, red beads of pom-pom fire ran out in livid streams, each to fade in a small white burst. Strange bursts of high-angle fire spasmodically dotted the sky, and still we ploughed on steadily and silently, and our guns poinred mutely towards the flashes ready to crash out again.'

For a time *Scharnhorst* was steering south-west, almost towards *Duke of York,* and the range closed rapidly. Just before 7 pm *Duke of York* and *Jamaica* turned ninety degrees to starboard to open 'A' arcs and at 7.01pm, *Duke of York* opened fire again at a range of 10,400 yards. According to the Gunnery Report, the enemy 'did not appear to observe the approach of *Duke of York*' and the first salvo 'created enormous havoc aft'. This first broadside of *Duke of York*'s second engagement in fact seemed to strike *Scharnhorst*'s quarter deck complete. 'Direct fire was now possible and 25 broadsides were fired, 21 straddles and many hits being observed'. The final demolition of *Scharnhorst* had begun.

This was now becoming clear to the men in exposed positions in *Scharnhorst*. 'During the ensuing exchange of fire and occasional pauses, 'wrote Gödde, 'I gathered from the telephone reports that more and more enemy units were joining the attack. Meanwhile came the report that a shell had landed on the plane hangar deck and that the place was in flames. Because a destroyer had approached us from our wake to within 400 meters, the after 15-cm. turret and the after 10.5 flak guns had to be turned to defend against these enemy attacks. I have a poor recollection of the times and of certain incidents, but the ship at this point took several hits from heavy guns. Among others, the ship ran squarely into one hit that tore up the forward section and lifted me into the air by sheer air pressure, throwing me on the deck. The Captain, who had left, was wounded by a fragment from this shell.'

'Actually, the Captain, having left his command station on the port side to get a view of all sides (glasses in station were all destroyed or unusable because of the pounding) was wounded in the face. This did not prevent him from coming to my post and helping me up. He asked me if I was wounded. Outside of a few scratches I was unhurt. He sent me to the starboard range-finder station to find out why no one was answering our calls. I found only dead men, and the station demolished. After about twenty minutes, at 1845-1900, we were hit by a torpedo which seemed to stop us for a moment in our tracks. Again there was a medium calibre hit forward, from which a shell fragment ripped out the apparatus behind which I was standing. Although the cords of my headphone were sliced through, I was unhurt. A quarter-master, who had been sent by the Captain and reported the situation, passed me the word to come into the command station, since there was no point in remaining outside any longer. I made my way into the command station, where I became the witness of the devastating and desperate death struggle of our ship against overwhelming odds. We were doing twenty knots. The third engine was out of action because of a damaged steam line. The men were working desperately to repair the damage. The Chief Engineer reported that he was hoping to get things in order to twenty to thirty minutes. The Captain called out to the L.I. (Chief Engineer): 'Well done, engine-room! Ship's officers and crew thank you for your work.' The ship changed course to the north in order to escape the threatening clinch'.

But there was no escape. From the north, *Norfolk* opened fire with main armament, but checked after two salvoes because the situation was so confused she had difficulty in finding the right target. *Belfast* also opened fire at a range of 17,000 yards at 7.15 in Visual Control and claimed at least two hits.

The signals and announcements from Bey and Hintze betray an increasing desperation. As early as 5.32, Admiral Northern Waters received *Scharnhorst*'s signal 'Surrounded by heavy units'. At 6.25, 'Flag Officer Cruisers and CO of *Scharnhorst* report: To the Fuhrer. We shall fight to the Last shell' and at 6.02 pm, to Admiral of the Fleet and C-in-C Fleet, 'Most Immediate. *Scharnhorst* will ever reign supreme. The Commanding Officer'. It seems the worse *Scharnhorst*'s predicament became the more defiant were the signals. But Hintze's announcements to his ship's company had a more ominous note. At about 7 pm., he broadcast that 'the heavy unit astern is overhauling us' and some time later, 'I shake you all by the hand for the last time.'

That probably was Hintze's last message. Possibly *Scharnhorst's* last transmission was at 6.30 pm., that she was 'steering for Tana Fjord, her position 71 57°N, 28 30° E., speed 20 knots.'

Scharnhorst's 'C' Turret kept firing almost to the end, though latterly in local control. But as *Duke of York* and *Jamaica* turned to administer the *coup de grace* there was a curious lull. 'No shell came near us for almost twenty minutes,' said Ramsden. 'We turned to starboard, the turrets following round so that both ships presented a full broadside. I think I yelled "Stand by again!" over the telephones, but my words were drowned by the deafening crash of gunfire. The tracer now appeared almost horizontal, so flat was the trajectory as they rushed like fireflies to converge at a point in the darkness.'

'Suddenly — a bright-red glow, and in it the enemy was to be clearly seen for a brief moment. "She's hit! My God, we've got her!" I was yelling like one possessed. We were cheering in the director. All over the ship a cheer went up, audible above the gun-fire. I had risen half standing in my seat as the wild thrill took hold of me. Again the dull glow, and in its light the sea was alive with shell-splashes from an out-pouring of shells. Great columns of water stood out clearly in the brief instant of light, and I could see smoke hanging above her. I was mad with excitement until I realised that my ravings must be an incoherent babble of enthusiasm to those below, as the telephones were still hanging round by head. I straightened my tin hat, sat down, and told them as calmly as I could that we could see that our shells had set her on fire, and that both the *Duke of York* and ourselves were hitting, and hitting hard. She must have been a hell on earth.'

Matrosengefreiter Helmut Boekhoff, whose action station was loading number of the starboard twin 37mm. gun mounting, was one of the close range guns crews taking shelter in the superstructure: 'A star shot came right across us. We were lit up from stern onwards and they landed on the deck and I was in the tower and I was certain that armament had hit and the armour plate was absolutely red and there was something whissling round in the middle of it, like it coming through. And I grabbed to my, you know, and I thought "Oh here it comes", but it didn't come through, it went outside and there was haywire all over'.

None of *Duke of York*'s 14″ shells penetrated the armoured deck, which remained intact, although a large number of shells penetrated the decks above it, exploding on contact with the armoured deck, causing great havoc and many casualties. The forward port 150mm twin turret was hit, and the gun and its hoist put out of action. The aircraft hangar was hit, the aircraft destroyed and a large fire started, which was extinguished in about ten minutes. Some Luftwaffe personnel on board had tried to launch the remaining aircraft but there was no compressed air to operate the catapult machinery and the aircraft and catapult were hit and wrecked shortly afterwards.

Further hits landed on the starboard side forward 105mm mounting; on the starboard side near the funnel; in the Tween Deck port side, in Section X; in the battery deck, port side, in Section IX; on the starboard after single 150 mm gun; and on one quadruple 20mm. mounting starboard side, which was seen to fly through the air and crash on the deck.

The survivors' accounts of their experience were often poignant *vignettes*, as vivid as the flashes of the shells. The Torpedo Officer, Oberleutnant Bosse, was seen running along the upperdeck in a hail of shrapnel to train the port side set of triple torpedo tubes onto their aftermost bearing. He actually fired all three torpedoes but only two went over the side. The third stuck and hung in the tube. It was still there when *Scharnhorst* sank.

A shell carried away the starboard anchor, and another parted the anchor cable on the fo'c'sle. *Scharnhorst*'s Bosun heard the roar of the released cable going out through the hawse-pipe and was last seen going forward on to the cable deck to inspect the damage when a heavy sea swept him overboard.

Although the armoured deck was not penetrated, the number of shells exploding on the Tween and Battery decks caused terrible scenes of carnage there. Mangled bodies swilled around in a mixture of blood and sea-water, while stretcher parties picked their way through the damage with ever-increasing numbers of wounded.

The ventilation system of 'B' Turret was hit and put out of action. The sole survivor from that turret, Matrosengefreiter Rudi Birke, described the conditions inside the turret which rapidly became intolerable. Every time the breeches were opened, thick black smoke belched out, blinding and choking the guns crews. In spite of the powerful lamps inside the turret, it was impossible to see anything more than a yard away. The crews had to bellow orders at each other, filling their lungs with choking cordite smoke.

This, with the motion of the ship, made almost every man in the turret violently sea-sick. When the ship altered course, so that their guns would no longer bear, they had a temporary respite by opening the hatch through which empty cartridge cases were dropped, thus getting some fresh air through it, and easing their smarting eyes and lungs. But, as time went on, most of the portside guns were put out of action and their crews lay in grotesque attitudes all over the deck, slowly being washed overboard, as the ship heeled.

By contrast, Wing Cdr Compston noted the scene in the Admiral's Plot in *Duke of York* where 'the voice pipes were conveying vital information to the staff, each voice was answered very quietly and distinctly by one or other of the officers concerned. In the short periods between our own broadsides and the enemy's salvoes, there was complete quiet in this little space high up in the superstructure — the cranium as it were of the brain behind the action. So quiet were the discussions that one might have imagined they were carrying out an ordinary practice shoot at the battle practise target.'

'These men, controlling the destiny of some eighteen hundred souls and in the act of writing a page in the annals of history gave the impression that they were able to make time wait for them.

'The enemy was now almost down to only a few knots — she was glowing on the bridge and quarterdeck but she continued to fire all the guns she could bring to bear on us as well as using her secondary armament against the destroyers which were running past her at very close range after their attack. Now was the time as the Chief of Staff said, "to slap her down", the *Duke of York* closed the range to give the *coup de grace*. It was a smashing blow. The tracer bands of her fourteen inch shells enabled one to follow five little circles of light thrown, like illuminated quoits, on to the glowing target now less than three miles away. As each salvo registered, flames and sparks flew up as high explosive disintegrated, piece by piece, the great structure that had been the *Scharnhorst*'.

Standing beside Compston, and close to Fraser, Vernon Merry, the Flag Lieutenant noticed the same pyrotechnical effect: 'Every time we hit her, it was just like stoking up a huge fire, with flames and sparks flying up the chimney. Every time a salvo landed, there was this great gust of flame roaring up into the air, just as though we were prodding a huge fire with a poker. Tremendous, unforgettable sight.'

Cdr. Maunsell, the Fleet Torpedo Officer, also had a very good view of *Scharnhorst* from the flag bridge, as 'she was in the centre of the arena, luminated by the star shells and outside that particular circle of light there was complete blackness. Towards the end she obviously had a very bad fire raging in her superstructure which was red and glowing, and stood out as an extremely good aiming point for our fire. Above her was a great ball of smoke. The effect of our gun fire when we achieved hits was a bright glow at the point of impact which disappeared fairly quickly, followed by a sheet of flame from an explosion. At other times we only saw an immediate glow at the point of impact and then nothing else which meant that our shells were exploding inside her. It was very quiet on the bridge of the *Duke of York*, there was only the noice of the guns and the noise of the falling *Scharnhorst* shells and the roar of our guns often obliterated the scream of the shell' (with the greatest respect to the Fleet Torpedo Officer, all that hardly merits the phrase 'very quiet on the bridge').

According to *Duke of York*'s gunnery narrative, 'at 1922, when the 72nd broadside fell, it was noticed on our Radar tubes that the echo, after first appearing as a normal straddle, developed into a great 'bunch' of width 800 yards either side of the target, at the same time a considerable explosion occurred aft in *Scharnhorst*. Fire was checked at 1929 after 80 broadsides, by which time *Scharnhorst* was a blazing wreck very low in the water ... '

Scharnhorst might have been battered into a blazing wreck (although she was not yet as low in the water as *Duke of York*'s gunners claimed) but she had not *sunk*. In fact, the closer *Duke of York* approached her target, and the flatter the trajectory of her shells, the less effective were her broadsides. Her heavy calibre shells did most damage against an armoured enemy at longer ranges, with 'plunging fire' of the shells falling almost vertically from a great height onto the target. Despite her 80 broadsides, *Duke of York* had yet to land a really damaging blow (indeed, *Scharnhorst*'s survivors said they could have withstood that sort of fire 'for two *days*').

Fraser was well aware of this and at 7.19 he ordered *Jamaica* to 'Finish her off with torpedoes'. Captain Hughes-Hallett had been observing that *Jamaica*'s 'six-inch guns were hitting her good and proper. The *Scharnhorst* was then burning with a sort of dull red and greenish glow and much smoke. She kept disappearing in smoke.'

By then *Scharnhorst* had turned north again, and then sharply to port to south-west. She was almost stationary, but not quite, and this probably disconcerted *Jamaica*'s torpedo tube crews, who fired three torpedoes to port at 7.25, at a range of 3,500 yards. One torpedo misfired. No hits were claimed.

As *Jamaica* closed the target, Ramsden was still waiting to engage with his 4-inch. 'Train round, train round, Stop. No, a little more. There she is! Guns follow director. Enemy in sight. No deflection. You've got the range, haven't you? O.K. Stand by then.'

'It had come. At last we were going to open fire, and I was controlling. I was cool now, and desperately grim in concentration. I mustn't lose this chance. We were turning, turning to starboard, and again came the flicker of gun-fire right in front of us, but much more vivid and far nearer. I caught sight of a red blob, then another, which rose in front and then curved down, and it seemed to come straight for us. No, it had gone over. Again everything blurred, and was shaken as one 6-inch broadside and then another was fired — straight into her. We couldn't miss at that range — three thousand yards. I could smell the sweetish smell of burning. It must be the *Scharnhorst*. I yelled above the din for permission to open fire. We waited and waited for an answer, but none came. They probably never received it on the bridge. And then we turned away and ceased firing. My 4-inch hadn't even opened up, and we were bitterly disappointed.'

'Star-shell from nowhere burst over our heads, bathing the whole ship in light. Surely she will open up now. We were naked, illuminated in every detail. But nothing came.'

Jamaica turned for another run to fire her starboard torpedoes; three torpedoes at a range of 3,750 yards, at 7.37 pm. Two very heavy explosions were heard but the target was hidden in smoke. However, Hughes-Hallett noticed that 'when we fired our second lot of torpedoes she was still firing her secondary armament. The *Scharnhorst* Oerlikon fire was very good indeed. There were quite a number of hits by us in the second phase. Between torpedo broadsides we were hitting her very hard with our secondary armament. We certainly stopped their Oerlikon fire.'

Jamaica's Torpedo Officer Lt.Cdr. Paul Chavasse saw 'a lot of smoke' as they closed the enemy at high speed. 'By starshell we saw the black mass of the *Scharnhorst* and as we closed with her we let fly with our torpedoes. At the 'moment critique' the target was blacked out with smoke. We then did another 'swing' and fired three more from our starboard tubes. The enemy seemed to resent this, and blazed away with his secondary armament and close-range weapons, but most of his stuff went over our heads. When the smoke cleared we saw the *Scharnhorst* lying on her side. She looked like a whale that had just come up for air, except that she was ablaze from stem to stern.'

Petty Officer Mahoney was in charge of the starboard torpedo tubes and 'could see a fire just off the starboard bow and a long way away. Shells were still going in that direction. The tubes were ready and the crew were singing their favourite song "Star Dust". I didn't feel like singing, but I joined in, as it broke the spell of waiting. A starshell broke over us which turned night into day ... the ship turned to bring the port tubes on, and then I heard them fired. I thought to myself — starboard tubes next — that's me. The ship swung round and I could see the *Scharnhorst* not very far away. Two columns of smoke were rising from her, one on each side of her funnel. Our torpedoes were fired one after the other. My work was finished, so I ordered the tubes trained fore and aft, and then waited for the explosions — if we hit. Then one explosion, and then another ... '

One minute after *Jamaica*, at 7.20, Fraser ordered *Belfast* also to attack with torpedoes. *Belfast* fired three torpedoes to starboard at 7.27 and claimed one hit, although nobody saw it and Fraser said it was 'considered unlikely' (an opinion hotly disputed by Burnett, who was convinced ever afterwards that it was *Belfast* who administered the final blow.) *Belfast* turned to fire another salvo to port at 7.35 but found such a mètée of ships and fire round the target that she altered round to the southward to await a more favourable opportunity' (which in fact never came again).

The 'melee' around the target was caused by the arrival of the 36th

Destroyer Division. Fisher and his destroyers had had a very long stern chase ever since the action just after tea. Fisher was a believer in the classical principle of destroyers coordinating their attacks and had earlier tried to synchronise his division's attack with *Savage*'s but had not been able to get into W/T touch with Meyrick.

In the event, the 36th Division arrived some forty minutes after *Savage*'s attack. 'After the *Duke of York* got into action,' wrote Fisher, 'I streaked at 32-33 knots to the east, keeping outside *Scharnhorst*'s radar range to the north of her, trying to gain bearing for a torpedo attack should she break away to the north-east, the only 'gap in the net'. I knew that there were four destroyers with the C-in-C and that the Senior Officer of the eight of us ought perhaps to try to co-ordinate a combined attack, but my Navy List showed the other four to be commanded by a chap senior to me so kept quiet. In fact Michael Meyrick was junior to me and nothing was done.'

By the time the 36th Division reached *Scharnhorst*, she was steering south-west but was virtually stopped. The destroyers closed from the north; 'At the end we were coming up fast astern of the *Scharnhorst* and as starshell cast an orange glow over the scene we could smell the fires raging in her as she was pounded by the *Duke of York's* guns. it was a sight never to be forgotten as these salvoes of shells showing red tracer lights in their bases curved through a graceful arc in the night sky, some of them to produce a great, slowly rising red glow in the target'.

The Division, steering almost the same course as *Scharnhorst*, split into two, the 71st Sub-Division, of *Musketeer* and *Matchless,* led by *Musketeer* ('fervently hoping that the *Duke of York* realised we were there') running upon *Scharnhorst*'s port side. At 7.33 *Musketeer* fired four torpedoes to starboard, at a range of 1,000 yards 'and saw the columns of white spray go up alongside the target as some of them hit' — two, possibly three hits, between the funnel and the mainmast. 'Turning away after firing *Musketeer* very nearly collided at high speed with *Matchless* who had had to turn the opposite way on account of the training gear of her tubes being jammed'.

Matchless had had the most wretched luck. Shortly before she made her attack a heavy sea had hit the torpedo tubes while they were being trained outboard and strained the tube mountings, including the training gear. During the attack the tubes had to be trained from port to starboard. As Petty Office Harold Walker, *Matchless*' Torpedo Gunner's Mate, explained: 'During the high speed turns in the run-up we shipped a heavy sea which wrenched our tubes round and twisted the training gear. It also filled our sound-powered telephones with water. Consequently the order "Ready Starboard" for the torpedo attack was never received and we turned away with all our fish still in the tubes. We were naturally very disappointed not to have made a more positive contribution in the action, though the final objective had been achieved'. However, as Midshipman Garnons-Williams, who joined *Matchless* from *Belfast*, later observed, she 'had fired a good proportion of 4.7" ammo from her forward battery, Sub.Lt. Napierala wreathed in smiles, but Gunner (T) Dudley Goodhugh not so joyful.'

The 72nd Sub-Division, of *Opportune* and *Virago*, attacked from *Scharnhorst*'s starboard side, *Opportune* firing four torpedoes at a range of 2,100 yards at 7.31. She claimed one hit, turned, made another run, fired a second salvo of four torpedoes at a range of 2,500 yards, and claimed a second hit. *Virago*, as her captain Lt.Cdr. White said, was a brand-new ship, less than two months out of the builders' yard. Seventy per cent of her raw ship's company had never been to sea before and their work-up had been completed in four weeks. They had had a foul day, rough and wet, with seas breaking right over the bridge and Director Control Tower. But now was their chance, and they took it. *Virago* followed *Opportune* in and, at 7.34, fired seven torpedoes at a range of 2,800 yards, and saw two hits. As she retired to the west, *Virago* opened fire with her 4.7″.

With three cruisers and eight destroyers in the target area, (*Duke of York* herself steered north to avoid the scrum), it was difficult to decide later which ship's torpedoes had hit. But it seems that five of the torpedoes did hit at this time. Three of the hits were from one destroyer, possibly *Savage* earlier, or *Musketeer* later. *Savage*, *Scorpion*, *Stord* and *Opportune* all fired eight torpedoes each; *Virago*, seven; *Jamaica* five, with one misfire; *Musketeer* and *Saumarez*, four each; and *Belfast*, three, making 55 torpedoes in all. Of those, eleven were considered to have hit. Whoever fired those, they certainly brought about *Scharnhorst*'s end.

It is clear that, just as her survivors boasted, gunfire alone would never have sunk *Scharnhorst*. By the time *Duke of York* ceased fire at 7.29 pm, after 80 broadsides, *Scharnhorst* had suffered at least thirteen 14″ shell hits. But she was certainly not about to sink. She also bore perhaps a dozen other hits of smaller calibre, 8″ from Norfolk, 6″ from *Belfast*, *Sheffield* and *Jamaica*, 5.25″ from *Duke of York*'s secodary armament, 4″ from *Belfast* and *Jamaica*, as well as uncounted hits from *Savage*'s 4.5″ and the other destroyers' 4.7″. Excluding 155 rounds of starshell fired by *Duke of York*'s 5.25″s, and the unknown number of rounds fired by the destroyers, Forces 1 and 2 fired no less than 2,195 shells of various calibres at *Scharnhorst* during the day.

After the torpedo hit starboard side in No.1 Boiler room, the water rapidly reached the level of the floor-plates and the boiler-room watch were ordered to leave. The fires were put out and the boiler-room was shut off. Despite König's best efforts, this had a permanent effect on the ship's speed. It picked up to 22 knots, dropped later, picked up again some ten minutes before the end, but dropped almost immediately. But, significantly, all the lights on board were still burning and did so until the very end.

The torpedo hits had a cumulative effect, aggravating the damage caused by previous explosions before it could be rectified. One torpedo hit Section III starboard side, when the after damage control party was already fully employed. The midships damage control party had to be sent to deal with the situation. They found the section so badly damaged the passageway was impassable, so they shut the watertight doors, while they tried to reach the scene from the port side. That proved just as unsuccessful so again they had to shut off the Section, trapping some 25 men in the after part of the ship.

A torpedo hit finally knocked out 'B' Turret, jamming its elevating and training mechanism so that 'B' Turret, like 'A', was immovably trained out to its limits to starboard. The handling crews from the magazine climbed up into the turret to find the outer door jammed. After the most frantic efforts they got one door open just as the ship was sinking and water was flooding into the turret from below. Rudi Birke was the only survivor from all the men in 'B' Turret, guns and magazines.

Gödde has soberly recorded *Scharnhorst*'s last moments: 'Then came the crushing report from the heavy artillery: 'Munitions exhausted. Turret 'B' still has three shells. Turret 'C' nothing.' 'C' Turret had fired to the end, latterly in local control, and using its own range-finder. There were several survivors from this turret and one of them said they had fired 'all but 60 shells in the two shell rooms'. The captain of the gun gave the order to abandon ship and led the way out of the turret. They could see men on the upper deck struggling with floats and rafts, many of which had been damaged by gunfire. One Petty Officer with a cooler head was warning the others not to blow up life-jackets too hard, or they would be wrenched off as they jumped into the water. Somebody saw two or three of the cadets under training jumping from the upper bridge. They had misjudged the angle of heel and crashed on to the upper deck.

The final memory of some survivors was of Hintze making what must have been his last broadcast: 'I shake you all by the hand for the last time. I have sent this signal to the Fuhrer: We shall fight to the last shell. *Scharnhorst* onwards!'

'Turret 'C' received the order to pass the ammunition from 'A' Turret aft,' said Gödde. 'The Captain had radioed headquarters before things got to this pass: 'We are fighting to the last shell. Long live the Fuehrer! Long live Deutschland!' Several torpedoes hit us, shaking the ship from stem to stern and leaving her with a bad list. Then came the order: 'All hands carry out preparatory ship sinking orders'.'

Abandon ship routine in *Scharnhorst* seems to have been hardly exercised and was only rudimentary at best. Many men seemed not to have been allocated abandon ship stations, nor to have life-jackets issued to them. On the order, the first part of 'Manoeuvre V' was carried out, involving shutting certain watertight doors to ensure that *Scharnhorst* sank more slowly and allowed more men more time to escape. The second part of Manoeuvre V involved the destruction of secret books, documents and equipment.

'The orders passed rapidly from one station to another,' said Godde. 'Several more torpedo hits, nearly all on the starboard side. We were heeling over more and more. Last ship's operational order was in plain language. Captain's order: 'Abandon ship!' All hands topside! Put on life jackets! Prepare to jump overboard!' The Captain then urged us, the 25 or so men in the command station, to secure and think of saving our skins.'

A curious rumour about Bey and Hintze circulated later, and even found its way into Fraser's dispatch: prisoners had stated that Bey and Hintze had shot themselves on the bridge. Certainly one survivor heard the Commander, Dominik, using the broadcast at the very end, and perhaps assumed he was the only survivor. In such ways do such rumours begin.

Gödde's account does not support any such rumour. 'Most of us refused to abandon the command station without the Captain and Admiral Bey. A young quartermaster said simply: 'We are staying with you.' The two of them, however, succeeded in getting us one after another out of the station. Outside the Captain gave the order through the voice transmitter, located on the upper deck, to jump overboard. Still more torpedoes tore into the ship, giving her a stronger list. On deck, order and discipline reigned. You could scarcely hear a single loud word. During the last half-hour the Executive Officer, Commander Dominik, had also been in the command station. Now he was with us on the flying bridge. I saw him later, a tall figure on the upper deck as he calmly helped the hundreds of seamen who had reached the deck to climb over the railing. Above, the Captain checked our life jackets once more and then Captain and Admiral clasped hands in a final farewell. 'If anyone gets out of this mess alive,' they said, 'he should say hello to the home folks and tell them that everybody has done his duty to the last moment.'

A large number of men were on the starboard side, waiting to jump. Many of them were sucked under, or knocked out by falling debris. There was one more torpedo explosion on the starboard side; survivors estimated it was the seventh or eighth on that side of the ship. *Scharnhorst* heeled over very rapidly, sinking almost immediately. One survivor's watch stopped at 7.40 pm which was when he thought he had jumped overboard.

Gödde's account is broadly corroborated by Günter Sträter, who got safely away from his after 4.1″ gun: '1930: Captain to damage control: 'Prepare for sinking!' Shortly thereafter a shattering blow shook the vessel. We began listing to starboard. Command from the bridge: 'All men overboard!' Then there was another staggering detonation. The ship began capsizing to starboard. Up to then, we were still firing: port 2 cm. from main A.A. foremast station and port 4.1″ turret guns. The turret had not been disturbed or damaged until the heavy list caused the ammunition hoist to jam. The men from the handling rooms could not leave the ship nor could in general any from the lower spaces. On leaving the turret I found the deck covered with dead and wounded. Chief Wibbelhoff and gun captain Senior Mate Moritz had not left the turret. The first had said: 'I am staying where I belong.' The other said: 'I am staying in the turret.' Chief Wibbelhoff ordered us to leave the turret. In parting he called to us: *'Es lebe Deutschland!'* (Long live Germany). *'Es lebe der Fuehrer!'* We replied with the same cry. Then he lighted a cigarette and sat down on the gunner's seat. He and Senior Mate Moritz were in the turret as the ship turned over.'

"1945: The ship was heeled over on her side and sank by the bow. The screw propellers were still turning as they came out of the water. Indeed all three screws were turning rather fast [this could not be: the starboard screw at least was stopped]. There was way on the ship up to the end. In the water, the soldiers were now trying to get rafts. Those who found a place on the rafts sang both stanzas of the song: 'On a sailor's grave no roses bloom.'

'I heard no cries for help in the water. Everything went off smoothly and without the slightest panic.'

In the confusion of the great ship's last throes, survivors had to escape as best they could. 'By quarter to eight,' said Helmut Boekhoff, 'we were alight from stern right over the ship and we had these last torpedo hits on starboard side and it came "Abandon Ship". With that I went up to the tower, into the crow's nest, to get out and by the time I get out there the ship already was starboard side lying, so we had to have a hard shaking us to pull us out. And there was the Admiralty captain up top and he pushed his hands out to us and we made a chain to pull each other out and as I get out I see the blokes jumping right from the searchlight tower right down onto the ship. By the time they hit the water they were already instantly killed because they hit the iron right beneath the water. I went over to the starboard side and by the time I got over to the starboard side she just went flop right over and I was slung right out into the water, away from the ship. And the first thing I thought about was raft. I've got no life jacket. Well I hadn't time to get one. And I saw all bits floating around, and the next thing I saw there was a piece of wood, and I just grabbed for it and it was one of the gunnery rafts from the pom-poms.'

Scharnhorst's last moments were obscured by a dense cloud of smoke, so that nobody was sure when she actually sank. *Belfast*, who had three torpedoes left, had intended to make another attack but broke off, and signalled at 7.32 that there were too many ships present to complete a second attack. In *Duke of York* the target suddenly disappeared off the P.P.I. in the Plot and there was what Dawnay called 'a sharp altercation' between the Plot and the Admiral's Bridge, in which the Plot was told to find the target again, and quickly. In fact, as Cox, who was watching the screen, said; 'you could see the echo that had been the *Scharnhorst* gradually getting smaller and smaller; a little golden streak. And as we watched it going smaller, it eventually just disappeared, and we knew that the *Scharnhorst* had sunk.'

But this was by no means so clear at the time, especially to Fraser, who became quite uncharacteristically perturbed over the lack of hard news that *Scharnhorst* had definitely sunk. Normally the most unruffled of men, he began to pace the Admiral's Bridge impatiently, firing off signals, for the 'nearest destroyer to illuminate the enemy', asking Burnett to keep him informed of *Scharnhorst*'s location, and demanding of *Scorpion* 'Has *Scharnhorst* sunk?'.

By that time, actually 8.18 pm., *Scharnhorst* had been sunk over half an hour and eventually Fraser was able to write in his Dispatch: 'All that could be seen of *Scharnhorst* was a dull glow through a dense cloud of smoke, which the starshell and searchlights of the surrounding ships could not penetrate. No ship therefore saw the enemy sink but it seems fairly certain that she sank after a heavy underwater explosion which was heard and felt in several ships at about 1945. *Jamaica, Matchless* and *Virago* were the last ships to sight her at about 1938; at 1948 when *Belfast* closed to deliver a second torpedo attack she had definitely sunk in approximate position 72°16′N., 28°41′E.'

At 7.48 pm *Belfast* fired a starshell to locate the target but in Burnett's words 'to the chagrin of the torpedomen, the affair was completed.' Just after 8 pm, thick oil was seen on the water, with a strong reek of burnt oil 'very noticeable'. Several rafts containing survivors were seen, and shouts were heard. According to Parham, looking down from his bridge, 'we came across a raft full of shouting, if not screaming, German sailors. Rather a horrid sight, really.'

Meanwhile, in the freezing water, those of *Scharnhorst*'s survivors who had a mind to live were fighting to do so. 'By the time I was lying on the raft,' said Helmut Boekhoff, 'I had somebody got hold of my boot which I let go, because if you don't let the boot go you go with them. And because you couldn't save anybody because the moment you were in the water all you think about was yourself.'

Wilhelm Gödde has vouched for the high morale and the exemplary state of discipline which prevailed in *Scharnhorst* to the end, and beyond, although his account contains some inconsistencies; for example, that the Captain had given orders for scuttling, and damage control parties were placing explosive charges — surely counter-productive when other parties of men, carrying out Manoeuvre V, were shutting water tight doors to enable the ship to float longer. According to Gödde, men were also destroying or rendering inoperative valuable or secret machinery and installations.

However, with the authentic ring of an eye-witness, Gödde describes the listing of the ship until the bridge wings were touching the water, and the largest waves were breaking over the base of the mast. Hintze gave orders for a plain language signal to be transmitted, giving the ship's final position (no record of this signal ever being received exists).

The men on the bridge continued to behave with commendable calm. Hintze removed his life-jacket and gave it to a young sailor who had said he would not leave because he had no life-jacket. Hintze said he himself was a good swimmer. Bey and Hintze shook every man by the hand as he left.

On the upper deck, men were coming up from decks below and assembling in silent, ordered parties to await instructions. Through a megaphone Hintze advised them to abandon ship by the port side — 'slide from the rail into the water'. Gödde said he saw the two Gunnery Officers, Bredenbreuker and Wieting, go down the port gangway ladder to the upper deck; they had quarrelled in life, but were together in death. On deck Dominik, 'towering a head above the others' was organising 'abandon ship' as an evolution, ensuring that every man had his life jacket done up correctly, helping men over the rail. Inferring from survivors' accounts, it seems that several hundred officers and men must at least have got away from *Scharnhorst* and into the water.

Gödde himself was helped into his life-jacket by another petty officer from his own division, Bootsmannsmaat Deierling. The deck was already slanting at a very steep angle as the two made their way careful across the icy metal down to the water. The port side was crowded so they went over to the starboard side, where they both lost their footing and were at once swept away into the sea. Gödde was pulled down by the suction of the ship for some way, until he felt an intolerable pressure on his ear-drums, but surfaced. He never saw Deierling again.

Gödde first struck out for an 'otter' float belonging to the ship's mine-sweeping gear (clearly the oropesa float which streamed the cutting wire out from the ship). The man already sitting astride it tried to help him up but the float overturned and both men slipped into the water. Gödde next tried an 11-inch brass cartridge but this filled with water and sank. He came across a wooden grating and actually managed to haul himself across it and lie flat on its surface. But he could not hold on, as the grating tossed about, and once again he was swimming.

There is an almost poetic hint in Gödde's account of his feelings, as he swam slowly and steadily away, turning his head towards the capsizing *Scharnhorst*. 'It was a gruesome scene that met his eyes as Gödde, lifted on the long crest of a wave, looked about him, a scene illuminated by starshell and the chalk-white beams of searchlights. Where their light met the blue-black ice-cold water it shone in flashes of dazzling silver.' It had begun to snow again and through the whirling veil of great snowflakes he saw *Scharnhorst* lying practically on her side and, in a surrealist shaft of imagination, 'it flashed through his mind that a fighter plane, banking, would have seen *Scharnhorst* like that. Everything was oblique, foreshortened, contradicting the laws of gravity.'

Gödde noticed how very few men were swimming with him on *Scharnhorst*'s starboard side. It transpired that Hintze's advice, to escape from the port side, was unsound; nearly all the men who were picked up were on the starboard side. Gödde saw the flickering light from a raft containing a young officer and several men. As he swam towards them, he said the young officer suddenly stood up and shouted 'Three cheers for the *Scharnhorst*!' The cheer was taken up by the men swimming and by Gödde himself. One of the sailors also shouted: 'Three cheers for our families, our homeland!' Again, the cheers sounded from all sides.

Gödde said he heard more shouts from men who said they had seen Hintze, swimming without a life-jacket (which seems to dispose of the suicide rumour) and another shout 'clearly audible through the driving snow which, mingling snow with hail, continued to fall in the yellow-white glare of starshell: 'Save the First Officer, he's swimming close to the ship and can't keep himself above water.' Another swimmer, Gödde said, told him that Hintze and Dominik had both given their life-jackets to men who had none.

Two or three hundreds yards from *Scharnhorst*, Gödde said he could look back and actually see down her funnel, as into a dark tunnel. He and many other survivors, he said, could still hear the turbines revolving within her hull. By then oil had begun to spread across the sea, which at least as Gödde noticed, had some effect in flattening the waves. He tried to reach one raft which had some twenty men on board but saw that their weight was forcing the raft itself underwater, so that it had no freeboard at all. Instead he swam to some baulks of heavy timber, used by damage control parties to shore up weakened bulkheads.

Clinging to the timber, Gödde saw another survivor, Mechanikergefreiter Johann Merkle, a Quarters Armourer and one of 'Caesar' Turret's crew, actually walking on the bottom of *Scharnhorst*'s hull, which had turned turtle, before he swam off to a raft.

The cheering, singing and shouting was a common factor of all *Scharnhorst*'s survivor's stories. Speaking many years afterwards, Helmut Boekhoff took a detached view of it:-

'I saw all the blokes screaming and shouting *Scharnhorst*, hip hip hurray, hip hip hurray" and then I was certain that the song was coming up "On the seaman's grave there is nothing but no roses". By that time I looked round I saw the ship turn right round and I saw the propellor still turning, because by that time the English had shot a starshot right across us. Then all of a sudden I saw her going down, come back up again, then all of a sudden finally she went down. And as she went down I heard this tremendous trummel in my stomach and my legs, you know. There was a big explosion below. And by that time all I thought about was to get away. Get, you know, get saved. You know, when I looked round I see these blokes, they're swimming between all these bits and still shouting "Heil our Fuhrer" you know and "*Scharnhorst*, hip hip hurray" again and again and I thought" Pscht, what a waste".'

CHAPTER 10

Back to Scapa Flow

TOWARDS 8 pm. Fraser, still not satisfied that *Scharnhorst* had really sunk, was growing impatient for news. 'Clear the area of the target, 'he signalled, at 7.57, 'except those ships with torpedoes and one destroyer with searchlight.' In other words, illuminate the target area, and if she was still there, sink her. One ship still with torpedoes was *Matchless*, who was hoping for another attack. But at 8 pm. her ship's company went to 'Rescue Stations' instead. A large scrambling net was hung over the ship's side, and the sailors stood ready with lines, boat-hooks and life-jackets.

There was still a huge sea running and, as the ship neared the spot, the men on deck could see that any sort of rescue was going to be difficult. There was a great deal of wreckage, a few tiny winking red lights, attached to life-jackets, and some cries coming out of the blackness. (It seems that what the Germans said was cheering and singing, the British thought was shouting and screaming).

One of *Matchless*'s radar ratings, John Horton, was looking out of his radar office and after he had seen 'a great glow where the *Scharnhorst* was' and heard 'a large explosion', he saw 'the search-lights switched on, and a search made for survivors and I heard the orders being given for hands to stand by and man the ship's side to pick up survivors. We started our search. There was wreckage and bodies everywhere. A few cries were heard and I saw ratings at the side of the ship take in survivors off a Carley float or similar. There were six ratings picked up, in a dirty condition, wet through, also covered in oil. Their behaviour was reasonable as they were glad to be saved and glad to get on board. They were treated like any other survivors that were picked up, taken to a messdeck, given rum to fetch up any oil they may have swallowed, given dry clothing and put into hammocks in the forward mess.'

About a cable away from *Matchless*, while the rescue was going on, was *Scorpion*, who had her searchlight sweeping the scene. Her sailors, too, could hear cries and see the rafts and pieces of wreckage, with a sprinkling of lights, rising and falling in the tremendous waves sweeping past their ship's side. *Scorpion* was as brand new as the other destroyers; even her name was quite unknown to the British general public until it was mentioned for the very first time in newspaper accounts after the battle. For some 50 of her younger seamen, this was their first ship and they were now about to gain first-hand experience of the aftermath of a naval battle.

The sea seemed to be covered with debris and men, most of them dead, but some still alive. Lt.Cdr. Clouston later reported that Hintze had been seen in the water, close to *Scorpion*, with his Executive Officer, Dominik, both men badly wounded. It seemed that Hintze died before he could be reached, but Dominik actually had his hands on a line before slipping away out of reach, and he was not seen again. Clouston said that his rescue parties had the greatest difficulty in getting survivors inboard because of the mass of wooden wreckage through which they had to be pulled by heaving lines and ropes' ends.

One sailor, Coder Farr, said he saw, when 'the searchlight hit the water, its beam picked out a Red German flag spread out in the water over some wreckage to which some men were clinging'. *Scorpion*'s sailors also heard the chilling screams from the blackness, some of them despairing because many of *Scharnhorst*'s men must by now have been able to see that they were not going to be rescued. *Scorpion* picked up thirty survivors, although, as Clouston said, 'there must have been about a hundred near the ship at one time'. But it simply was not possible to save them all. Many must have just drifted away, out of sight and reach.

Even when they had been hauled on board, the survivors had one more spine-tingling shock. It transpired that Clouston bore a very marked facial resemblance to Admiral Bey. As the interrogators reported later, 'to be received on a board a British destroyer by someone they took to be their admiral nearly proved the last straw for these frozen and exhausted men.'

Amongst those rescued by *Scorpion* were Merkle, Sträter, and Willi Gödde, who had been in the water just over an hour when he was dragged, half-frozen, by Merkle into a small raft with three or four other men. Despite his condition, Gödde was able to observe, with professional interest, the two destroyers approaching them, and the skilful way in which they were handled. The nearest destroyer stopped up wind, leaving their raft in her lee, and then drifted down towrads them.

By that time, Gödde was physically unable to grasp a rope and haul himself to safety. Nor could he get the bowline loop over his elbows and let the rescuers drag him up. After four attempts, he says, the line hit him directly across the mouth, so he bit into it, and was hauled up, literally, by the skin of his teeth. 'As he reached deck level he felt a pair of giant fists grasp the collar of his uniform and pull him over the rail. Those were all *Scharnhorst*'s survivors: thirty in *Scorpion*, six in *Matchless*. Gödde was the senior survivor. There were no officers.

Now, at last, an exchange of signals convinced Fraser that he had won. *Scorpion* had made, at 8.04: "Am picking up German survivors." At 8.18, Fraser asked: Has *Scharnhorst* sunk? Clouston replied: Survivors are from *Scharnhorst*, and then, at 8.30: Survivors state that *Scharnhorst* has sunk.

Burnett also signalled: "Satisfied that *Scharnhorst* is sunk." Thus, at 8.35, Fraser was able to broadcast, thunderously, to Scapa W/T and to the world: '*Scharnhorst* Sunk." To which the Admiralty replied at 9.36 'Your 26/2035. Grand. Well done.'

Stord had asked at 8.22 if she could help in picking up survivors — a most magnanimous signal. But nobody seems to have answered her. In any case, Burnett was then signalling to Fraser: 'Several survivors samples being taken.' It may seem a callous and clinically cruel term to use of human beings, a 'sample', but it was quite true that only a 'sample' was needed. The rescuing ships could afford to spend only the minimum amount of time in an area where a U-boat was likely to appear. McCoy had already broadcast that there were U-boats to right and left, and ahead, of his convoy. In fact a 'Most Immediate' ULTRA sent to Fraser and to Burnett at 11.51 pm that night reported that the Eisenbart Group of U-boats had been ordered, at 6.15 that evening, to steer at top speed for an area bounded from 72°00′N to 72°18′N, and 26° E to 27°E. As late as 10.45 pm, the Germans evidently still only had an approximate position for *Scharnhorst*'s sinking, because the U-boats were asked to report the exact position. They were also to search for survivors in a 70-mile sweep, on a course of 140°, starting from 72°57′N, 28°30′E and carrying on to a position at about 72°39′N, 26°50′E.

ULTRA also reported, at 6.25 am on the morning of 27th December, that the U-boats had been permitted to attack warships and were warned of the possible presence of Russian submarines. At 7.05 that morning, the U-boats were ordered to steer back along the way they had come, on a reciprocal course of 320° after finishing their 70-mile sweep. Thus ULTRA confirmed what everybody on the spot knew: that where *Scharnhorst* had gone down was no place to linger. The search for survivors was called off at about 8.40 pm.

Although there were stories of at least one of *Scharnhorst*'s survivors being 'stroppy', there was never any animosity towards any of them in any ship. On the contrary, the widespread feeling in the British ships was one of genuine sympathy, tempered with the thought that 'it could have been us'. Fraser himself said that 'it was really very unpleasant having to go on shooting at her, because we didn't know whether she had surrendered or what she had done. But we had to sink her, unpleasant as it was.' In fact, *Scharnhorst* never surrendered. Her flag was never struck and some of her guns, especially the smaller calibres, appear to have been manned and fired to the end, until their crews were literally swept over the side.

The feelings of the onlookers were well put by Ernest Purdy, one of those who 'stood around more or less just watching her go down, seeing those chaps jump overboard, thinking "Well they've had their lot" and thought to ourselves "Well it could have been us, instead of them". It's not a nice death to go through, you know, but I thought "Well, it's either them or us".'

Over by the convoy, in *Onslaught*, where they had been following the battle on the R/T, Sub.Lieut Adrian Carey caught the elegiac mood on board, when, 'after a brief cheer at the final sinking, our sailors fell silent reflecting with real pity on the fate of so many of that green ship's company consigned, in the Arctic twilight and with little hope of rescue, to the wintry and unwelcoming sea. There was almost tangible compassion (born partly, of course, of our own consciousness of the constant danger of ourselves being sunk by submarines) and the winter solstice had not altogether blotted out the message of the Christmas angels, "Peace on earth, goodwill towards men".'

The feeling was the same in the cruisers of Force 1. 'All that was left of a 26,000 ton ship, 'wrote Lieut. Stanley Walker, of *Sheffield*, in a letter home, 'was some 36 survivors and a few pieces of shrapnel. One couldn't help feeling a little sorry for those who had perished. It was a cold dark night with little chance of survival in those icy waters. However, it might just as easily have been one, or indeed all of us.'

The same point occurred to *Sheffield*'s junior doctor, Surgeon Lieut. J.C.H. Dunlop RNVR, when he wrote home: 'I wouldn't be surprised if she had had nearly 2,000 men on board, and of course its the thought of those poor miserable wretches that makes the whole thing rather nauseating, especially when you know what these Arctic waters are like. If it had been like a football match after which one can unreservedly rejoice in the well-deserved victory of one's own side, it would have been much nicer'.

Another of *Sheffield*'s officers was quoted as writing: 'It was absolutely horrible. I was greatly relieved when two dull explosions and a cloud of smoke told us that all was over. None of us saw the ship disappear. She simply passed out of sight, fighting to the end.' Possibly that officer was influenced by what others told him later, because in fact *Sheffield* did not rejoin Force 1 until 9 pm. Although her engine-room department did their utmost to gain lost time, in Addis' words *Sheffield* 'doggedly pursued the battle and enjoyed a remarkable though sadly detached view of *Duke of York* in action some ten miles distant'. Dunlop called it 'a ringside seat' just like a gigantic "Brock's Benefit". But Captain Addis' steward took a much more phlegmatic view. When called the next morning, Addis remarked to him: 'That was rather a good little show we had yesterday, wasn't it?' To which he replied: 'Well sir it makes a change'.

Sheffield had one casualty, 'a minor scalp wound' which it fell to Dunlop to repair — 'so that I did have something, although not very much, to do!' *Belfast*'s only casualty was Olga the reindeer, who was terrified by the gunfire, and was found to be in a demented state in her hangar. Her custodian, the Royal Marine ship's butcher, was summoned to put the wretched animal out of her misery with his cleaver.

For Captain Parham, it had been 'a very long day indeed. The best way to get the feeling of that day would be to read the dispatches in a refrigerator, being heavily rocked, by the light of a single candle, with occasionally someone banging on the outside with a very large hammer.'

Belfast's sailors, like *Sheffield*'s, were not easily impressed. *Belfast*'s main engines had performed superbly throughout the day and, towards the end, the Senior Engineer, Lt.Cdr. W.L.G. Porter, allowed one stoker to go on deck to give an eye-witness account. 'He said it was completely dark, snowing hard, and the sea smelt of oil fuel. I think he was glad to return to the heat and light of the Engine Room.' Some of *Belfast*'s sailors were actually disappointed — like Banderillero, when in due course 'Splice the Main-brace' was piped. 'Alas! I am under twenty-one and only get lime.'

In *Jamaica*, the only damage was self-inflicted, by the blast of her own guns. The hinges of the rear door of Ramsden's director were blown in and at one time he had to train the director hurriedly round, on the beam, just before 'A' and 'B' turrets fired, with their shells, he calculated, passing only a few feet away from him.

The guns of *Jamaica*'s 'B' Turret, firing on their aftermost bearing, were very close to the Aircraft Direction Room. In the middle of the action, *Jamaica*'s Fighter Direction Officer Lieut. Dudley Blunt RNVR 'saw move-ment in the dead-light over our foremost scuttle. I jumped on to a table, followed by Midshipman Traherne, and we tried to secure the wing-nuts which held the dead-light in place. The seating, however, had been frac-tured by the gun-blast and it was only seconds before the whole scuttle was blown in, leaving a gaping hole adjacent to the muzzles of the guns. All hell broke loose as boards were blasted off our bulkheads, the trunking twisted like paper and anything loose blown from its seating; the noise was deafening in this inferno while the guns were firing. I gave orders to evacuate the A.D.R. and it was a miracle nobody was injured.' In fact, a piece of the scuttle struck the retreating Blunt on the back-side and, as he says, 'I must have been *Jamaica*'s only casualty!'

For *Jamaica*, as for everybody else, it had been a very long day. 'After an alfresco meal of ham and beer,' wrote Ramsden, 'and still feeling dirty and dishevelled, I went down to my cabin to turn in before the morning watch. My bedding was still on the deck, and after ripping off my oilskin and outer clothing I rolled myself up in the crumpled blankets fully dressed, and fell into an exhausted sleep. My last memory was a faint sweet smell of burning which still hung to my clothes.'

The feeling was much the same in *Duke of York*. 'One's feelings?' wrote Henry Leach. 'Almost a blankness or shock at what had been done. Some relief that it had gone the way it had. Little exultation — the closing scenes were too grim for that and the remoteness of actions at sea precludes hate between sailors. Pride in achievement. And a great weariness. It had been a long day's night'. Vernon Merry said, 'I just felt, there were two thousand Krauts, gone to a cold and miserable death, while we were going to supper.'

But before supper, and to the consternation of his communications staff, Bruce Fraser expressed a wish to speak personally to Bob Burnett on the R/T TBS (Talk Between Ships). Neither flag officer had had any training in the use of the R/T equipment. Fraser was given instruction by the Fleet Wireless Officer. 'First, sir, you press this thing when you want to speak,' said Peter Dawnay. 'When you have finished speaking, you say 'Over', release it, and listen to what Admiral Burnett has to say. Finally, sir, you must use callsigns, or you will make it easy for the Germans to make use of what you say. Admiral Burnett's callsign is REMBRANDT, sir. Yours is WIGLEY.'

'*Wiggly?*' Fraser could hardly believe his ears. '*Wiggly?* Who gave me this ridiculous name? Did *you?*'

Bob Burnett had no inkling of the coming conversation and had had no instruction at all, thus Peter Dawnay's description of the exchange was 'frightfully unsuccessful'. Courage said 'the only people who understood every word must have been the Germans.'

'Bob? Is that you?'

'Bob, can you hear me?'

From Dawnay: 'Say "*Over,* sir" and release that handle'.

'Bob, are you clutching your thing? I'll send you *Jamaica.* I'm off to Russia, Follow me when you can ... '

From Dawnay, seizing the microphone: '*Out.*' '... It made us laugh, which is always a good thing,' said Courage.

Next, Fraser wanted a large glass of whisky. He had a bottle ready in his sea-cabin. But when Merry went down to fetch it, he found two Paymaster Lieutenants (the emergency cyphering team, in case the others were killed) whose Action Station it was. They had been there all day, seeing nothing and hearing only the sound of the guns (the ship's broadcast system was not installed in the Admiral's cabin), and the whisky bottle was empty. 'So I twigged what had happened to the whisky and accused them of scoffing the lot,' said Merry. 'They owned up, and offered to reimburse the Admiral. He was highly amused ... In the event the Wardroom Bar was, uniquely, opened for half an hour for a "quick one" all round!'

Apart from the obvious enemy damage to both masts, *Duke of York* also had extensive though superficial blast damage from her own guns, or possibly from near-misses. The Admiral's barge was not much more than match-wood, with two accompanying engines, and most of the other ship's boats, including those stowed on the catapult deck, were unseaworthy. The roller shutter doors to the two hangars looked 'as if they had been hit in the middle by a giant battering ram', and the fireproof blankets which hung behind them were each torn in shreds from top to bottom, though still hanging in place. One ladder from the 5.25″ gundeck to the catapult deck was twisted through 90° so that its bottom rung was nearly vertical. A heavy wash-deck locker nearby, secured to the deck by six stout bolts, had vanished. In the sickbay, blast had done extensive damage and one bath 'made a surprise appearance some feet from its stowage position'.

Every mushroom head on the fo'c'sle leading down to the ventilation system was missing and sea water poured into the main deck below. The 14″ gun crews were working in two watches, pumping out the messdecks. Nobody could get to the forward 'heads' without wearing deck boots, or at least a waterproof pair of shoes. The cork parts of many Carley floats had been reduced to crumbled dust and spent ammunition was still cluttering up compartments near the turrets. (When the ship eventually reached Rosyth, four railway wagons were filled with the empty Clarkson cases which had held the half-charges for the 14″ shells, and another eight wagons were needed for the spent brass cylinders of the 5.25″ fixed ammunition).

The ventilation to some turrets had been inadequate and some of the guns crews were so fatigued it affected their rate of fire towards the end of the action. One rating was overcome, and collapsed. There were other defects in the guns. A3, for example, due to a shell-cage defect compounded by poor drill, only fired six shells during the whole action, and missed 71 broadsides. 'Y' Turret had three guns fail all at once and 17 broadsides were missed in 15 minutes, due to bad luck, with 'a roll plus a violent lurch plus extremely careful ramming at the wrong moment'. But all four guns were fit to fire again by the end of the action. Altogether *Duke of York*'s guns achieved 68% of output, the best performance being by B1 gun, which fired 77 shells and missed only three broadsides.

However, as *Duke of York*'s gunnery narrative said, the ship's armament and radar combined together to 'find, fix, fight and finish off the *Scharnhorst*'. Fraser gave the ship full credit in his Dispatch: '*Duke of York* fought hard and well having drawn, for over an hour and a half, the whole of the enemy's fire. She was frequently straddled with near misses, ahead, astern and on the beam. That she was not hit was probably due to masterly handling aided by accurate advice from the plot [everybody who saw it, and many of those who only appreciated its results, commented upon Guy Russell's skilful ship-handling]. There is no doubt that the *Duke of York* was the principal factor in the battle. She fought the *Scharnhorst* at night and she won. This is no way detracts from the achievements of the 'S' Class destroyers who with great gallantry and dash pressed in unsupported, to the closest ranges, to deliver their attacks, being subjected the while to the whole fire power of the enemy'.

It was, of course, possible to give a different and far less reverential emphasis to the flagship's achievement, which was widely shared in the other ships and very succinctly put by Dunlop, the junior doctor in *Sheffield*: 'They fought each other for about three hours — and fought extremely well — and, as a matter of fact, at the end of that time the old *Duke of York* hadn't achieved a great deal (in spite of all the blah in the papers).' In Dunlop's opinion, it was the destroyers, and especially *Stord,* who turned the battle.

While most of the ships of Forces 1 and 2 headed for Kola Inlet at 20 knots, *Saumarez* was some distance astern, metaphorically still feeling herself all over for damage, and feeling lucky to be still alive. By 7.30 pm *Saumarez* was steering east at 8 knots, on her port main engine. Just after 8 pm Walmsley made a very brave 'state of efficiency' signal to Fraser, saying that the maximum speed available was 16 knots (an optimistic estimate at that time), two of his main armament guns were still in action, three torpedoes remained and 'CO is in action'.

Saumarez' director control tower and range-finder were wrecked and bodies had to be removed from a shambles of metal, tangles of wires, and smashed equipment. The near-misses on the starboard side had flailed the upper deck with a squall of shrapnel, cutting down most of the after torpedo tubes' crew, preventing the ship firing her full outfit of torpedoes. *Saumarez* had made smoke as she broke away, to cover her escape, but a smoke float had also been ignited accidentally on 'X' Gun deck. From the bridge this had appeared to be a bad fire raging where the ship had been hit, so Walmsley ordered the after magazine and shell room to be flooded, as a precaution.

Saumarez was shortly joined by *Savage*, as escort, and later by *Scorpion*. Her speed was gingerly raised by stages until by 11 pm. she was doing some 15 knots. Walmsley and his ship's company buried their dead at sea at noon on 27th December. But their adventures were not quite over. That evening, when *Saumarez* was inside Kola Inlet, Able Seaman Mervyn Salter came on deck to ditch a bucketful of gory remains which he had cleaned out from the damaged messdeck below. In the dark he lost his footing, and fell overboard through a hole in the main deck.

At first, Salter's inclination 'was not to bother to struggle'. But a life-belt was thrown to him, and *Scorpion* lowered a boat which picked him up, after a period of time in the icy water which only a very fit young man could have survived. *Saumarez* came alongside Vaenga Pier at 10.24 that night. After temporary repairs she left for Scapa, with *Scourge* in company, on 6th January.

The rest of the story of JW55B is briefly told. There were several U-boats still in contact on the evening of 26th December and by midnight *Wrestler, Onslow, Iroquois,* and *Wrestler* for the second time, had carried out sweeps to look for U-boats after H/F D/F detections ahead, astern or on the starboard beam of the convoy. But nothing was found. By the morning of 27th, only one U-boat was definitely in contact, still shadowing from the convoy's starboard quarter. The rest appeared to have left, to search the area where *Scharnhorst* had been sunk.

During the early hours of 27th, and for the rest of the day, several aircraft made reconnaissance reports and a Fw 200 made a sighting report, giving a position for the convoy at 5.55 pm. that day. A group of Heinkel He.155 seaplanes was ordered to be at one hour's notice from 8 am to 12, but no attack developed. Also, at 2.30 on 27th, the Luftwaffe in North Norway and in Finland were informed that German W/T intelligence showed a westbound convoy at sea, on the way from Russia. This seemed to have been the only intimation ULTRA ever provided that the enemy was ever aware of RA 55A.

At dawn on 27th, two ships were found to be missing, (one of them inevitably *Ocean Gypsy*,) who had both missed a course alteration during the night. *Ocean Valour*, one of the stragglers, was detected by radar and safely gathered into the fold again on the morning of the 28th. The convoy entered Kola Inlet at 10.30 am. on 29th December. *Ocean Gypsy*, a straggler to the last, came in alone several hours later. That was the end of Operation FV, the passage of the convoy JW55 to Russia.

When Fraser and his ships arrived at Kola Inlet on 27th to refuel, Golovko was as grudging as ever with his praise. 'The destruction of the German warship is, indisputably, a major success for the British. It should be added that they were assisted by preliminary basing on the Kola Inlet and the fact that their journey here and visit went undiscovered by the enemy'. However, Golovko did congratulate Fraser, who, he said, 'described the action briefly. The details are not yet complete, since not all the destroyers have arrived. This must be a pretext, as the British Admiral spoke mainly about his own losses and was very distressed about them. British losses were 26 killed and a number wounded, of whom two died today.' Golovko said that there were 2,029 men on board *Scharnhorst*. 'Only thirty-eight (sic) were picked up from the ship, none of whom according to Fraser was an officer. I did not raise the question of officers. In all probability the British Admiral mentioned this on the assumption that we should request the opportunity of talking to captured Nazis from the *Scharnhorst*'s crew. Here it came to light that the German ship was hit by eleven torpedoes (four of them on the port side) according to the British, and by eight (all on the starboard side) according to the prisoners.' Golovko complained that he had been told 'the fuel requirements of the British squadron — about 10,000 tons of oil are needed for the whole of this 'Armada'.'

While *Duke of York* was fuelling, 'Barehand' Bates did go up the mast — the mainmast, to repair the 281 Radar set damaged in the action. The cables were all metal lead-cased, and the lead had to be removed, the cable tested with electrical meters and the individual wires identified. 'This could only be done with bare hands' wrote Bates, and perhaps this is how the legendary nickname was acquired. Bates and his team climbed the mast in turn, in an outside temperature of 16°F and with a strong wind blowing, working on the cables until their fingers were numb and then returning to a small office at the base of the mast to warm body and hands in front of electric fires.

The work was carried on non-stop for several hours. The urgency was because air activity could be expected on the return journey and Fraser had said 'Bates, I am not leaving here until you have repaired that aircraft warning radar'. The damaged mast was repaired by welding (by a Russian welder) and the 281 was restored to working order by Bates and his assistants. In fact, there was no danger from air attack all the way back to Scapa.

That evening, Fraser gave a celebration dinner party for Captains of ships in company, after which everybody went to their bunks, tired out. But, at 2 am, when Courage happened to be on *Duke of York*'s quarterdeck after dealing with some signals problems, he saw 'an enormous black motor boat loom alongside the starboard gangway. Out stepped two Russians carrying parcels. They told the Officer of the Watch that they wanted to see the Commander-in-Chief in person. Nothing the Officer of the Watch said would dissuade them — so poor Vernon Merry was hauled out of bed to handle the matter. The Russians had express orders from the Supreme Soviet to present the Commander-in-Chief in person with two presents, one a large fur hat and the other an enormous fur coat. The Admiral had to turn out and drink a glass of whisky with them before returning to his bed. Vernon Merry conducted them round the *Duke of York* at 0400!' (Fraser, who had no use for the coat, subsequently tried to sell it to Gieves, the well-known naval tailors, who regretted they could not assist, because the coat was of such poor quality).

Golovko was much less hospitable. 'We are not being told anything more', he complained, in his diary for 28th December, 'although it must be clear to Admiral Fraser and his staff that the information obtained from the Nazis fished out of the water interests us keenly — not, of course, the details of the action, but the situation at Altenfjord and Lang Fjord which form the pivot of the Nazi naval forces operating against us in the Northern theatre. Hence the annoyance caused by the way the allies on this occasion confined themselves to radiant smiles and lengthy declarations that they and we are allies. Never mind, we will manage on our own information. I wished Admiral Fraser a good trip and at 18.00 the *Duke of York*, *Jamaica* and seven destroyers left for England'.

While at Kola, the 'Nazis fished out of the water' were transferred to *Duke of York* — by Russian tug, which greatly alarmed them, thinking they were to be turned over to the Russians. Some said they would sooner jump overboard. However, they were reassured, and according to Gödde, Merkle (who, it seems, was German-Canadian by birth and spoke good English) actually called for three cheers for the men of the British destroyer *(Scorpion)*. All joined in. Gödde reflected on such a strange circumstances: German cheers for British seamen in a Russian port.

According to Peter Whittley, of *Duke of York*, 'to us they were not prisoners-of-war, they were survivors. Our own ship's company included men who had been survivors of previous naval engagements'. Four seriously wounded survivors were taken to the sick bay, the rest accommodated in one of the lower forward messdecks, appropriately in the ship's cell flat. They were guarded by six Royal Marines with whom, according to Gödde, they were soon on friendly terms. Every day on passage to Scapa they took exercise on the catapult deck, and 'were much photographed by war reporters and members of the crew'.

The survivors had to pass through several flats and messdecks to reach their bathroom and toilets and so were able to see a good deal of the ship. They professed themselves amazed at the small amount of damage in *Duke of York*. By Gödde's account, their captors were remarkably chatty, especially a 'young ship's doctor', who acted as their interpreter and who told them that after the battle Admiral Fraser had called the ship and staff officers together and told them that if they ever were' called upon to lead a ship into action against an opponent many times superior, you will command your ship as gallantly as the *Scharnhorst* was commanded today'. Also, the 'young doctor' told Gödde after he had asked about battle damage that 'we hadn't a dry spot anywhere on the battery and lower decks (which was true enough) we had to keep the electric and hand pumps going day and night.'

Nevertheless, it is difficult to decide how much of Gödde's account (prepared after he was released from captivity and given to Kapitan Giessler) can be believed. Some of it is pure legend, notably his version of Fraser's visit to the survivors' messdeck, during *Duke of York*'s passage to Scapa. Fraser was preceded (according to Gödde) by bugle calls and when the survivors saluted 'the British Admiral took up his stance about three feet in front of our ranks, his officers behind him. The Commander-in-Chief raised his hand to his cap and all the officers, among them the Captain of the *Duke of York*, followed his example. For a full minute they honoured thus in silence their vanquished opponents. We all realised that this mark of respect applied not to us personally, but to our proud ship and her gallant dead.'

'Then Admiral Fraser reviewed each rank — because of the restricted space we were drawn up five ranks deep — and, accompanied by an interpreter, talked to practically every man, asking him his age, profession, where he lived, why he had joined the navy etc.'

'Finally he stepped in front again and said: 'We honour a brave opponent even if he has been beaten. The British people harbour no hatred against you. Have no misgivings about being taken to England. Just do as you are told and you will be all right'.'

'We repeated our salute, the British Commander-in-Chief and his officers returned it and left the room. Never shall I forget the solemnity of that moment.'

Vernon Merry's account is much less highly-coloured. He accompanied Fraser, who had said he wanted to look at the survivors, 'after all, he had been a prisoner-of-war himself. We prevailed upon him to wear a pusser's raincoat over his uniform, so that his gold lace was hidden, and he did not wear a cap, so nobody could guess he was the admiral. He just moved amongst them, looking into their faces. He didn't speak to any of them.' Gödde also described a 'great wreath' being dropped from *Duke of York* at the spot where *Scharnhorst* had gone down. Merry's comment on this was even pithier: 'Absolute *balls*.'

However, some aspects of Gödde's narrative are completely believable — such as, that he could not sleep for six whole days and nights after his rescue, even with sedatives. Some of the other survivors did eventually give some useful information. Matrose (Ordinary Seaman) Gerhard Lobin, for instance, whose action station was Lookout in the Forward Director Tower, said that he had watched the fall of shot and *Duke of York*'s ability to follow *Scharnhorst*'s every move was 'uncanny'. In spite of *Scharnhorst*'s zig zags, *Duke of York* straddled her time and again, with columns of water drenching Lobin and the other men up in their crow's nest.

Scharnhorst's survivors might have given much more valuable intelligence, then and later, had they not been prematurely and inexpertly interrogated on board. The questioning, as the questioners admitted, was mishandled, though from the best of intentions. Lt.Cdr. Crawford, *Duke of York*'s gunnery officer, was understandably keen to establish whether, and when, *Duke of York*'s gunfire had slowed *Scharnhorst* down. He prevailed upon the Chief of Staff, who prevailed upon Fraser, to have the survivors interrogated.

Fraser's Staff Officer (Intelligence) Lieut. Edward Thomas RNVR, a fluent German speaker, objected. He wished to obseve the tried and trusted rule that interrogation should *not* be attempted until the prisoners of war could be questioned by experts. Thomas was then accused of having a short-sighted attitude and warned that the prisoners' memories would be blunted if they were let alone for another week. Eventually, Thomas was ordered to get on with the interrogation.

Thomas did so and, just as he feared, was able to get very little out of the prisoners: 'they were punch drunk with their terrible experience and if ever there was a case for leaving prisoners alone to be competently dealt with in due course this was it'. Later, the real interrogators complained that their pitch had been queered. *Scharnhorst*'s survivors were a tough proposition in any case and it was as though this bout of questioning had in some way 'inoculated' them against future interrogation. 'Fraser was officially re-buked for it,' said Thomas.

Whilst Fraser and his staff were sailing home, Doenitz and his staff were mulling over the disaster and its implications. Doenitz promulgated his conclusions in a directive to the German Navy on 29th December (which was, incidentally, read, decoded and redistributed to authorised recipients by ULTRA on the same day). Doenitz began by stressing the imperative need for *Scharnhorst* to make some sort of intervention to help to relieve the situation of the Army on the Eastern Front.

Doenitz's directive said that prospects for attack had been favourable. Air reconnaissance had established that the convoy was escorted only by light forces. Any limitations imposed by the weather would be to *Scharnhorst*'s advantage (as indeed they were). Doenitz had also relied upon an element of surprise, because two recent convoys had passed unmolested to north Russia (actually, it was the very fact that these two convoys had not been attacked which made Fraser even more suspicious that the third convoy would be threatened).

Doenitz then gave a brief summary of the engagement, explaining that *Scharnhorst*, after making her first contact with the cruisers, had been engaged by a 'heavy enemy unit'. She had therefore broken off the action in accordance with her orders. But when she tried to withdraw, she was located and tracked by R.D/F. More heavy forces were brought up. *Scharnhorst* was encircled, and sank at about 7.30 on 26th, after fighting heroically. (In other words, the German Admiralty concluded that there had been a battleship present at the first, morning, encounter with CS.10's cruisers).

Doenitz guessed that this very powerful concentration of heavy British ships was possibly connected with the homeward journey of a *second* convoy, hitherto undetected. He emphasised that the most important lesson by far to be drawn from the battle was that the British ships had been able to detect *Scharnhorst* at more than thirty miles range, and with R.D/F, to shadow and then 'bombard her unseen at a range of 19,500 yards'. Doenitz's summary showed that the Germans had no idea of the damage they had inflicted upon *Norfolk* and *Sheffield,* or on *Duke of York.*

The sinking of *Scharnhorst* was a great operational success for ULTRA. Until the time the two forces made contact with each other, ULTRA supplied Fraser and Burnett with a steady flow of accurate up-to-date information on the movements of German surface, air and U-boat forces. The information was provided astonishingly quickly; the interval between the German time of origin of a message, and the dispatch of the ULTRA signal based on it, varied from twelve down to five hours. ULTRA had provided the only source of information on *Scharnhorst*'s departure from Alta Fjord. It had also shown how ignorant the enemy was of the odds against him.

Duke of York arrived at Scapa early on New Year's Day, 1944. The war correspondents (who were not permitted to sail with the ships) had been waiting since before dawn at the entrance to the fleet anchorage in fishing drifters which were bobbing about in a sea that 'was more than rough'. One of them, Arthur Oakeshott, described with excusable hyperbole how 'suddenly out of the murk to the norrard appeared the *Duke of York* with smoke-blackened fourteen-inch guns flying her shell-torn (sic) battle ensign and cramming on almost every piece of bunting in the ship. Astern of her came the cruiser *Jamaica* and then the long line of destroyers [seven in all] all flying battle ensigns and bunting and over their torpedo tubes trained outboard the 'Affirmative' signal and beneath it the numeral signals showing the number of hits on the *Scharnhorst*'.

Ramsden described the homecoming in *Jamaica*. 'The southward trip to Scapa was eventful only in the weather. A typical gale force wind from the north-west set up heavy seas, and most of our seaboats on the boat deck were severely damaged. It was an uncomfortable journey and bitterly cold. Four days later we made Hoxa Gate and steamed slowly into the Flow, battle-ensigns flying, the *Duke of York* ahead and our destroyers astern. Despite its remoteness from civilized habitation it was an impressive and unforgettable experience passing through the Fleet to our anchorage, each ship's company massed on deck cheering as we came abreast of them. And then the flood of congratulatory telegrams and signals from all parts of the world, including one most dearly prized from Admiral Fraser's mother, who had launched the *Jamaica*.'

'Well Done *Jamaica*,' said Mrs. Monica Fraser's telegram, 'I am proud to have launched you' and it was, as Ramsden said, part of a flood of congratulations. From His Majesty, King George VI, to Fraser, 'Well done, *Duke of York,* and all of you. I am proud of you', and from Mr Churchill,

'Heartiest congratulations to you and Home Fleet on your brilliant action. All comes to him who knows how to wait.'

These were followed by congratulations from the War Cabinet and the First Lord, from the First Sea Lord, from the President of the United States, and from Stalin. Some of the heartiest plaudits came from quarters which might not have been expected to have been so personally concerned with *Scharnhorst*'s fate. 'Your guest of a month ago sends his heartiest congratulations to you,' said Abdul Illah, the Regent of Irak, 'and your gallant officers and men in a magnificent exploit and wishes to all under your distinguished command continued success and a very Happy New Year.'

There were salutes from Crown Prince Paul of Greece, from Admiral Fisher in Russia, from the C-in-C US Fleet, from the C-in-C Royal Norwegian Navy, and from Fraser's professional peers, the C-in-C Mediterranean, the C-in-C Eastern Fleet and the C-in-C Levant, amongst others. There were signals from the French battleship *Richelieu* and the American carrier *Ranger*, from Rear Admiral (Destroyers) and Flag Officer 15th CS, from the Air Officer Commanding 18 Group RAF, from all the officers and men of the Orkneys and Shetlands Defence Force, from the President of the Merchant Navy Officers Association, from the Confederation of Shipbuilding and Engineering Trades Production Committee and Shop Stewards, Belfast, and from the Thames Lightermen and Barge Owners of London.

Individual ships had signals: *Duke of York* from the Provost and the City of Glasgow who had adopted the ship; *Norfolk* from Fairfield Shipbuilding and Engineering Co, Ltd. who had built her; and *Jamaica* from the Lord Mayor and City of Bristol, and from the West India Committee. It was, as somebody said 'rather like a very splendid Christmas card list'. Fraser replied gracefully and appropriately to them all, as, for instance, in his response to Marshall Stalin: 'We were much honoured to receive your message particularly as it coincided with the great advance of the Russian Armies. We have all appreciated the help received from C-in-C North Russian Fleet.'

Fraser had written in his Report of Proceedings 'The conduct of all officers and men throughout the action was in accordance with the highest traditions of the Service' and in delivering his dispatches Fraser determined that another old Service tradition would be observed. The Dispatch itself was taken to London by air by the Fleet Navigating Officer, Cdr. E.H. Thomas, known always by the old title of 'Master of the Fleet', accompanied by Courage, who was due to go on leave and hence cadged a lift in the aircraft.

After an eventful and uncomfortable journey by aircraft and by RAF truck from Hornchurch (where they had landed, instead of Hendon) the pair arrived at the Admiralty at about seven in the evening 'full of importance', as Courage said, and demanding to see the First Sea Lord in person. 'A somewhat cross looking A.B.C. came out of his Office and took the 'Master' inside and left me outside without even saying "How do you do". *Very* unlike the real A.B.C.'

While waiting, Courage engaged A.B.C.'s secretary in light conversation. 'Seems a bit gloomy up here?' he said, 'Something gone wrong?' 'Yes it had,' said the Secretary 'It may be Christmas Day in Scapa but it certainly isn't in Archway Block North' (the First Sea Lord's office).

It transpired that, because the sailors had missed their Christmas Day, Fraser had decreed that the first full day in harbour would be Christmas Day for everyone who took part in the action. He himself enjoyed his own Christmas lunch party, at which somebody had said 'I think Dicky ought to arrive at the Admiralty carrying the despatches on a horse — it would make a wonderful photograph 'Apparently the Commander-in-Chief had that look in his eye which said — "Good *Idea*".' Arrangements were made with the Metropolitan police, for Courage to bring the good news, not from Hendon (which was too far) but from Charing Cross (although Fraser said 'Much too close, the horses must arrive steaming, better pour some hot water over them!)'

But the arrival at Hornchurch threw the police arrangements out, while A.B.C. got to hear of the affair. 'No wonder we got a frigid reception,' said Courage, 'even though we were in complete ignorance of the whole affair. Anyhow I was glad we ended up at Hornchurch — I'm sure I would have capsized on the way from Charing Cross Station to the Admiralty — I was in no state to ride a sharp two furlongs across Trafalgar Square in the dark especially under blackout conditions with no lights showing anywhere.'

No matter how they were delivered, the contents of Fraser's dispatches were unimpeachable. 'I have forwarded separately,' he said, 'my recommendations for honours and awards as a result of this action'. The first results bore fruit in a signal of 4th January (released to the public the next day) which made Merry hasten to 'Barehand' Bates' cabin, where he was just shaving, to tell him he had won a DSC. ('He very nearly cut himself'). In the same signal were a GCB for Fraser, a KBE for Burnett, DSOs for Addis, Bain, Parham and Russell, a Bar to his DSC for Walmsley, DSCs for Fisher, in *Musketeer* and Clouston of *Scorpion,* and DSMs for the two Able Seamen, Badkin and Whitton, who had been in the radar office with Bates when the shell struck. (It was, in its own way, very probably a unique honours signal, starting at the top with a GCB for a full admiral, and ending, only twelve names and seven lines later, with DSMs for two Able Seamen.)

Characteristically, Fraser was disappointed. He would much have preferred a DSO, although, as he knew, he was too senior for such an award. He would have liked some sort of special dispensation to allow him to have a DSO because, as he said, 'I would probably have got the GCB anyway. But I've got no other medals, nothing to show I've ever been in action. A DSO would at least prove that I'd been fired at.' But it was not be, and Fraser was denied his medal (although, many years later, he discovered in a trunk a

Croix de Guerre and a Legion D'Honneur which the French had awarded him and which he had completely forgotten).

Bates' DSC must have been one of the first, if not the very first, naval award for 'radar service'. As Bates himself said, Fraser made the point 'that the immediate award of this decoration had wider reflections. Radar officers and ratings in the Royal Navy, the then Admiralty radar scientists and designers, the shop-floor workers manufacturing the radars, will not have been fooled by the publicity but will have gleaned their just reward of reflected glory. They would know it was a *radar* success ... '

Later, of course, there were many other awards: DSOs for Hughes-Hallett, and Meyrick; a Bar to his DSC for Storheil in *Stord;* DSCs for Merry, Courage, Dawnay, and Crawford in *Duke of York*, for Wainwright in *Jamaica*, for Lt. J.E. Dyre, *Saumarez'* First Lieutenant. Also in *Saumarez,* there was a CGM for Petty Officer F.W.J. Wilkes, the Torpedo Gunner's Mate, seven DSMs, including Chief Stoker Cadwallader and Ordinary Seaman Bostock, and nine Mentions in Dipstaches. *Norfolk,* besides Bain's DSO, had eight DSMs, including Leading Canteen Assistant G.H.L. Jewitt and Marine C.G. Hardy, (see Appendix III).

The only sour note was struck back at Scapa, when Le Fanu and Parry, two staff officers who had missed the battle, were presented with cardboard medals, adorned on one side with a picture of a rat in full flight and on the other with the words 'Shipmates Ashore Dec. 26 1943'. The ribbon was made of yellow bunting and on it, instead of the oak leaves symbolising 'Mention in Dispatches', there was a little white feather. This seemed to be a joke, if it could be called a joke, in the very worst possible taste. But as Coney, the Fleet Gunnery Officer says, it was *'not* as beastly as it may sound. Le Fanu himself was a prime perpetrator of that sort of schoolboy joke to keep us sane'. (Le Fanu had already won a DSC, as Gunnery Officer of the cruiser *Aurora* in the Mediterranean).

Captain Russell Grenfell, the naval correspondent of the *Sunday Times,* writing on 2nd January 1944, commented that the sinking of the *Scharnhorst* was 'a model operation of its kind, in which all concerned on our side seem to have played their parts with almost text-book correctitude'. He had much harsher words for *Scharnhorst*: 'By comparison with this masterly British performance, the *Scharnhorst*'s conduct seems extraordinarily vacillating and irresolute. She should have been quite strong enough to break through the British cruiser screen and play havoc with the convoy. Yet she wasted about three vital hours between two half-hearted and ineffectual advances, and finally went down with great loss of life without achieving anything at all.'

But the last word should be left to Admiral Luetzow, a naval spokesman, speaking on German radio on the evening of 29th December 1943: 'We pay tribute to our comrades who died the death of seamen in heroic battle against enemy superiority. The *Scharnhorst* is now on the field of honour'.

Chapter Notes

CHAPTER 1

P.1, Merry's quote on Scharnhorst, from Interview of 30.7.81; p.12, Raeder, quoted from Doenitz' Memoirs, p.371; p.14, Doenitz, from Memoirs, p.373.

CHAPTER 2

P.17, Merry's quote on Fraser from *Bruce Fraser: The Man and the Admiral;* p.17, Parham's anecdote, from Interview of 5.8.82; Kimmins' anecdote, from *Half Time,* p.281; pp.21/22, Fraser's daily routine, Merry, ibid.; p.22, Thomas' account of Fraser and ULTRA, from letter of 16.10.82; p.23, Fraser's table, from Merry, ibid.; p.24, Leach on Russell, from letter and enclosure of 25.9.81; p.25 Coney's comment, from letter of 20.10.81; p.26, Pound's comment to Churchill, from CAB 69/5; p.26, Fraser's opinion on Arctic convoys, from his letter to Pound DO.1325 of 30.6.43, quoted in Roskill, *The War at Sea,* Vol. III, Part I, p.59; p.30, leave for *Duke of York,* from Peter Woodhouse, 'The North Atlantic Fleet in Wartime'; p.31, Woodhouse, ibid.; Garnons-Williams, from 'Experiences of a Midshipman during the Russian Convoys – 1942-1944'; p.32, Woodhouse, ibid.; p.33, King George VI's visit to *Duke of York,* Peter Cree's Midshipman's Journal; p.34, Scapa, from *The Story of Scapa Flow,* p.182; p.35, R.O.L. Thomas, from HMS *Duke of York,* 1941-44; p.36, Merry, ibid.

CHAPTER 3

P.45, Fraser's refusal of First Sea Lordship, Churchill, *The Second World War,* Vol.V, p.145, Humble, *Fraser of North Cape,* in T/S, p.239; Campbell on Russia, The *Kola Run,* Ch.16 and 17, p.49; Doenitz' comment on Bey, Memoirs, p.374, p.49, Busch's description of Bey, *The Drama of the Scharnhorst,* pp.49-50.

CHAPTER 4

P.53, Campbell on Kola, op.cit., Ch.17; p.54, Campbell, op.cit.; p.55 Golovko on Fraser, *With the Red Fleet,* p.180-181; p.56, 'Buns' incident, Golovko, op.cit., p.181, and Soviet White Sea Glee Party; p.57, Golovko, op.cit., pp.181-2; p.57, Garnons-Williams, ibid.; p.58, Parham on Burnett, Interview of 5.8.81; p.61, Parham on Addis, ibid.; p.62, Fraser's Dispatch, para. 3 and 4; p.63 Fraser and Russell ashore in Iceland, Humble, ibid. p.252; p.64, Courage's signal exercise, *The Sinking of the Scharnhorst,* in T/S; p.65, Blunt on Hughes-Hallett, 'Recollections of Jamaica's Fighter Direction Officer, 19.10.82; p.70, Ramsden, *Blackwoods* Maga. Nov. 1944, p.344; p.70 Musician Ernie Heather, tape of 9/81.

CHAPTER 5

P.71, Doenitz at Fuhrer Conference, Brassey's 1948, p.374; p.72, Schniewind's orders, from Doenitz' Memoirs, p.375; p.73, teleprinter conversation, from Bekker, *Hitler's Naval War,* p.347; p.76, *Scharnhorst* getting ready for sea, Busch, op.cit., p.63; p.77, letter from one of *Scharnhorst*'s officers, from Vuilliez and Mordal, *Battleship Scharnhorst,* p.210; p.79, text of Doenitz's signal, from Bekker, op.cit. p.352.

CHAPTER 6

P.85, quote from 'Banderillero', *The Naval Review,* February 1944, p.25; p.87, Godde's account of loudseaker message, from Busch, op.cit., p.106; p.88, Doenitz's comments, from Memoirs, pp.380-1; p.89, Parham on Burnett, Interview of 5.8.82; p.90, Roskill's comment, op.cit, p.84n.; p.90, Fisher's account from 'Some personal recollections' of 29.5.81; Parham's version, from letter of 5.6.81; p.92, Dawnay, from 'The sinking of Scharnhorst' in T/S; p.92, Dawnay, ibid.;

p.94, Godde's account of Hintze's broadcast, Busch, op.cit., p.114; p.95, comment from Ltd.Cdr Wainwright, from letter of 27.9.82; p.95, Food, Welby-Everard, 'Action of 26th December', Ramsden, op.cit., p.345, Leach, ibid, Merry, Interview of 30.7.81; p.96, Courage's comment, from explanatory tape of signal log of 6.11.81.

CHAPTER 7

P.97, Carey's comment on Captain Selby, from letter of 7.7.82; p.98 Parham's comment, ibid., Banderillero's quote, op.cit., p.98, Godde's account, from Doenitz's Memoirs, pp.382-3 p.100, Stoker Moth's account, from 'The *Scharnhorst*' by David Woodward, BBC Home Service; p.100, Eng.Lt.Cdr. Reed, from *The King's Cruisers*, by Gordon Holman, p.164, CERA Cardey, Holman, op.cit., p.162; CERA Davies, Holman, op.cit., p.163, Cansfield, p.163; p.101, Fisher, ibid.; p.102, Fisher, ibid.; Doenitz' comment, from Memoirs, p.383; p.105, description of flag bridge, from *The Battle of North Cape,* by Lt.Cdr. Michael Ogden, p.129; p.105, Cox's comment on Fraser, 'The Life and Death of the Scharnhorst', BBC TV Tuesday Documentary, by Ludovic Kennedy; Courage on Blohm & Voss, signal log tape of 6.11.81; p.107, Tovey to Parham, from HMS *Belfast;* p.107 Courage, signal tape, ibid.; p.107, Dawnay, ibid.; p.108. Fisher, ibid.; p.109, Parham's comment, tape of 5.8.82; p.151, Cdr. Hitchens, of *Jamaica,* Woodward, ibid.; p.111, Ramsden, op.cit., pp.345-6; Parham and Welby-Everard, ibid.; p.112, Ramsden, The *Naval Review,* November 1947, p.311.

CHAPTER 8

P.114, Ditcham's quote from letter to Roskill of 10.8.56; Leach, ibid.; Courage, ibid.; p.115, Crawford, from *The Daily Telegraph,* 3 Jan. 1944; Ramsden, op.cit., p.346; p.115 kitchen clock, Courage, The sinking of the Scharnhorst, 7.6.77; Ramsden, op.cit., p.346; p.116, Ramsden, op.cit. p.347; p.117, ROL Thomas, '*HMS Duke of York* 1941-44'; p.118, Compston, 'An account'; p.119, Bates, letter of 2.9.82; p.119, CS Forester, *Sat. Eve. Post,* 25th March 1944; p.120, Ramsden, op.cit., p.347; p.121, Fraser giving up hope, Humble, ibid., p.290; Leach, ibid.; Meyrick, 'The Life and Death of the Scharnhorst' Documentary; p.121, Leach, ibid.; p.123, Godde's account of the action, from Karl-Hinrich Peter, 'The Sinking of the

Scharnhorst', *USNI Proc.* Jan. 1956, p.51; p.125, Lt. Dennis, Woodward, op.cit.; Mr. Berner, Woodward, op.cit.; Ldg. Tel. Catlow, Woodward, op.cit.; p.126, Cdr. Maunsell, Woodward. op.cit.; p.127, Ditcham, ibid.; p.128, Yeoman Mills, letter in Imperial War Museum; p.128, Berner, ibid.

CHAPTER 9

P.130, Ramsden, op.cit. p.348; Homan, *The War Illustrated,* Vol.7, p.570; Godde, USNI Proc., p.52; p.132, Ramsden, p.349; Boekhoff, Kennedy, BBC Documentary; p.134 Compston, ibid. Merry, interview of 30.7.81; p.134, Maunsell, Woodward, op.cit.; p.135, Ramsden, op.cit., p.350; p.136, Chavasse, *The Daily Telegraph,* 3 Jan. 1944; p.184A, Mahoney, Woodward, op.cit.; p.137, Fisher, ibid.; p.137, Walker, *Scharnhorst* Action, in T/S; Garnons-Williams, ibid.; p.139, Godde, ibid.; p.140, Strater, USNI Proc. p.53; p.191A, Boekhoff, ibid.; p.140, Fraser's Dispatch, para.76; p.141, Boekhoff, ibid.; p.143, Godde's account, Busch, op.cit., p.164; p.144, Boekhoff, ibid.

CHAPTER 10

P.145, Horton, letter of 16.9.81; p.146, Coder Farr, letter in Imperial War Museum; p.147, Fraser, Kennedy, BBC documentary; Purdy, Kennedy, BBC documentary; p.148, Dunlop, letter in Imperial War Museum; p.148, quote from one of *Sheffield*'s officers, Vuilliez and Mordal, op.cit., p.239; p.148, Dunlop, ibid.; Parham, letter of 5.6.81; Porter, letter of 5.10.81; p.149, Blunt, Recollections; Ramsden, op.cit, p.351; Leach, letter of 25.9.81; Merry, interview of 30.7.81; p.150, Whisky anecdote, Humble, op.cit., p.300; p.151, Dunlop, ibid.; p.206, Golovko, *With the Red Fleet,* p.186; p.153, Golovko, op.cit., p.187; p.154, Golovko, op.cit., p.188; p.154, Peter Whittley, letter of 21.9.82; Godde's account, Busch, op.cit., pp.171-174; p.155, Merry's account, interview of 30.7.81; p.156, Thomas' comment on POWs, McLachlan, *Room 39,* p.165; p.157, Ramsden, *The Naval Review,* Nov. 1947, p.312; p.158, 'Horse back' anecdote, Courage, 'Sinking of the Scharnhorst'; p.159, Fraser's reaction to awards, from Merry, interview of 30.7.81; Bates, letter of 2.9.82

APPENDIX 1

Operation 'FV'

BRIDGE CARD

HMS *Duke of York*	Vice Admiral (acting Admiral) Sir Bruce Fraser KCB, KBE Commander-in-Chief, Home Fleet
	Captain The Hon. G.H.E. Russell CBE
HMS *Belfast*	Vice Admiral R.L. Burnett CB, DSO, OBE, Flag Officer commanding 10th Cruiser Squadron
	Captain F.R. Parham
HMS *Jamaica*	Captain J. Hughes-Hallett DSO
HMS *Norfolk*	Captain D.K. Bain
HMS *Sheffield*	Captain C.T. Addis
HMS *Ashanti*	Lt. Cdr. J.R. Barnes
HMCS *Athabaskan*	Ltd. Cdr. J.H. Stubbs DSO RCN
HMS *Beagle*	Lt. Cdr. N.R. Murch
HMCS *Haida*	Cdr. H.G. de Wowlf RCN
HMCS *Huron*	Lt. Cdr. H.S. Rayner DSC RCN
HMS *Impulsive*	Lt. Cdr. P. Bekenn
HMCS *Iroquois*	Cdr. J.C. Hibberd DSC RCN
HMS *Matchless*	Lt. W.D. Shaw
HMS *Meteor*	Lt. Cdr. D.J.P. Jewitt
HMS *Milne*	Captain I.M.R. Campbell DSO (Capt. D)
HMS *Musketeer*	Cdr. R.L. Fisher DSO OBE
HMS *Onslaught*	Cdr. W.H. Selby DSC
HMS *Onslow*	Captain J.A. McCoy DSO (Captain (D) 17)
HMS *Opportune*	Cdr. J. Lee-Barber DSO
HMS *Orwell*	Lt. Cdr. J.A. Hodges DSO
HMS *Saumarez*	Lt. Cdr. E.W. Walmsley DSC
HMS *Savage*	Cdr. M.D.C. Meyrick
HMS *Scorpion*	Lt. Cdr. W.S. Clouston
HMS *Scourge*	Lt. Cdr. G.L.M. Balfour
HMNor. S. *Stord*	Lt. Cdr. Skule Storheill RNorN
HMS *Virago*	Lt. Cdr. A.J.R. White
HMS *Westcott*	Cdr. H. Lambton
HMS *Whitehall*	Lt. Cdr. P.J. Cowell DSC
HMS *Wrestler*	Lt. R.W.B. Lacon DSC

HMNorS. *Acanthus*	
HMS *Dianella*	Temp. Lt. J.F. Tognola RNR
HMS *Honeysuckle*	Lt. H.H.D. MacKilligan DSC RNR
HMS *Oxlip*	Lt. Cdr. C.W. Leadbetter RNR
HMS *Poppy*	Temp. Lt. D.R.C. Onslow RNR
HMS *Cleaner*	Lt. Cdr. F.J.S. Hewitt DSC
HMS *Seagull*	Lt. Cdr. R.W. Ellis DSC
Scharnhorst	Kontradmiral Erich Bey, Commander Battle Group
	Kapitan zur See Fritz Julius Hintze
Z.29	Kapitan zur See Rolf Johannesson
	Korv. Kapitan Theodor von Mutius
Z.30	Korv. Kapitan Karl Heinrich Lampe
Z.33	Kapitan zur See Erich Holtorf
Z.34	Korv. Kapitan Karl Hetz
Z.38	Korv. Kapitan Gerfried Brutzer
R.56	Kap. Lt. Wilhelm Maclot
R.58	Ober Lt.z.S. Werner Hauss
R.121	
U.277	Kap. Lt. Lubsen
U.314	Korv. Kap. Basse
U.354	Korv. Kap. Herbschleb
U.387	Korv. Kap. Buchler
U.601	Kap. Lt. Hansen
U.716	Ober Lt.z.S. Dunkelberg
U.957	Ober Lt.z.S. Schaar

APPENDIX II

Survivors of *Scharnhorst*

Name	Rating	Action Station	Date of Birth
GODDE, Wilhelm	*Oberbootsmannsmaat (Acting Petty Officer)*	Look-out Port forward Searchlight Control	1.12.10
KASTENHOLZ, Johann	*Oberbootsmannmaat (Acting Petty Officer)*	No.3 Port 5.9″	18.3.17
SCHERER Franz	*Bootsmannmaat (Leading Seaman)*	Starboard after A.A. Director controlling No.3 Stbd. 4.1″ twin mounting & centre after 4.1″.	20.1.21
LOFFENLHOLZ, Heinrich	*Bootsmannmaat*	No.4 Port After 5.9″	22.8.22
HOVEDESBRUNKEN, Wilhelm	*Matrosenhauptgefreiter (A.B.)*	No.1 Stbd. 5.9″ Communications Number	13.3.18
STEINIGANZ, Hans	*Maschinenhauptgefreiter. (Stoker, 1st Class)*	Not given	28.1.21
ZANGER, Rolf	*Maschinenhauptgefreiter*	No.1 Boiler Room	4.12.19
RAUSCHERT, Max	*Maschinenhauptgefreiter*	Engineers Stores, Section IX 'Tween Deck'	11.10.19
PFEIL, Heinz	*Matrosenobergefreiter (A.B.)*	CAESAR Turret Ammo, Hoist	24.7.19
WIEBUSCH, Nicolaus	*Matrosenobergefreiter*	After 37mm. Stbd.	10.7.22
BOHLE, Gunter	*Metrosenobergefreiter*	No.4 Port 4.1″	14.1.22
ALSEN, Willi	*Matrosenobergefreiter*	Ammunition Supply Section IX	27.11.23
BACKHAUS, Helmut	*Matrosenobergefreiter*	Forward 4.1″ Communications Number	15.8.24
TRZEMBIATOWSKI, Hans	*Matrosenobergefreiter*	Not given	20.2.23
SCHUTZ, Hermann	*Matrosenobergefreiter*	No. Stbd. Twin 4.1″	13.8.24
WITTE, Hubert	*Matrosenobergefreiter*	Messenger on Admiral's Bridge	24.12.22
GROENEWOND, Heinz	*Matrosenobergefreiter*	No.2 4.1″ Ammon Supply Number	3.9.22
ACHILLES, Johann	*Maschinenobergefreiter (Stoker 1st Class)*	No.1 (After) Turbine Room	29.10.20

SCHAFFRATI, Paul	*Maschinenoberge freiter*	Repair Party ("Storungswehr") Section IX 'Tween Deck'	30.3.20
MARKO, Franz	*Maschinenoberge freiter*	Auxiliary Boiler Room	10.2.23
FEIFER, Helmut	*Maschinenoberge freiter*	Damage Control Party Messenger	26.5.23
LAISZ, Franz	*Maschinenoberge freiter*	Engine Room Messenger Section IX, Port side	10.5.22
WALLEK, Martin	*Zimmermannsoberge freiter (Shipwright A.B. Rating)*	Damage Control Party	28.10.21
BIRKE, Rudi	*Matrosengefreiter (A.B.)*	BRUNO Turret	18.2.22
HAGER, Fritz	*Matrosengefreiter*	Stbd. For'd. twin 5.9" turret Loading Number	9.8.24
KOSTER, Wilhelm	*Matrosengefreiter*	No.1 Stbd. 4.1"	8.2.21
SCHAFER, Max	*Matrosengefreiter*	No.2 Stbd. 4.1"	28.4.24
STRATER, Gunter	*Matrosengefreiter*	After 4.1"	31.12.23
BOEKHOFF, Helmut	*Matrosengefreiter*	Stbd Twin 37mm. loading Number	6.4.24
KRUSE, Wilhelm	*Steursmannsgefreiter A.B. (Navigator's Yeoman)*	Admiral's Staff	14.5.23
ZAUBITZER, Horst	*Mechanikergefreiter (A.B.) Quarters Armourer*	CAESAR Turret	2.4.24
REIMANN, Ernst	*Mechanikergefreiter*	CAESAR Turret Hydraulic Pump	4.1.24
WIEST, Johann	*Mechanikergefreiter*	Port A/A guns	3.8.24
MERKLE, Johann	*Mechanikergefreiter*	Port Twin 5.9"	4.10.23
LORKE, Gunter	*Matrose (Ordinary Seaman)*	After twin 4.1" A/A	24.7.19
LOBIN, Gerhard	*Matrose*	Forward Director Tower Lookout	22.12.22

Thirty-six survivors, average age 22 years.

APPENDIX III

Honours and Awards

Supplement to *The London Gazzette,* of Wednesday, 5 January 1944

CENTRAL CHANCERY OF THE ORDERS OF KNIGHTHOOD

St. James's Palace, S.W.1

5th January, 1944

The KING has been graciously pleased to give orders for the following promotion in the Most Honourable Order of the Bath, for good services rendered in the pursuit and destruction of the Scharnhorst on the 26th December, 1943:

To be an Additional Member of the Military Division of the First Class, or Knights Grand Cross, of the said Most Honourable Order:

Vice-Admiral (acting Admiral) Sir Bruce Austin Fraser, K.C.B., K.B.E.

CENTRAL CHANCERY OF THE ORDERS OF KNIGHTHOOD

St. James's Palace, S.W.1

5th January, 1944

The KING has been graciously pleased to give orders for the following promotion in the Most Excellent Order of the British Empire, for good services rendered in the pursuit and destruction of the Scharnhorst on the 26th December, 1943:

To be an Additional Knight Commander of the Military Division of the said Most Excellent Order:

Vice-Admiral Robert Lindsay Burnett, C.B., D.S.O., O.B.E.,

for great determination and skill throughout the action and in twice driving off the enemy thus saving the convoy.

ADMIRALTY

Whitehall

5th January, 1944

The KING has been graciously pleased to give orders for the following appointments to the Distinguished Service Order and to approve the following awards:

For great gallantry, determination and skill while serving in H.M. Ships Sheffield, Norfolk, Belfast, Duke of York, Savage, Saumarez, Musketeer, Scorpion, Jamaica, Opportune, Virago and Matchless, throughout the action in which the German Battleship Scharnhorst was sunk:

To be Companions of the Distinguished Service Order

Captain Charles Thorburn Addis, Royal Navy.

Captain Donald Keppel Bain, Royal Navy.

Captain Frederick Robertson Parham, Royal Navy.

Captain the Honourable Guy Herbrand Edward Russell, C.B.E., Royal Navy.

Commander Michael Donston Capel Meyrick, Royal Navy.

Bar to the Distinguished Service Cross

Lieutenant-Commander Eric Norman Walmsley, D.S.C., Royal Navy.

The Distinguished Service Cross

Commander Ralph Lindsay Fisher, D.S.O., O.B.E., Royal Navy.

Lieutenant-Commander William Stratford Clouston, Royal Navy.

Temporary Lieutenant Harold Raymond Kingsmill Bates, R.N.V.R. (Guildford).

The Distinguished Service, Medal

Able Seaman Horace Victor John Badkin, D/JX.273451 (London).

Able Seaman Geoffrey Witton, P/JX.257392 (Manchester).

Mention in Despatches

Captain (Commodore First Class) John Hughes-Hallett, D.S.O., Royal Navy.

Commander John Lee-Barber, D.S.O., Royal Navy.

Lieutenant-Commander Archibald John Ramsay White, Royal Navy.

Lieutenant William David Shaw, Royal Navy.

Such further Awards as the KING may be graciously pleased to approve for this action will be published in due course.

Supplement to *The London Gazette* of 29 February 1944

The KING has been graciously pleased to give unrestricted permission for the wearing of the Insignia of the following Honours conferred by the Presidium of the Supreme Council of the USSR

For distinguished services in the action which resulted in the sinking of the German Battleship Scharnhorst:

Order of Suvorov, First Degree

Admiral Sir Bruce Austin Fraser, G.C.B., K.B.E.

Fourth Supplement to *The London Gazette* of Tuesday, 7th March, 1944

CENTRAL CHANCERY OF THE ORDERS OF KNIGHTHOOD

St. James's Palace, S.W.1.

7th March, 1944

The KING has been graciously pleased to approve the award of the British Empire Medal (Military Division) to:

Fireman Kenneth Richard Hellyer, R.234240, for outstanding services in salvage and repair work on board a damaged Merchant Vessel.

ADMIRALTY

Whitehall

7th March, 1944

The KING has been graciously pleased to give orders for the following appointment to the Distinguished Service Order and to approve the following awards:

For gallantry, distinguished service and devotion to duty on the staff of the Commander-in-Chief, Home Fleet, and in H.M. Ships Duke of York, Belfast, Norfolk, Sheffield, Jamaica, Savage, Saumarez, Scorpion, Musketeer, Matchless, Virago and Opportune during the action in which the Scharnhorst was engaged and sunk:

To be a Companion of the Distinguished Service Order

Captain (Commodore First Class) William Rudolph Slayter, D.S.C., Royal Navy (Dunsfold, Surrey).

Bar to the Distinguished Service Cross

Captain Christopher Theodore Jellicoe, D.S.O., D.S.C., Royal Navy (Pulborough, Sussex).

Commander William Alan Frank Hawkins, D.S.O., O.B.E., D.S.C., Royal Navy (Mevagissey, Cornwall).

Commander Earle Hathway Thomas, D.S.C., Royal Navy (Newbury).

Commander (E) Kenneth Morland Symonds, D.S.C., Royal Navy (Bowdon, Cheshire).

Lieutenant-Commander Graham James Alexander Lumsden, D.S.C., Royal Navy (Edinburgh).

Lieutenant-Commander Paul Morrison Bushe Chavasse, D.S.C., Royal Navy (Lyme Regis).

Lieutenant John Edwin Dyer, D.S.C., Royal Navy.

The Distinguished Service Cross

Commander Peter Dawnay, M.V.O., Royal Navy (London).

Commander (E) Hugh Wilson Findlay, Royal Navy.

Commander (E) Harold William Mole, Royal Navy (Portsmouth).

Commander (E) James Hartley Brandon Dathan, Royal Navy (Tavistock).

Acting Commander (E) Charles Peter Graham Walker, Royal Navy (King's Lynn).

Instructor Commander John Fleming, B.A., Royal Navy (Blackburn, West Lothian).

Lieutenant-Commander James Hamilton Crawford, Royal Navy (Bude).

Lieutenant-Commander John Aubrey Meares, Royal Navy (Hossell, Surrey).

Lieutenant-Commander Reginald Alfred Philips Mountfield, Royal Navy (High Salvington, Sussex).

Lieutenant-Commander Rupert Charles Purchas Wainwright, Royal Navy (Portsmouth).

Acting Lieutenant-Commander (E) Robert Charles Heartley Reed, R.N.R. (Saltash).

Lieutenant Stephen Marcus de la Poer Beresford, Royal Navy.

Lieutenant Frank Douglas Holford, Royal Navy (Wylam, Northumberland).

Lieutenant George William Muirhead, Royal Navy (Plymouth).

The Reverend Arthur Kenneth Mathews, O.B.E., M.A., Temporary Chaplain, R.N.V.R. (Bath).

Acting Lieutenant (E) William McCullough Livingston, Royal Navy (Co. Down).

Temporary Sub-Lieutenant the Honourable Simon George Warrender, R.N.V.R. (London).

Mr. Kenneth William Cobley, Gunner, Royal Navy (Salcombe).

Mr. Alexander John Berner, Gunner (T), Royal Navy (Wootton Bridge, Isle of Wight).

Mr. Leslie James Napper, Gunner (T), Royal Navy.

Mr. Percival O'Kell, Gunner (T), Royal Navy.

Mr. Sidney Tom Henry Winkworth, Warrant Engineer, Royal Navy (Gillingham).

The Conspicuous Gallantry Medal

Petty Officer Frederick William John Wilkes, D/J.111017.

On the 26th December, 1943, when his ship, H.M.S. Saumarez, was being heavily engaged by the Scharnhorst, sprayed by splinters, and members of his torpedo tube's crew were killed or wounded, Petty Officer Wilkes, Torpedo Gunner's Mate, by his leadership, coolness and splendid example ensured the firing of the torpedoes.

Bar to the Distinguished Service Medal

Chief Petty Officer Arnold Lee Baldwin, D.S.M., P/J.100380 (Wolverhampton).

The Distinguished Service Medal

Chief Petty Officer William Patrick Foulger, C/JX.127397 (Shotesham, Norfolk).

Chief Petty Officer Frederick Warren Potter, P/J.115332 (Frimley Green).

Chief Petty Officer John Edward Yeo, P/J.78799 (Bournemouth).

Acting Chief Petty Officer Donald Carmichael, D/JX.135164.

Chief Yeoman of Signals Ralph Charles Fuller, B.E.M., C/J.109411.

Chief Petty Officer Telegraphist Edward John Cornford, C/J.93419 (Gillingham).

Chief Engine Room Artificer Frederick John Grimmer, C/MX.47134 (Caister-on-Sea).

Chief Engine Room Artificer Roy Walter Frederick Le Page, D/MX.49902 (Plymouth).

Chief Engine Room Artificer Arthur Leslie Lucking, D/MX.46551.

Chief Engine Room Artificer Francis Frederick Claud Nelmes, D/M.6281 (Plymouth).

Chief Engine Room Artificer Ronald O'Brien, C/MX.48425 (Glasgow).

Chief Engine Room Artificer Sydney Charles Rundle, D/MX.47860.

Chief Electrical Artificer Edward Albert Beard, C/M.37731 (Weymouth).

Chief Electrical Artificer Frederick Horace Frank Hornblow, D/MX.45679 (St. Ives).

Chief Mechanician Frederick Arthur May, C/K.53205.

Chief Stoker William Cadwallader, D/KX.76007.

Chief Stoker Harry Edwin Shawyer, C/K.61844 (Nelson, Lancashire).

Engine Room Artificer Third Class Rodger Walker, D/MX.59981.

Engine Room Artificer Third Class Denis Richard Western, P/MX.60438 (Godalming).

Petty Officer Walter Stanley Smith, C/JX.218306 (Deptford).

Petty Officer Robert Lewis Walkey, D/JX.130366.

Temporary Petty Officer Hugh John Miscimmons, D/JX.139034 (Bangor, Co. Down).

Temporary Petty Officer Frederick Charles Leslie Thompson, C/JX.145400 (Woodbridge, Suffolk).

Yeoman of Signals John Young, C/JX.131436 (Gillingham).

Petty Officer Telegraphist James Ebrey Clare May, D/SSX.15940.

Engine Room Artificer Fourth Class James Duncan, D/UD/X.1495 (Bootle, Lancashire).

Engine Room Artificer Fourth Class Victor Charles Nicholls, C/MX.55193 (Southend-on-Sea).

Electrical Artificer Arthur John Hazell, D/MX.47213 (Axminster).

Stoker Petty Officer William Leslie Growden, D/K.64236 (St. Austell).

Stoker Petty Officer William Alexander Hammond, C/K.65196 (Cloues, Eire).

Stoker Petty Officer James Harvey, D/KX.88415 (Kilrush, Eire).

Stoker Petty Officer Alfred Levi Cecil Harvey, C/K.61951 (Charing, Kent).

Stoker Petty Officer George Pilkington, D/K.64474 (Manchester).

Petty Officer Wireman Ronald Jack Pettitt, D/MX.63108 (Bristol).

Acting Petty Officer Radio Mechanic Ronald William Colton, P/MX.99675 (Bulpham, Essex).

Sergeant William Eggar Jenkins, Ply.X.756, R.M. (Plymouth).

Bandmaster First Class Douglas Zenas Colls, R.M.B.2631 (Birmingham).

Bandmaster Second Class Clifford Joseph Burley, R.M.B.X.160 (Kempston, Bedford).

Leading Seaman Cornelius McCarthy, D/J.96991 (Baltimore, Co. Cork).

Temporary Leading Seaman William Anderson, C/SSX.21081 (Possilpark, Glasgow).

Acting Leading Seaman Roy Nightingale, P/JX.223023 (Darwen, Lancashire).

Leading Telegraphist John Caldwell Campbell, P/JX.171002 (Renfrew).

Temporary Acting Leading Telegraphist Leonard Walker, D/JX.233352 (Monkseaton, Northumberland).

Temporary Leading Stoker John Cranston, C/KX.90123 (Limehouse, London).

Temporary Acting Leading Stoker Arthur Harry Perkins, D/KX.103481 (Bath).

Leading Canteen Assistant Gordon Horton Leonard Jewitt, Ch/NX.1980 (Grimsby).

Corporal (Temporary) David Charles Henry Eason, Ch.X.120 R.M. (Walthamstow).

Ordnance Mechanic Fourth Class Gerald Frederick Turney Burgess, P/MX.98384 (Leighton Buzzard).

Able Seaman Francis Breen, D/JX.170909.

Able Seaman Herbert Joseph Burgess, C/JX.301469 (Sevenoaks).

Able Seaman Norman Lambert, C/JX.420245 (Salford).

Able Seaman Edward McKay, D/MX.100044 (Burnley).

Able Seaman William Raymond Sanders, P/JX.240599 (Swansea).

Able Seaman Edward Walter Starck, D/JX.260221 (London).

Able Seaman Sidney Arthur Stevens, D/JX.328015.

Able Seaman Leslie Richard Stone, C/SSX.20920 (Rushden, Northants).

Signalman William Lewens Ray, D/JX.191380.

Telegraphist Kenneth Anthony Chanot, P/JX.246323 (Aldershot).

Stoker First Class John Ferguson Clements, D/KX.108110.

Stoker First Class Arthur Frederick Fursland, P/KX.116120 (Bridgewater).

Stoker First Class Leslie William Moody, C/KX.166007 (East Dulwich).

Mechanician Albert Henry Mortimore, D/K.30327 (St. Austell).

Marine Cecil George Hardy, Ply.X.2104, R.M. (Walton-on-Thames).

Ordinary Seaman Kenneth Leslie Bostock, D/JX.416732.

Ordinary Signalman William Clifford Howard, D/JX.340853.

Mention in Despatches (Posthumous)

Chief Stoker William Lynch, D/K.62876 (Preston).

Leading Seaman Bernard Gilham Hall, P/JX.255202.

Mention in Despatches

Constructor Captain Neville Green Holt, R.C.N.C. (Bath).

Commander George David Archibald Gregory, D.S.O., Royal Navy (Perth).

Commander Terence Augustus Ker Maunsell, Royal Navy (Henley, Surrey).

Commander (E) John Roland Patterson, D.S.C., Royal Navy (Lanark).

Surgeon Lieutenant-Commander John Denis Lendrum, M.B., Ch.B., D.P.H., R.N.V.R. (Harpenden).

Acting Paymaster Lieutenant-Commander Peter White, Royal Navy (Amersham).

Lieutenant John Alexander Jeffreys Dennis, D.S.C., Royal Navy (West Kirby, Cheshire).

Lieutenant Michael Patrick Pollock, Royal Navy (Pontesbury).

Lieutenant Llewellyn Fred Scillitoe, M.B.E., Royal Navy (Gillingham).

Lieutenant Denis Furnivall Swithinbank, D.S.C., Royal Navy (Eltham).

Lieutenant John Leslie West, D.S.C., Royal Navy (London).

Lieutenant (E) Kenneth Richard Montague Sandford, Royal Navy (Usaka, N. Rhodesia).

Lieutenant (E) George Lefroy Yorke, Royal Navy (Nantwich).

Acting Lieutenant (E) Charles Weston Frederick Bass, D.S.C., Royal Navy.

Acting Lieutenant (E) Leonard Horace Colwill, Royal Navy (Plymouth).

Temporary Lieutenant Laurence Herbert Longley-Cook, M.A., R.N.V.R. (Tunbridge Wells).

Temporary Lieutenant William Watson McGillivray, R.N.V.R. (Maidenhead).

Temporary Surgeon Lieutenant John Philip Whitby Grant, M.B., Ch.B., R.N.V.R.

Temporary Instructor Lieutenant Leonard Thomas Draycott, B.Sc., Royal Navy (Nuneaton).

Temporary Instructor Lieutenant Donald MacDonald MacPhee, M.A., Royal Navy (Oban).

Temporary Acting Lieutenant Keith Julyan Day, R.N.V.R. (Fritton).

Captain John Allen Gilks, Royal Marines (Leamington Spa).

Sub-Lieutenant Gordon John Dodd, Royal Navy (York).

Temporary Sub-Lieutenant Anthony Thomas Napierala, R.N.V.R. (Dorking).

Temporary Sub-Lieutenant Peter James Spicer, R.N.V.R.

Temporary Acting Sub-Lieutenant Denis Frederick Wicks, R.N.V.R. (North Finchley, London).

Midshipman William Victor Spiers Green, R.N.R. (Liverpool).

Mr. Alfred George Hancock, Gunner, Royal Navy (Stoke, Devonport).

Mr. Frederick Reginald Northam, Gunner, Royal Navy (Ermington, South Devon).

Mr. Gilbert Simpson, Gunner, Royal Navy (Fyffe).

Mr. Cecil William Daniels, D.S.C., Gunner (T), Royal Navy (Dagenham).

Mr. William Horace Withy, Gunner, Royal Navy (Sheerness).

Mr. Edwin John Webber, Warrant Telegraphist, Royal Navy (Okehampton, Devonshire).

Mr. Percy Ernest Jordan Quantick, Temporary Warrant Shipwright, Royal Navy (Plymouth).

Chief Petty Officer James Albert Collis, C/J.108896 (Rochester).

Chief Yeoman of Signals Edward Alfred Stanley Steere, D/J.69320.

Chief Petty Officer Telegraphist Hugh Mario Mitcalfe Dale, D/J.100371 (Stratford-on-Avon).

Chief Petty Officer Telegraphist Alfred John Reader, P/JX.129192 (Pretoria, South Africa).

Chief Engine Room Artificer Alfred Leslie Barnes, C/M.38748 (Crawley Down, Sussex).

Chief Electrical Artificer David McConnachie, P/MX.53651 (Ayr).

Temporary Acting Chief Electrical Artificer Frederick Claude Pattinson, D/MX.48602 (Shipley, Yorkshire).

Chief Stoker Oswald Bamber, D/K.64238 (Preston).

Chief Stoker Leslie Charles Guy Woon, D/KX.75423 (Plymouth).

Chief Petty Officer Cook (S) George Henry Rowswell, D/M.36523 (Greenford, Middlesex).

Engine Room Artificer First Class Charles Reginald Louton Clarke, P/M.14989 (Fareham).

Engine Room Artificer Second Class John Ernest Elias Penny, D/MX.51385 (Plymouth).

Engine Room Artificer Third Class William Humphry Spiller, D/MX.56724.

Electrical Artificer Fourth Class Norman John Francis, D/MX.93519 (Accrington).

Ordnance Artificer First Class Frederick Alexander Unwin, C/M.37068 (Ayston Hill, Shrewsbury).

Shipwright First Class Fred Axon, D/M.27433 (Callington).

Shipwright Fourth Class Wilfred Gerald Christopher, D/MX.73024 (Marlborough).

Petty Officer Albert Nathan Llewellyn Joy, D/JX.147478.

Petty Officer George Sheppard, D/JX.132698.

Petty Officer Peter Welsh, P/JX.130539 (Kirkaldy).

Petty Officer William Lewis Young, D/JX.137072.

Temporary Petty Officer George Dring, D/JX.141021 (Bodmin, Cornwall).

Temporary Petty Officer John William Mallaburn, D/J.89819 (Tooting, S.W.17).

Acting Petty Officer Thomas Robert McHaffey, C/JX.139241 (Chatham).

Temporary Acting Petty Officer Richard Donald Baldry, C/JX.145377 (Ipswich).

Temporary Acting Petty Officer Thomas Ronald Gridley, C/JX.140815 (Harwich).

Temporary Acting Petty Officer William Johnstone, P/SSX.23744 (Stranraer).

Temporary Acting Petty Officer Henry Hezekiah Smith, D/JX.157165 (Preston).

Yeoman of Signals Frank Broad, C/JX.132961 (Sittingbourne, Kent).

Yeoman of Signals William Horace Elford, P/JX.140721 (Brighton).

Yeoman of Signals Walter Harold Gadsden, C/JX.133004 (Strood).

Yeoman of Signals Alec William Thomas Raisey, P/JX.136739 (Gourock).

Temporary Acting Yeoman of Signals Sydney George Rhodes, P/JX.163019 (Laming, Sussex).

Petty Officer Telegraphist Cyril Dennis George Linkin, C/JX.133984 (Folkestone).

Stoker Petty Officer Wilfred Burke, D/KX.79140.

Stoker Petty Officer Alec George Dengate, C/K.62456 (Margate).

Stoker Petty Officer John Hadyn Gurmin, D/KX.83353.

Acting Stoker Petty Officer Enoch Davies, D/KX.76292.

Petty Officer Radio Mechanic Hubert Douglas Reynolds, P/MX.89122 (Lewes, Sussex).

Temporary Supply Petty Officer Sydney Garden Hutcheson, C/MX.67127 (Aberdeen).

Petty Officer Cook Albert Thomas Mills, C/MX.48116 (Parkestone, Harwich).

Electrical Mechanician Fourth Class William Cowan, C/MX.69282 (Kirkconnel, Dumfriesshire).

Electrical Mechanician Fourth Class Charles Gavan Duffy, D/JX.256743 (Liverpool).

Sergeant Daniel James, Ply.X.437, R.M. (Hawick, Roxburghshire).

Leading Seaman Ronald Green Lomax, P/JX.284302 (Oswaldtwistle).

Leading Seaman Harold Christopher Preece, D/J.43596 (Cardiff).

Leading Seaman Stanley Arthur Prince, C/JX.263267 (Carshalton, Surrey).

Temporary Leading Seaman Jack Beck, D/JX.152875 (Wakefield).

Temporary Leading Seaman George Howard Cutler, D/SR.620 (Walthamstow).

Temporary Leading Seaman Leonard Fisher, D/X.18239A.

Temporary Leading Seaman Sidney Edwin Thomas, D/JX.295753 (Preston).

Temporary Acting Leading Seaman Sidney Garston, D/JX.219970 (Stanmore, Middlesex).

Temporary Acting Leading Seaman Benjamin David Jones, D/JX.257613 (Greenford, Middlesex).

Temporary Acting Leading Seaman Charles Reid, C/JX.336061 (Dundee).

Leading Signalman Douglas Alan Smith, C/JX.185214 (East Runton, Norfolk).

Leading Telegraphist Wilfred Maitland Hicks, D/JX.309141.

Leading Stoker John Thomas Cormack, D/KX.92237.

Temporary Acting Leading Stoker Samuel Leslie Clark, D/KX.112517 (Plymouth).

Teemporary Acting Leading Stoker Thomas Welch, D/KX.120486 (Newport, Mon.).

Temporary Leading Coder Frederick William Train, D/JX.196301 (Plymouth).

Able Seaman Thomas Arnold Dearing, P/JX.310374 (Huddersfield).

Able Seaman William Gabbott Foster, C/SSX.32835 (Worcester).

Able Seaman William Thomas Knock, C/J.97678 (Tottenham).

Able Seaman Joe Lloyd, P/JX.303352 (Stockport).

Able Seaman Arthur Mack, P/JX.367306 (Cheadle).

Able Seaman Angus Macpherson, C/JX.351578 (Portree, Isle of Skye).

Able Seaman Gerald William Ricketts, D/JX.170987 (Barbourne, Worcs.).

Able Seaman David George Taylor, D/JX.213024.

Stoker First Class George Barker, D/KX.97504.

Stoker First Class Alfred Albert William Fry, C/KX.122385 (London).

Stoker First Class Thomas Hall, D/KX.132171 (Preston).

Coder Ronald Edward Tamlyn, C/JX.360600 (East Barnet, Herts).

Musician James Steward Cameron, R.M.B.X.1667 (Bebington, Cheshire).

Signal Boy Harry Ings, P/JX.292089 (Portsmouth).

Bibliography and Sources

A: Printed Sources

A.W.C., 'Admiral Sir Robert Burnett, GBE, KCB, DSO, LL.D. – Valediction', *The Naval Review*, Vol.XLVII, No.3, July 1959

BAKER, Richard, *Dry Ginger:* The biography of Admiral of the Fleet Sir Michael Le Fanu, GCB, DSC, W.H. Allen & Co Ltd., 1977, Ch.5 'Scapa Services'

'BANDERILLERO', 'Battle of Saint Stephen's Day', *The Naval Review*, Vol.XXXII, No.1, February 1944

BEESLY, Patrick, *Very Special Intelligence:* The Story of the Admiralty's Operational Intelligence Centre 1939-1945, Hamish Hamilton, 1977, Ch.13 'The End of *Scharnhorst* and *Tirpitz*'

BEESLY, Patrick, and ROHWER, Jurgen, '"Special Intelligence" und die Vernichtung der "Scharnhorst"', *Marine Rundschau*, 74 Jahrgang, Heft.10, October 1977

BEKKER, Cajus, *Hitler's Naval War,* Macdonald & Jane's 1974, Chs.5 'The Fall of Grand Admiral Raeder' and 7 'The end of the German Navy', App.9 'Doenitz' Plan of 2nd February 1943' and 12 'Complement of *Scharnhorst* for Operation OSTFRONT 25th-26th December 1943'

BROWN, Malcolm, and MEEHAN, Patricia, *Scapa Flow:* Reminiscences of men and women who served in Scapa Flow in the two World Wars, Allen Lane, The Penguin Press, 1968

BRASSEY'S NAVAL ANNUAL 1948, 'The Fuhrer Conferences on Naval Affairs', Clowes & Sons, 1948

BOOKES, Ewart, *The Gates of Hell,* Jarrolds, 1960, Ch.17

BROOME, Captain Jack, DSC RN, *Make A Signal,* Putnams 1955 (rev. and reprinted, William Kimber, 1973) III Naval History by Signal, *Scharnhorst* and *Gneisenau: Mutter* und *Tochter*

BUSCH, Corvette-Captain Fritz-Otto, *The Drama of the Scharnhorst:* A Factual Account from the German Viewpoint, Robert Hale Ltd., 1956

CAMPBELL, Vice Admiral Sir Ian, KBE, CB, DSO, and MACINTYRE, Captain Donald, DSO, DSC, *The Kola Run:* A Record of Arctic Convoys 1941-1945, Frederick Muller, 1958, Chs. 15 'Destination Dreadful' and 17 'Battle of Giants'

CHURCHILL, Winton S., *The Second World War,* Volume V: Closing the Ring, Cassell & Co., 1952, Chs. IX, 'A Spell at Home' and XV 'Arctic Convoys Again'

COUSINS, Geoffrey, *The Story of Scapa Flow,* Frederick Muller, 1965

CRESWELL, Captain John, RN, *Sea Warfare 1939-1945:* A Short History, Longmans Green & Co., 1950, Ch.14 'The Convoys to North Russia'

CUNNINGHAM, Viscount, of Hyndhope, KT, GCB, OM, DSO, *A Sailor's Odyssey,* Hutchinson, Ch.XLIII

DOENITZ, Gross Admiral Karl, *Memoirs: Ten Years and Twenty Days,* Weidenfeld & Nicholson 1959, Ch. 'My Tasks as Commander-in-Chief'

EDWARDS, Cdr. Kenneth, *Men of Action,* Collins, 1943, 'Robert Lindsay Burnett, CB, DSO, OBE, Rear Admiral in His Majesty's Fleet'

Seven Sailors, Collins, 1945, 'Sir Bruce Austin Fraser, GCB, KBE, Admiral in His Majesty's Fleet'

Reports in *The Daily Telegraph,* 28th and 29th December 1943

FORESTER, C.S., 'How the British Sank the *Scharnhorst*', *Saturday Evening Post,* 25th March 1944

FRASER, Admiral Sir Bruce A., KCB, KBE, 'Sinking of the German Battle-Cruiser SCHARNHORST' on the 26th December 1943', Supplement No. 38038 to *London Gazette,* of Thursday 7 August 1947

GARRETT, Richard, *Scharnhorst and Gneisenau: The Elusive Sisters,* David & Charles, Newton Abbot, 1978

GOLOVKO, Admiral Arseni, *With the Red Fleet,* Putnam, 1965

HEZLET, Vice Admiral Sir Arthur, KBE, CB, DSO, DSC, *The Electron and Sea Power,* Peter Davies, 1975, Ch. IX 'The Second World War 1942-3'

HOLMAN, Gordon, *The King's Cruisers,* Hodder & Stoughton, 1947, Ch. X *'Bismarck and Scharnhorst*

HUMBLE, Richard, 'Sinking the Scharnhorst', *Purnell's History of the Second World War,* Volume IV, p.1677

JAMES, Admiral Sir William, GCB, *The British Navies in the Second World War,* Longmans Green & Co., 1946, Ch. XII 'July 1943-Dec. 1943'

JAMESON, Rear Admiral Sir William, KBE, CB, 'Great Naval Leaders – 4: "Fraser and the *Scharnhorst*", *The Sunday Times*

KENNEDY, Ludovic, *Menace: The Life and Death of the Tirpitz,* Sidgwick & Jackson, 1979, Ch.8

KIMMINS, Anthony, *Half Time,* Heinemann, 1947

LONDON GAZETTE, 'The North Russian Convoys', Supplement of 13th October 1950

MCLACHLAN, Donald, *Room 39:* Naval Intelligence in Action 1939-45, Weidenfeld & Nicholson, 1968

MARTIENSSEN, Anthony, *Hitler and His Admirals,* Secker & Warburg, 1948

MONTAGU, Ewen, *Beyond Top Secret U,* Peter Davies, 1977

OAKESHOTT, Arthur, Report in *The Daily Telegraph* of 3rd January 1944
'The Post-Atom Admiral' (Fraser), *Illustrated,* 21st August 1948

O'NEILL, Richard, 'Scharnhorst', *War Monthly,* Issue 2, May 1974

PARKES, Dr Oscar OBE, AINA, *British Battleships,* Seeley Service & Co. (New Ed.1966) Chs.115 'The Washington Treaty Terminates', 116 'The New German Navy and British Contemporaries' and 117 'World War II'

POPE, Dudley, *73 North,* Weidenfeld & Nicholson, 1958, Ch.24 'A Bloodless Victory'

PITCAIRN-JONES, Cdr.L. RN, *Sinking of the Scharnhorst: 26 December 1943,* Battle Summary No.24, B.R. 1736 (17/50), Naval Staff History, Second World War, Tactical & Staff Duties Division (Historical Section), 1950 (also in ADM1/15691)

PETER, Karl-Hinrich, 'The Sinking of the *Scharnhorst*', *United States Naval Institute Proceedings,* January 1956

RAEDER, Gross Admiral Eerich, *Struggle for the Sea,* Weidenfeld & Nicholson, 1959

RAMSDEN, Lieut. Bryce, Royal Marines, 'Sinking the *Scharnhorst;* 26th December 1943' *Blackwood's magazine, No.1549, November 1944*
'Sinking of the German Battle Cruiser Scharnhorst on the 26th December 1943' (Commentary on Supplement to *London Gazette*) *The Naval Review,* Vol.XXXV, No.4, November 1947

ROHWER, J., and HUMMELCHEN, G., *Chronology of the war at sea 1939-1945,* Volume Two, 1943-1945, Ian Allan 1974

ROSKILL, Captain S.W., DSC RN, *The War at Sea 1939-1945,* Volume II The Period of Balance, HMSO, 1956, Ch.XVI 'Home Waters and the Arctic 1st January – 31st May, 1943', and Volume III Part 1 The Offensive, HMSO, 1960, Ch.IV 'Home Waters and the Arctic, 1st June – 31st December 1943'

SCHMALENBACH, Fregatten Kapitan a.D. Paul, *Profile Warship 33;* German Battlecruisers *Scharnhorst* and *Gneisenau,* Profile Publications Ltd., Windsor, 1974

SCHOFIELD, B.B., *The Russian Convoys,* B.T. Batsford 1964, Ch.12 'The *Scharnhorst's* Last Sortie'

THE TIMES, 13 February 1981, Lord Fraser's Obituary

TULEJA, Thaddeus V., *Eclipse of the German Navy,* J.M. Dent & Sons, 1958, Ch.8 'Last Sortie of the *Scharnhorst*'

VULLIEZ, Albert, and MORDAL, Jacques, *Battleship Scharnhorst,* Hutchinson, 1958, Part Three: 'The Sacrifice'

WAR ILLUSTRATED, Amalgamated Press Ltd., Vol.7, No.173, February 4th 1944, p.570, 'We Saw the Scharnhorst Hit in North Cape Battle'

WATTS, A.J., *The Loss of the Scharnhorst,* Ian Allan, 1970

WILKINSON, Norman, *A Brush With Life,* Seeley, Service & Co., 1969

WINGATE, John, DSC, *HMS Belfast,* Profile Publications Ltd., Windsor, 1973

WINTON, John, *Captains and Kings:* The Royal Navy and the Royal Family 1901-1981 Bluejacket Books, 1981

WOODWARD, David, *The Tirpitz,* William Kimber 1953, Ch.9 'The last great surface battle'

B: Unprinted Sources in Public Record Office

ADM 1/16833 Interrogation of *Scharnhorst* Survivors

ADM 53/117405 HMS *Duke of York* Fair Deck Log December 1943

ADM 53/117685 HMS *Jamaica* Fair Deck Log December 1943

ADM 53/117020 HMS *Belfast* Fair Deck Log December 1943

ADM 53/118307 HMS *Norfolk* Fair Deck Log December 1943

ADM 53/118532 HMS *Sheffield* Fair Deck Long December 1943

(No Fair Deck Logs for destroyers could be traced)

ADM 199/77 JW and RA Convoys, Documents on JW55A and B, RA55A and B

ADM 199/913 Documents on the sinking of *Scharnhorst*

ADM 223/36 Signals connected with sinking of *Scharnhorst* (ULTRA intercepts)

ADM 223/88 Review of Importance of ULTRA in Naval Operations in the War, by Cdr. Geoffrey Colpoys RN, Ch.VIII 'The Battle of the North Cape, 26th December 1943 – Sinking of *Scharnhorst*' and Ch.XI 'Movements of German Major Units From and To the Baltic, and Coastal Movements Between Norwegian Ports, 1942-1943'

CAB 69/5 Minutes of Defence Committee (Operations) 1943

Admiralty Chart, Folio No.2315, Söröy to Nordkapp, printed September 1981

C: Unprinted Private and Unpublished Sources

Special thanks and acknowledgements are due to the following: Captain Richard Courage, for providing a log of more than 500 signals relating to the sinking of *Scharnhorst:* Mrs Renee Duncan, for permission to examine the papers of Lord Fraser; Mr Richard Humble, for the loan of two chapters in typescript of his *Lord Fraser of North Cape;* Mr Ludovic Kennedy, for permission to obtain a transcript of his BBC-TV programme "The Sinking of *Scharnhorst*"; 'Peterborough' of *The Daily Telegraph,* for an appeal in 'London Day by Day' which traced Captain R.H.K. 'Barehand' Bates; W.H. Smith OBE, for the loan of the Type 271 Radar log of HMS *Matchless* for December 1943; Mr Edward Thomas, for comment upon the ULTRA aspects of this book; and Mr Peter Woodhouse, for tape recordings of Musician Ernie Heather, of *Duke of York,* Petty Officer Dennis Moore of *Duke of York,* Corporal George Mudd, RM, of *Duke of York,* Paymaster Captain Peter Weeks, of *Belfast,* and Leading Seaman Mick Weller, of *Savage;* and to Mr Dudley Blunt, Rear Admiral Fisher, Lt. Cdr Addis, Admiral Sir Frederick Parham, Mr K. Wintle for the loan of photographs.

AVCOTT, Tom, Letter of 29.11.82

BATES, Captain H.R.K. DSC RN, Letters of 2.9.82 and 24.9.82

BERRY, Lieut. C.R., DSC RN, 'The sinking of the *Scharnhorst* as remembered by one member of HMS *Jamaica*', in typescript, 26.10.82

BLUNT, Dudley J., 'Recollections of *Jamaica*'s Fighter Direction Officer', in typescript 19.10.82

BURNETT, Lt. Cdr. Keith, MBE, 'Sinking of *Scharnhorst*', in MS, 5.10.81

CAREY, Rev. Canon Adrian, 'The sinking of the *Scharnhorst* – in Distant Retrospect' in typescript, 7.7.82

CLOUSTON, Cdr. W.S. DSC RN, Letters, Journal, Log and Report of Proceedings, in Clouston Papers, Imperial War Museum, Access No. 74/89/1

COMPSTON, Wing Cdr. Robin, AFC RAF, 'An account of the sinking of the German battlecruiser *Scharnhorst*', in typescript, no date

CONEY, Captain G.T., OBE RN, Notes on service in REPULSE and DUKE OF YORK

COURAGE, Captain R.H., OBE DSC, RN, Notes on THE DRAMA OF THE SCHARNHORST, 1.3.77 THE SINKING OF THE SCHARNHORST, in Typescript, 7.6.77, letter of 25.10.81 and explanatory tape of 6.11.81 on *Scharnhorst* Signal Log

COX, Vivian, 'A Calculated Risk: The Story of the Battle of North Cape December 26th 1943', Play

CRAWFORD, Captain James, DSC, Interview of 20.11.82

CREE, Peter, Midshipman's Journal, December 1943

DAWNAY, Vice Admiral Sir Peter, KCVO, CB, DSC, 'The Sinking of the *Scharnhorst*', in typescript, no date, and Appendix on 'Communications'

DITCHAM, A.G.F., Letter to Captain S.W. Roskill, of 10.8.56

DUNLOP, Surgeon Lieut. J.C.H., Letter in Imperial War Museum

FISHER, Rear Admiral R.L. CB, DSO, OBE, DSC, Some personal recollections, in typescript, 29.5.81

GARNONS-WILLIAMS, Captain R.L., 'Experiences of a Midshipman during the Russian Convoys – 1942 to 1944', in typescript, 8.12.81

HAGUE, F., Letter of 2.11.81

HORTON, John, 'Who sank the *Scharnhorst* on Boxing Day 1943', Letter of 16.9.81

HUMBLE, Richard, *Fraser of North Cape*, Ch.17 C-in-C Home Fleet, and Ch.18 Sinking of the *Scharnhorst*, 23-26 December 1943, in typescript

KENNEDY, Ludovic, 'The Life and Death of the *Scharnhorst*', Tuesday Documentary, BBC-1, 26th December 1971

LEACH, Admiral Sir Henry, GCB, ADC, Letter of 25.9.81 and Enclosure

McGREGOR, John, Letter of 12.12.81

MERRY, Captain Vernon, DSC RN, 'Bruce Fraser – The Man and the Admiral', in typescript, Interview of 30.7.81

NORTHCOTT, Edward, Letter of 21.11.81

OAKESHOTT, Arthur, 'Admiral Burnett's Story', and 'A Captain's Story' (Parham), in typescript, no date

PARHAM, Admiral Sir Frederick, GBE, KCB, DSO, Letter of 5.6.81, Tape of 5.8.82

PETRIE, A., Letter of 10.9.81

PORTER, Captain W.L.G., RN, Letter of 5.10.81

THOMAS, Edward, OBE, DSC, Letter of 16.10.82

THOMAS, R.O.L., 'HMS *Duke of York* 1941-44' in MS, 10.1.82, and Letter of 17.10.71

THOMPSON, Rear Admiral J.Y., CB, Letter of 10.10.81

VAUGHAN-LEWIS, Lt.Cdr. John, Letter of 1.10.81

WAINWRIGHT, Rear Admiral R.C.P., CB, DSC, Letter of 27.9.82

WALKER, Cdr Stanley OBE, DSC, Letter in Imperial War Museum

WALKER, Lt.Cdr, H. MBE, '*Scharnhorst* Action', in typescript, no date, and Letter of 26.12.81

WATERFIELD, C.A.G., 'Memories of life aboard HMS *Belfast* June 1942-July 1944', 8.10.82, in MS

WELBY-EVERARD, Captain P.H.E., RN, 'Action of 26th December – Sinking of *Scharnhorst*, The story from HMS *Belfast*', in MS, no date

WEST, Cdr. John, DSC, 'Sinking of *Scharnhorst*: Recollections of Navigating Officer HMS *Jamaica*, in typescript, 24.11.82

WHITTLEY, Peter, Letter of 21.9.82

WINTLE, K., 'Narrative of Boxing Day 1943', in MS, 1.10.81

WOODHOUSE, Peter, 'The North Atlantic Fleet in Wartime', in typescript, 1.9.81

WOODWARD, David, 'The Scharnhorst', BBC Home Service, 10th March 1953, Produced by Maurice Brown

Index